HOW TO HANDLE YOUR

OWN CONTRACTS

by
Christopher Neubert
and
Jack Withiam, Jr.

Weathervane Books
New York

Table of Contents

About the Authors

Jack Withiam, Jr. graduated from Hamilton College in Clinton, New York in May of 1971 with an A.B. degree in economics. He then attended the Albany Law School of Union University in Albany, New York and received a J.D. degree in June, 1974. Currently residing in New York City, he is employed by the Mutual Life Insurance Company of New York and has been admitted to the practice of law in New York State since February 18, 1975.

Christopher Neubert attended the University of Notre Dame in South Bend, Indiana, graduating with a degree in Business Administration in June of 1970. Thereafter, he attended New York Law School in Manhattan and was awarded his J.D. degree in June, 1974. Chris lives in New York City and works for the Mutual Life Insurance Company of New York. Chris, however, is not admitted to any state bar. Although in preparation for the New York State Bar Exam, Chris is not an attorney, and it is not his intention to give that appearance in the publication of this book.

Preface

Any attorney or student of the law comprehends the complexity of contract law. To say that the topic is voluminous is an understatement. The layman, however, does not have the opportunity to study contract law and cannot expect to fully understand the consequences of his written or verbal acceptance of an offer.

Unquestionably, an attorney's function is to assist the layman in his legal transactions and it would be ludicrous to suggest that this book, or any publication, could competently replace an attorney's advice. The authors do not make that claim. This book is not a formal legal treatise, but rather a guide to the layman. Where an attorney offers solutions, this book instead hopefully highlights problem areas in contract law. If this objective is accomplished, then armed with an awareness of his rights, the layman can seek the advice of counsel, trained to advocate the law as it applies to the layman's particular situation. It cannot be stressed adamantly enough, that in any individual case, an attorney should always be consulted.

In closing, the authors offer this thought from the New York State Bar Association Lawyer's Code of Professional Responsibility, Canon 2, EC2-5: "A lawyer who writes or speaks for the purpose of educating members of the public to recognize their legal problems should carefully refrain from giving or appearing to give a general solution to all apparently similar individual problems, since slight changes in fact situations may require a material variance in the applicable advice; otherwise, the public may be misled and misadvised. Talks and writings by lawyers for laymen should caution them not to attempt to solve individual problems upon the basis of the information contained therein." The book was written in this spirit and the reader should keep this in mind while reading it.

Introduction

"Mephistopheles: . . .   But tell me Faustus, shall I have thy soul?
                        And I will be thy slave, and wait on thee,
                        And give thee more than thou hast wit to ask.

Faustus: Ay, Mephistopheles, I give it to thee . . .

Mephistopheles: But Faustus, thou must write it in a manner of a deed of gift . . .

Faustus: Now I will make an end immediately. (Writes)

Mephistopheles: O what will not I do to obtain his soul? (Aside)

Faustus: Consummation est: this bill is ended,
                        And Faustus hath bequeathed his soul to Lucifer."

Dr. Faustus (Marlowe)

What appeared to Dr. Faustus to be an intelligently conceived deal at the outset, moved inexorably into a nightmare. Although the doctor possessed a sense of his commitment at the time of signing his contract with Mephistopheles, it was the Devil who later possessed the more favorable position and in the end possessed Faustus himself.

Not all contractual agreements result in obligations as onerous and unforeseen as the pact between Lucifer and Faustus, but the signing of a contract where one party unwittingly commits himself beyond his immediate comprehension of the event is not an infrequent occurrence. Except under particular circumstances forbidden by statute or after-the-fact, court-imposed nullifications, parties can contract to perform or not perform any act. A person's promise, in return for a promise or an action on the part of another, binds the parties securely to each and every implied or expressed covenant in the agreement.

In today's world, people are required more and more often to put their signatures on the dotted line. Although a written contract is in most cases a mutual safeguard, since it may explicitly define duties and rights, it can just as effectively be an inescapable snare for the layman. The "fine print" or legal interpretation of the contract's bold-faced language can entrap the unwary and obligate him far in excess of his original intention.

Attorneys spend lifetimes mastering the law. The layman cannot expect to understand the complete legal ramifications of his actions, and yet so often he is in a position which demands a legal action on his part. Although the most prudent course to follow is to consult an attorney before entering into a contract, time or cost might not permit this—what some may consider a luxury. In the long run, however, the situation may become so burdensome that legal advice must be procured.

It would be propitious to avoid any position of having to seek legal assistance after the event in order to resolve the dilemma of an oppressive contract. The purpose of this book is to that end. By alerting the layman to his rights and to the patent dangers that can be inherent in legal provisions and clauses, before he subscribes to them, the expense and headaches associated with extricating himself from the entanglement can be averted. The layman, aware of his rights and possessing a perfunctory knowledge of the applicable law, will be able to avoid many problems by refusing to commit himself or by obtaining legal counsel to bolster his bargaining status and to protect his rights through a more equitable agreement.

This book attempts to outline the basic legal complications of contracts and certain other documents. The book is not an exhaustive or definitive treatise, nor does it purport to

be. It is a guide which explains the layman's rights and translates "legalese" into the vernacular, so that the next time he is confronted with a legal instrument, a dotted line and a pen, he will not sign in wonderment, or out of embarrassment.

Because the law is a constantly evolving discipline and because vagaries exist between states, the thrust of the legal conclusions in this book are general. The authors are themselves New York schooled, but clearly indicate where reference is made to peculiarities in their own state's law. In any event, because of these differences, where specific information is required, it is always recommended that the layman consult local law. Also, if the risk is great and the danger of later legal complications imminent, the layman should never hesitate to consult an attorney.

The first chapter will discuss the basic concepts of contract law. It is not intended to be exhaustive, but it is a guide to help the reader familiarize himself with the elements of contract law.

CHAPTER 1

General Principles of Contract Law

What is a contract? There are many definitions of a contract—the following is typical of most: A contract is a *promise*, or a set of promises, for breach of which the law gives a remedy, or for the performance of which the law in some way recognizes a duty. There are certain essential elements that are found in all valid contracts. These elements will be discussed in more detail later, but a quick mention of them here is helpful. They are as follows:

(1) Offer

(2) Acceptance

(3) Consideration

(4) Legal capacity of the parties to the contract.

(5) Legal subject matter.

(6) A writing if required by law.

Other factors might be taken into account in determining the validity and scope of the contract, but the above elements are essential for an enforceable contract and should serve as a good reference point for recognizing the existence, or absence, of a contract.

Elements (1) and (2) are dealt with together, since in order for an offer to culminate in a contract, there must be an *acceptance* of that particular *offer*. The theory underlying offer and acceptance is termed *mutual assent*. Mutual assent is frequently referred to as a "meeting of the minds" of the parties to the contract. In essence, it means that the parties are both agreeing to the same thing. This is an important aspect for the party of a contract to

remember; that is, it is not his subjective intent that governs the contract but rather the outward, objective expression of the intent that is looked to and is controlling. Just as a child cannot run until it begins to walk, the parties cannot have a contract unless there is an offer and an acceptance of that offer. It is most important that a person fully understands an offer and all of its ramifications, before accepting it. Subjective interpretations of the offer are not the controlling factor. If one is not sure of what is being offered, then the intelligent response is to ask "What does this mean?" and not to sign the dotted line and ask questions later.

Offer

What is an offer? An offer is a promise conditional upon an act, forbearance or return promise, which is being given in exchange for the promise of its performance. The essential components of an offer are:

(1) Intent to contract

(2) Definite and certain terms

(3) Communcation to the offeror

When these components exist, the person to whom the offer is made has the ability to accept, and thereby create a contract.

An agreement to agree is not a contract, because components (1) and (2) are lacking. However, there are instances whereby parties have entered into a binding contract orally, agreeing to reduce the oral agreement to writing at a subsequent date. The mere fact that one party cannot force the other party to sign the written contract at a later date does not render the oral contract unenforceable.

Once the offer is made, it is binding on the offeror until an agreed upon time expires, or until a reasonable amount of time passes. Generally, an offer may be revoked at any time before it is accepted. But if the offeror grants another party an option in writing, for a specified duration, the offer must remain open and cannot be revoked until that time has passed. The revocation may be effectuated by:

(1)   An offeror's revocation, which puts the offeree on notice of the revocation;

(2)   The offeree's rejection of the offer;

(3)   The offeror's death or insanity; or

(4)   The proposed contract becoming illegal due to some third party intervention, e.g., a statute passed by a government.

Except for (2), the forms that revocation can take are self-explanatory. Let us briefly consider (2). An offer may be rejected in three basic ways:

(a)   Express rejection

(b)   Counter offer—this changes the terms of the original offer, and as such, is regarded as a rejection of it

(c)   An acceptance which is conditional upon some act or promise which is not included in the original offer. Again, it works as a rejection of the original offer.

We now have proffered a general explanation of what is an offer, and how it may be terminated or rejected. Our focus should next be centered upon the acceptance of the offer.

Acceptance

Acceptance is simply saying "yes" to an offer—assenting to the terms of the offer. The terms of the acceptance must comply with the offeror's requirements of method of acceptance. Acceptance, like offer, has three essential elements that are necessary for it to be valid:

(1)   It must be absolute on its face;

(2)   It must conform to the conditions set out in the offer; and

(3)   a.   In the case of a bilateral contract, the offeree must inform the offeror of the acceptance or

b.   the undertaking and completion of the act requested for in the offer where the contract is unilateral.

A quick review of what has been discussed might now prove helpful. Offer and acceptance have been explored along with the essential elements of both. But what is this talk about "bilateral" contracts and "unilateral" contracts? A quick definition of these two terms might help in understanding what is expected of the offeree who is responding to an offer. A *unilateral contract* is one in which the promisor does not receive a return promise as consideration for his promise, but receives something other than a promise, generally performance of some act by the other party. A *bilateral contract*, which is the type with which the book will mainly concern itself, is one in which there are mutual promises between the two parties to the contract.

Consideration

The third element of a contract is consideration. A promisor (offeror) promises to do something for the promisee (offeree) and in return expects a return promise or performance. This return promise or performance is the consideration. Consideration takes the form of a legal benefit to the promisor or a legal detriment to the promisee. The consideration may be represented by something other than a promise; it may be a forbearance or the creation, modification, or destruction of a legal relationship; or simply a return promise.

Generally, a court will not inquire into the adequacy or fairness of the consideration in the contract unless it is unduly inadequate on its face. If this is found to be the case, the contract may be unenforceable. If the court finds that the parties bargained fairly and from equal positions, the parties will be bound by the consideration contained in the contract. Therefore it is imperative that a contracting party demand a fair return for his promise or performance.

Generally, the consideration is given to the party who is making the promise or performance. However, a consideration given to, or by a third person will constitute a valid consideration and support a promise and impose contractual liability. An example will be helpful. X promises to pay Y $1,000 in consideration for Y's transferring title of his car to Z, a third party. Y transfers the title to Z and demands the $1,000 from X. X refuses. Y can sue X on the contract because the promise is enforceable. As a rule, one promise is valid consideration for another promise. In a bilateral contract, legal enforceability of both promises must be present or the contract might be unenforceable.

Consideration can be viewed as the bargaining objective of the parties: "I promise to do something for you and in return for this undertaking, you promise to do something for me." In most instances, money is the consideration for the promised act. "I promise to transfer title of my car to you and in return for this transfer, you promise to pay me $1,000." Simply stated, the offeror will sell his car to the offeree for $1,000. When viewed from a contractual point of view, it is the exchange of two promises. The consideration given the seller for his promise to transfer title is the $1,000. The consideration given to the buyer for the $1,000 is the car.

There are some pitfalls of which the contracting party should be aware. Some promises on their face appear to be consideration but really are not. A moral obligation to do something is not consideration. However, a *moral duty* to pay, in addition to a pre-existing debt, will support a promise. An example would be a debt that has been discharged in bankruptcy. After being discharged in bankruptcy, the debtor makes a promise to pay the debt. It is valid and enforceable. This should be distinguished from a situation where a promise to do an act which is legally enforceable does not constitute consideration. The logic underlying this theory should be evident. If a person is legally obligated to do something anyway (if the act is legally enforceable), that person is not deemed to be giving any consideration in return for an additional promise. The original and legally enforceable promise (duty) is binding without the new contract. The party has given no new consideration for the return promise. However, if that once-legally enforceable promise is no longer viable, due to some reason such as discharge in bankruptcy, then we have the original cited situation. The promise to pay, which is no longer legally enforceable, is new consideration for a return promise or performance. It is a unique situation and one should be aware of its existence.

Capacity of the Parties

This fourth element of a contract (see list at the beginning of the chapter) is generally overlooked by contracting parties. Most parties impetuously sign their names on the dotted line and ask questions later. This practice should be avoided. Before signing any contractual agreement, a party should ask pertinent questions first, and make the proper inquiries as to with whom he is doing business. Generally, persons who are minors (in New York, under the age of 18), mentally ill or defective, under guardianship, or intoxicated are deemed incapable of entering into an enforceable contract. But, how can it be determined that a person is mentally ill or defective? There is no formula to be applied whereby it can be determined if someone is lacking capacity in some way. This fact is true and can be unfortunate. The result could be a contract that is unenforceable. The contract is voidable, or at least the parts of the contract that have not yet been performed are voidable. The rationale underlying the law is that the party does not have the capacity to understand the full nature of the transaction into which he or she is entering. In reality, the law is stepping in to protect these innocent parties.

In regard to capacity of the parties to the contract, the only concepts that will be covered are *void* and *voidable* contracts. If the contracting parties do have capacity and the other essential elements are met, there is a valid and enforceable contract. However, at times, one party may lack capacity. A voidable contract is a contract that one or more of the parties can get out of simply by electing to do so. Of course, the party may elect to honor the contract (ratification) and the parties will be legally obligated to perform. The latter situation causes no problem. It is when the party wants to avoid the legal relations created by the contract, due to lack of capacity, that a problem arises. Unfortunately, there is not much a party can do if he contracted with a person who lacks capacity. The contract is voidable and the party is out of luck. However, if the party who contracted with the party lacking capacity has already partially performed the contract, the court may award him the reasonable compensation for his services, especially in the case of supplying necessaries.

A void contract is a misnomer, because actually no contract ever existed. It is more like an unenforceable agreement. A void contract imposes no liability whatsoever on the incapacitated party making the contract. This dif-

fers slightly from the voidable contract in that a voidable contract can be ratified and treated as an enforceable contract. Even if the contract is deemed void, a party might be able to recover some compensation for services rendered. In summary, a voidable contract can be ratified (at least you have a slim chance); a void contract cannot be ratified.

Legal Subject Matter

The fifth element essential to a contract is a simple, logical concept dealing with the legality of the subject matter. In essence, what is meant is that two parties cannot contract to do something that is illegal. To put it another way, the parties may enter into a contract to do something illegal (e.g., sell marijuana), but it is not enforceable. The performance or formation of the contract is illegal, if what is contracted (bargained) for, is *tortious*, criminal or contrary to public policy. If there is a statute that prohibits certain conduct, then the conduct is unenforceable, by virtue of the statute. Public policy is more of an interpretation by the courts, and if the courts deem a transaction to be against public policy, then the contract is illegal and unenforceable. Common examples are gambling transactions. If a contract has been entered into and the subject matter is illegal, or is subsequently declared illegal by statute, the contract is illegal and unenforceable.

A Writing If Required By Law: The Statute of Frauds

This sixth and final element is self-explanatory. If a writing is required by law, there must be a writing or else the contract is unenforceable. For all practical purposes, a contract should always be reduced to writing and signed by the parties whenever possible. However, this does not mean that an oral contract is not enforceable. It might be harder to prove, but it still can be enforced by either party. But if the agreement can be reduced to writing and signed by the contracting parties, do it. Then, this element, the statute of frauds, will be automatically satisfied.

There are two general principles indicating whether or not a written contract is necessary. The two principles are: when the transaction involves (a) real estate or (b) a contract which will not be completed within one year from the date of the contract, a writing is required. Principle (a) is always applicable—any transaction involving real estate must be reduced to writing to be enforceable. Principle (b) is more of a rule-of-thumb which is used to judge the enforceability of an oral contract. Remember, an oral contract is as enforceable and as legally binding as is a written contract, if the contract is not required to be in writing, and can be performed within one year.

The six essential elements of a contract have been discussed briefly. These elements should be considered as a skeleton or foundation of basic contracts. As will be seen in our discussion and use of the blank contract provided in the text, sometimes other elements are contained within the contract that do not directly make up the framework of the basic skeleton.

Contract law is voluminous, and it is not the objective of this book to furnish a detailed history and all the legal ramifications of contract law. Rather, the book, and this initial section, in particular, have as the main objective, to describe the basic elements of any contract, so that the reader may understand his or her position more fully when entering into a contractual arrangement with another party.

We now take up some of the problems that will confront a contracting party. Usually, a person has certain rights and/or obligations of which he or she is not aware. The remainder of the text deals with some of these.

A Sample Contract

Let us begin by briefly looking at a blank contract, and let us fill it in with a hypothetical

transaction, in order to see that the six basic elements are satisfied.

In the sample, the two contracting parties are identified at the outset of the form. The offer and acceptance, which have been reduced to writing, are present. John Smith offers to transfer title of an automobile to Mary Jones, who accepts this offer, as is evidenced by her signature on the contract. The consideration given by John Smith is the transfer of title of the automobile. The consideration given by Mary Jones is the $1,000. Therefore, mutual assent exists (offer and acceptance), supported by consideration from both parties. It is assumed that both parties have the legal capacity to enter into the contract and that the contract's subject matter (i.e., transfer of title for $1,000) is not illegal or void by statute. Finally, since the contract is in writing, and is signed by both contracting parties, the six elements are met.

On its face, the contract is enforceable. However, something might happen. Suppose the car is stolen before delivery? What happens if the parties want to get out of the contract because fraud was involved? What happens if the parties left some element of the agreement out of the contract and have now realized this fact? These and other problems can and do arise. These problems are covered in the book.

A good starting point is to refer to the last sentence of the sample contract, above the clause "IN WITNESS WHEREOF". The sentence states, "This instrument may not be changed orally.", which leads us to the *Parol Evidence Rule*.

Parol Evidence Rule

The Restatement of Contracts, § 237, states the parol evidence rule in this manner: ". . . the integration of an agreement makes inoperative to add to or vary the agreement all contemporaneous oral agreements relating to the same subject matter; and also, unless the integration is void, or voidable and avoided, the integration leaves the operation of prior

Articles of Agreement,

Between   JOHN SMITH, WHO RESIDES AT
10 XYZ STREET
NEW YORK, N. Y.

of the first part,

and   MARY JONES, WHO RESIDES AT
20 ABC STREET
NEW YORK, N. Y.

of the second part.

The party   *of the first part, in consideration of*

ONE THOUSAND DOLLARS ($1,000.00)

covenants and agrees to

SELL TO THE PARTY OF THE SECOND PART A 1970 BLACK FORD
AUTOMOBILE. PARTY OF THE FIRST PART WILL TRANSFER TO
THE PARTY OF THE SECOND PART THE CERTIFICATE OF TITLE
AND ANY OTHER DOCUMENTS NECESSARY TO EFFECTUATE A
COMPLETE TRANSFER OF TITLE FROM PARTY OF THE FIRST PART
TO THE PARTY OF THE SECOND PART.

How to Handle Your Own Contracts

The party of the second part, *in consideration of* COMPLETE TRANSFER OF TITLE OF THE 1970 BLACK FORD AUTOMOBILE FROM THE PARTY OF THE FIRST PART TO THE PARTY OF THE SECOND PART.

covenants and agrees TO TENDER PAYMENT OF ONE THOUSAND DOLLARS ($1,000.00) TO THE PARTY OF THE FIRST PART. THE TENDER SHALL BE IN THE FORM OF CASH AND WILL BE DUE ON THE DATE OF DELIVERY OF SAID AUTOMOBILE.

This instrument may not be changed orally.

𝕴𝖓 𝖂𝖎𝖙𝖓𝖊𝖘𝖘 𝖂𝖍𝖊𝖗𝖊𝖔𝖋, *the parties hereunto have set their hands and seals the day of in the year one thousand nine hundred and*

Sealed and delivered in the presence of

_____

_____

General Principles of Contract Law

agreements unaffected." What does this mean? When a contract is expressed in a writing which is intended to be the complete and final expression of the rights and duties of the parties, parol evidence of prior oral or written agreements of the parties or of contemporaneous oral agreements which varies or contradicts the written contract is not admissible. *Parol evidence* means evidence *not* contained in the particular written contract. Think about it for a minute. The purpose of the parol evidence rule is to have all the elements of the contract contained within one document. The rule is attempting to eliminate the possibility that there will be two parties presenting numerous agreements which contradict each other. The purpose of the parol evidence rule is to provide a means by which parties to contracts can secure certainty and finality in defining their rights and obligations, and exclude fraudulent claims.

Does the rule accomplish its purpose? Yes and no. It accomplishes its purpose in so far as prior and contemporaneous agreements are concerned, if the contract meets certain requirements. These requirements are: (1) there is a writing; (2) it has legal efficacy (effectiveness of the contract itself); (3) the writing must be an integration (the writing is adopted as incorporating within itself finally and completely all prior and contemporaneous plans, deliberations, negotiations and agreements); (4) and it is the intention of the parties that all terms of the agreement are included within the contract that were intended to be included. With these requirements met, no other prior oral or written agreements on the subject matter are admissible.

Here is an illustration of this principle. In fact, the reader might have had this unfortunate experience already. Peter Purchaser wants to buy a used car. He goes to Shakey Sam the Used Car Man. Peter informs Sam that he wants a 1970 Ford. Sam says, "I have just the car for you." In fact, Peter and Sam converse for the better part of an hour discussing white-wall tires, radio, air conditioning and other "so-called" extras for the car. The extras discussed are never reduced to writing. Peter and Sam

finally agree to the price. Sam asks Peter to step into the office where he produces a written contract. The essential element needed is Peter's signature on the contract and the car will belong to him. Peter is excited. All he can think about is the car and the drive-in movie that night with his favorite girl friend, Sally Sweetlips. Peter does not take the time to read the contract; he just signs it. Unfortunately, the contract that Peter signed with Shakey Sam is an agreement that requires Sam to transfer to Peter a 1970 Ford and nothing else. None of the extras are included in the contract that Peter believed would be included. On the bottom of the contract, above the signatures, is a clause which states ... "the parties agree that this agreement signed by them contains all prior written and oral agreements between the parties and it is the understanding of the parties that this agreement is intended to merge all prior agreements as to the sale of said automobile. The contract is deemed to be a total and complete integration of all the intentions of the parties ..."

Sam produces a 1970 Ford and says to Peter, "Here is the car. Where is my money?" Peter is shocked; he shouts "this is not what I wanted; where are the extras that we discussed and agreed upon?" Sam pulls out the contract which calls for transfer and delivery of a 1970 Ford and says, "We contracted for a 1970 Ford, nothing more, and this is what you get." Peter is out of luck under the parol evidence rule. However, under the UCC dealing with the sale of goods, he might be afforded a remedy. In a later chapter the rights and remedies of a purchaser of goods in a sales transaction will be discussed.

But what about subsequent agreements by the parties? Referring back to our sample contract between Smith and Jones, the clause "This instrument may not be changed orally" is contained within the contract. What effect does the rule have on the clause? In general, the parol evidence rule does not prevent proof of an oral or written agreement which varies or contradicts the terms of a prior written agreement. Just because parties enter into a contract does

8

not mean that they cannot get out of it if they desire to. Parties should be allowed to change prior contracts if they wish. So the rule fails in its purpose when dealing with subsequent agreements. Some states (e.g., California, Montana, and others) have enacted statutes to secure complete finality by providing that contracts can be changed only by another written contract or by a completely-performed oral agreement. So, in the above example, a subsequent written modification, signed by the parties to the original contract, would be admissible. Again, statutes of the particular locality must be consulted to determine if and when the rule is applicable.

The purpose of briefly discussing the parol evidence rule is so that the reader will be aware that an oral modification of prior contracts is very dangerous. If the parties desire to modify the contract, then it should be done in writing and should be signed. This subsequent writing is admissible and will effectuate a modification of the original contract terms.

In concluding discussion on the parol evidence rule, it is worth noting that there are situations which could be classified as exceptions to the rule; more accurately, they can be said to be outside the scope of the rule. For example, parol evidence is admissible to show that no contract was made or that the contract executed by the parties was voidable for fraud, mistake, duress, undue influence, incapacity, or illegality. Parol evidence also is admissible to show that the writing to which the parties assented was only a part of their complete contract. If it is established that this is true, a collateral oral agreement is provable and enforceable, even without additional consideration.

Ambiguity of expressions contained in the contract can be interpreted by the use of parol evidence. Parol evidence also is admissible to prove usage and custom, to define the meaning of words used in the writing and to add terms of performance in accordance with usages not inconsistent with the terms expressed in the writing.

This section by no means covers the parol evidence rule in depth. However, there are two important points that the reader should retain:

(1) A writing that is legally effective, integrated and intended as such by the parties will not be affected by prior oral or written agreements between the parties. That writing (contract) will be deemed complete on its face. So make sure that all the duties and obligations of the parties are contained in the contract.

(2) Subsequent oral agreements affecting the contract and its subject matter should be entered into only if the party knows that it is enforceable. If confronted with this problem, a person should consult an attorney since enforceability of the oral modification is governed by state statute. The safest approach is to have the subsequent agreement reduced to writing and signed by the parties.

Duress, Unconscionability, and Fraud

A contract induced by *duress* is either void or voidable, and therefore unenforceable. Duress basically consists of threats of bodily or other harm, or means which coerce the will of another, inducing him to do an involuntary act. Duress also can consist of illegal imprisonment or legal imprisonment used for an illegal purpose which induces a person to act against his will.

One must be exercising free will when a contract is entered into. The parties must be acting voluntarily. Duress is concerned with the state of mind of the party who is entering into the contract. Certain situations are not considered to be duress. For example, where a party enters into a contract on account of embarrassment, this emotion will not be deemed duress and the contract is valid. Moreover, a person entering into a contract because he feels that there is a moral obligation to do so is not under duress. One last point to remember is that agreements procured by duress may be ratified but not while the duress which induced the original transaction is still present. A species of duress—undue influence—is very similar and is another expression for the restraint of free will. Generally, in order to invalidate a contract, undue influence must operate to deprive a party of his free agency or will.

Unconscionability is an elusive concept. Conduct could be considered unconscionable if it appears that one party is at a considerable disadvantage in bargaining with another who takes advantage of his superior bargaining status. If a court deems that a contract is unconscionable, it will refuse to enforce the contract. In the absence of any mistake, fraud, or oppression, however, the courts are not interested in the impolicy, or injudiciousness, of contracts voluntarily entered into between the parties. Such parties have the right to insert any stipulations they wish to, provided that the contracts are not unconscionable, illegal or against public policy. Just because the bargain entered into appears onerous, it is not invalidated, if entered into voluntarily and fairly.

Unconscionability concerns itself with the fairness of the bargaining positions of the parties to the contract. For example, Mrs. Jones is on public assistance and receives $200.00 monthly from the government. She purchases a $1,000 refrigerator and freezer from Mr. Smith who owns a retail store. She puts $10.00 down and signs a retail installment agreement whereby her furniture is pledged as security for the loan. Mr. Smith knows that Mrs. Jones is on welfare and knows what is her monthly income. The retail installment agreement calls for $100.00 monthly payments and in the event of default (of payment), Mr. Smith may take all of her furniture. The court might find this agreement unconscionable and unenforceable due to the unfairness of the bargaining position of the parties. (Note: in New York, price alone can be deemed unconscionable in a retail installment agreement.)

The general theme which runs throughout contract law, is that there must be full and free consent between the parties to the contract. The law will generally not inquire into a contract to see if it is a wise and reasonable bargain. However, the courts will inquire into

whether fraud was present and material to the signing of the contract. Fraud is material where the contract would not have been made if the fraud had not been perpetrated.

Fraud means misrepresentation, concealment, or non-disclosure where there is no privilege to withhold information. If a material element of the contract is concealed, or misrepresented to a party when there is a duty to disclose, that party has been defrauded—the contract is voidable and unenforceable. The facts surrounding the contract are the determining factor to which the courts look. If the courts feel that a material element relating to the subject matter of the contract has been misrepresented, concealed or not disclosed when there was a duty to do so, the courts may deem this conduct to be fraudulent, in which instance the contract is unenforceable.

Impossibility of Performance

The general rule is that impossibility of performance is not a defense for one under a contractual duty. There have been a great many cases in which courts have inquired into the question of impossibility of performance and acted to resolve it. Impossibility of performance is generally divided into two areas: *original impossibility* and *supervening impossibility*. Original impossibility exists where the contract entered into was impossible to perform from the outset. Supervening impossibility develops sometime after the inception of the contract.

There are two other distinctions between the kinds of impossibility of performance—*subjective impossibility* and *objective impossibility*. Impossibility of performing a promise that is due wholly to the inability of the individual promisor is subjective. Subjective impossibility neither negates the validity of a contract nor discharges a duty created by the contract, and the party may be held liable under the contract. Objective impossibility is distinguished by the fact that the promise or performance contracted for cannot be done by anyone and is not due to the fact that only the promisor cannot do it.

Impossibility of performance, if it is to

10

release a party from his obligation to perform, must be real and not just an inconvenience. If a party is excused for the reason of impossibility of performance, it is imperative that the performance contracted for cannot be done by any means.

Generally, facts existing when a bargain is entered into or which occur subsequently and make the performance more difficult or expensive than originally anticipated by the parties, does not discharge the parties from their obligations to perform.

There are exceptions to the general rule and in such instances, impossibility of performance is a defense for non-performance of the contract. This transpires where the contract subject matter has been destroyed or ceases to exist through no fault of the performing party to the contract. Also, if the contract is for personal services, then death, illness, or incapacity of that essential person will constitute a defense for non-performance. Suppose a lawful contract was entered into, but subsequently has been deemed illegal, by statute or as against public policy. Future events prevent the intended purpose of the parties to the contract. The classic case dealing with this last exception is where X rents Y a room in her house. X and Y both believe that a parade will be along the road on which X's house is located. The room is rented so that Y can see the parade. That is the purpose of the rental agreement. However, the parade's route is altered and does not proceed on X's street. X wants the rental money and Y claims the accomplishment of the purpose became impossible. This is valid defense for Y's non-performance.

Temporary impossibility of performance may not excuse a party from performing; his performance might be delayed only temporarily. These are questions of fact to be evaluated by the courts.

Similar to the other sections of contract law which have been covered here in this chapter, impossibility of performance is investigated on a very elementary level without going into depth. The main purpose has been to familiarize the reader with these areas so that he may

understand more fully his contractual position. Impossibility of performance is a difficult concept of contract law, and as such, is based on interpretation of each individual set of facts. However, in conclusion, a couple of points might be worth noting:

(1) Upon entering into a contractual situation the parties should always ascertain that the performance for which the contract calls is possible at the time the contract is signed.

(2) There is nothing illegal with placing a "saving" clause in the contract. The "saving" clause is an added protection for the contracting party and simply states that if performance of the thing or act contracted for is rendered impossible due to some act, event, or other intervening factor not caused by the fault of the performing party, such party will be discharged of his duty to perform.

Statute of Frauds

The Statute of Frauds is operative in procedural law rather than in substantive law. A contract which fails to comply with the statute of frauds is not void, but merely unenforceable (in some states the contract is void).

The Statute of Frauds concerns itself with the requirement of a writing in certain contractual situations. Where a writing is required, absence of such writing violates the Statute of Frauds and the contract is unenforceable.

A list of major classes of cases covered by writing requirements (UCC excluded; some of these types of contracts will be covered later in the book) in New York State.

(1) Promise to answer for the debt, default, or miscarriage of another. (G.O.L. Sec. 5-701 (2)).

(2) Promise of an executor or adminis-

trator to answer for damages or debts owed by decedent out of his own pocket. (E.P.T.L. Sec. 13-2.1).

(3) An executory contract to establish a trust, make a will, or a testamentary disposition. (E.P.T.L. Sec. 13-2.1).

(4) A promise made in consideration of marriage except mutual promises to marry (mutual promises to marry are unenforceable in N.Y.). (G.O.L. Sec. 5-701 (3)).

(5) A contract to pay a commission or finder's fee for negotiation of a loan or of a sale of real estate, or of the sale of a business or business opportunity. (G.O.L. Sec. 5-701 (10)).

(Not applicable to auctioneers, lawyers, and licensed real estate brokers.)

(6) A contract to transfer an interest in real property, or an actual transfer. So also is a lease for more than one year. (G.O.L. 5-703).

(7) A contract which, by its terms, is not to be performed within one year from the making thereof. (G.O.L. Sec. 5-701 (1)).

(8) A contract which, by its terms, is not to be completed before the end of a lifetime. (G.O.L. Sec. 5-701 (1)).

Accord and Satisfaction

One last area of consideration that the reader should note is *accord* and *satisfaction*. At common law, an accord and satisfaction was a technical instrument. It was not until the 1800's that an executory accord, based on sufficient consideration came to be recognized as a valid contract. In operation, an accord and satisfaction replaces the obligation of the original contract with a new contractual obligation. The

accord and satisfaction becomes effective when there is:

(a) an accord (which is the new agreement the parties enter into);

(b) subject matter of the accord (generally the amount of money owed) and

(c) an obligee who accepts the tender by the obligor.

Upon satisfaction of the accord, the original contract is discharged and the obligor is no longer liable on either contract. This is not an easy concept. The reason for mentioning it is that accords and satisfactions are used everyday by people who do not realize that they are involved in such a transaction. An example might illustrate the point. **X** has a legitimate claim against **Y**. **Y** agrees to pay **X** $1,000 and **X** agrees that when he receives the money, he will accept it in satisfaction of his legitimate claim. The agreement is in writing, signed by the parties. **Y** gives the $1,000 to **X** and **X** accepts the money. In New York State this is an accord and satisfaction. As stated in the foreword of the book, many of the rules of contract that are discussed in the book might be unique to New York. The reader should always consult the laws of his locality to determine if the rules are similar.

Upon breach by the party who promises to pay or render performance, the promisee has two options. The promisee may elect to enforce the accord, or sue on the original obligation. The written accord only suspends, it does not discharge the original claim. As an example of accord and satisfaction in daily affairs, consider this situation (which does occur frequently): there is an unliquidated amount owed to one party. The debtor sends a check to the creditor, marking on the check "payment in full." If the creditor cashes the check, an implied accord and satisfaction occurs, and the creditor is *estopped* from asserting that his claim is not discharged. So, one should be wary, if a check is received on a debt in which the amount is still in dispute, and if the debtor has added the notation "payment in full" on his check. The check should not be cashed before consulting an attorney.

Conclusion

Other aspects of contract law, such as breach of contract, remedies, and discharge of the contract will be discussed in later chapters.

Hopefully, the reader has gained an understanding of basic contract law from this introduction. An attempt should be made to apply these concepts while reading the book. Through application of any principles discussed, the reader may better understand his position when he enters into a contract. Hopefully, the reader will not find himself in a situation as unfortunate as that of Dr. Faustus.

CHAPTER 2

Leases . . . The Renter's Predicament

Introduction

Of all legal agreements, the one that is perhaps most steeped in history is the lease. Although in essence a contract for personal property, its roots are so intertwined with real property law that a lease possesses problems peculiar unto itself which cannot be cured solely by contract law remedies. For this reason, a prospective lessee should be most cautious when signing a lease, scrutinizing every paragraph for clauses which later could result in unanticipated hardships. This is not to say that recognition of an unfavorable sentence and a curt request to the landlord to erase the undesired language will be your panacea. In most urban areas, apartment letting is a seller's market and little can be done to secure the upper hand on the landlord. If you will not sign, another lessee awaits in the hall, ready to accept the landlord's terms.

However, all is not lost. Ideally, you wish to keep disagreeable clauses out of the lease entirely, and your awareness of possible problems is to your advantage. Depending upon the city or state in which you reside, you may not need to resort to the courts for relief. State or municipal agencies will often assist an apparently tortured tenant. In many instances, tenant unions have been formed by irate lessees to better promote their bargaining position in disputes. If all else fails, one can always turn to the judicial system, but legal relief can prove to be both time-consuming and expensive. A wary, alert and informed lessee can sidestep many of the common lease pitfalls without resorting to outside assistance.

To put the situation in proper perspective, a cursory comprehension of landlord-tenant law, its common-law origins and its current statutory status, is helpful. At its incipience, the concept of a leasehold was both contractual and personal. By creating convenants the landlord and tenant agreed to the performance or non performance of certain acts, the most obvious examples being the tenant's promise to pay a predetermined rent for which the landlord pledges not to oust the tenant from the leased property. As law progressed, the tenant's rights became more extensive until his defensible rights stemmed not just from the covenants, but from the possession of the land. Thus if the landlord sold the property to a third person or if an outsider forced the lessee from the leasehold, the tenant could maintain an action to recover possession against the third person, since his lease had developed into an estate, albeit a non-freehold estate.

It was this recognition by the law of a lease as an estate in land and not a contract in personalty that was the foundation of modern landlord-tenant law. The tenant now obtains an estate in the leasehold for a specified term; a position just short of actual ownership. For the length of the term the tenant has absolute control over the property—control so absolute, in fact, that it is good even against the landlord.

If this be the case, however, then why is the present-day tenant at such a disadvantage? The answer lies in simple supply and demand. Because of the serious shortage of adequate housing in most metropolitan areas, lessees are willing to subscribe to a lease with covenants granting the landlord the ultimate upperhand.

In this sense, contract law does prevail, and a tenant, suddenly oppressed with a typical letting disaster, will find that he has unwittingly signed away his rights, under the lease. Although the time may not be too late to secure a final resolution in his favor, prevention at the outset could prove to be the saving grace in time, money and aggravation.

One covenant which any prospective tenant must sign is the one stating the rent which he must pay in order to have the possession of the property pass to him. The covenant to pay rent is usually the thorn in the tenant's side when a dispute arises. The reason for this is that the rent payment is not conditioned upon performance by the landlord under any of the other lease provisions. In most states, as long as the landlord has delivered the leasehold and thereafter does not commit any act of absolute or constructive eviction, the tenant is compelled to pay rent to the landlord as it accrues. The tenant, in other words, cannot rescind the lease once he commits himself to a term, whatever the period of time might be.

Because the covenant to pay rent is independent in its own right, the landlord enjoys the privilege of collecting rent from a vacated tenant without bearing any responsibility to mitigate damages by seeking a replacement tenant. In fact, unless the lease specifically provides to the contrary, the landlord need not accept a third party offered by the original tenant, regardless of the reasonableness of the request. The tenant has contracted to pay a predetermined amount of rent for possession of the leased premises and pay it he must.

Tenancies

Although the typical apartment lease runs for a set term as agreed to by the parties, there are basically four types of less-than-freehold estates. Since each type of tenancy carries with it its own legal quirks, it would be prudent to recognize the one under which you, as tenant, possess the land.

Signing a lease for two months, two years, or for any specified period of time, creat-

ed an estate for years, an historical misnomer which might be better described as a *term tenancy*. This leasehold can come into existence only through an agreement between the landlord and tenant; an agreement which in most states must be reduced to writing if the term exceeds a year in length. At common law the major distinction between term tenancies of different lengths was the duration of the period in which a vacating tenant or landlord had to inform the other of the termination of the lease. Statutory law in most states now dictates that notice must be given which is equal to the period of the lease, except for leases for one year or more. Thus, in the case of a month-to-month tenancy, one party had to notify the other at least one month prior to his termination. Obviously such a requirement would place an undue burden upon parties to lengthier leases, so statutory law permits six months notice for termination of a year-to-year lease.

In some cases the parties to a lease agree to the rental, but do not establish a specific duration. The arrangement is known as a *periodic tenancy* which continues automatically from period to period until one party notifies the other within the prescribed time. That time is measured usually by the length of time covered in each rent payment. The major distinctions between a periodic tenancy and the third type of tenancy, a *tenancy at will*, is that in the latter the landlord and tenant must specifically agree to its creation and either can terminate at will. Otherwise, without expressed understanding, the payment of rent on any orderly, measurable period of time will lead to a periodic tenancy as an operation of law.

The fourth type is *tenancy at sufferance*. This situation occurs when a tenant who was originally in lawful possession of the premises under a prior lease does not vacate the leasehold at the end of the term. The landlord now has an option. If he wishes to continue letting the premises to the tenant and the tenant presents him with the rent payment, he can accept the offer and in effect reestablish the original lease. Thus, a tenant must be cautious not to unknowingly commit himself to another year term by holding over one month on the previous one year lease and paying one month's rent. In such a situation, all provisions of the earlier lease are carried over and both parties become bound. One usual exception to this holdover rule applies to a seasonal lease where the landlord has no election to establish a period tenancy because the tenant holds over. The landlord, however, need not accept the rent and can consider the tenancy terminated. Still, to remove the holdover tenant, in most states, the landlord must inform the tenant of his intentions. Remember, however, that the landlord does not have this option where he expressly permits you to remain on the property, or for some other unforeseeable reason, you are unable to leave. Although you are still liable for rent prorated to the length of hold-over period, you are not binding yourself to another lease unless otherwise agreed to.

Covenants

A tenant might often hear the phrase, "covenants which run with the land." Covenants are the basic duties and obligations of the parties to the lease. Since they arise from the execution of the lease and actually delimit the scope of the landlord-tenant relationship, they become as much a part of the land as the landscaping. Should either party decide to pass his rights on, the subsequent taker is as readily bound by the terms of the lease as were the original parties. Because most leases now include "the parties, their heirs, executors, administrators, successors and *assigns*" for practical purposes all covenants "run with the land".

Covenants are the contractual elements of the lease, and as such, can be both expressed within the provisions of the lease or implied as a matter of law. In either case, the parties or their assignees or grantees are bound to honor them in order not to become liable for breach of a covenant. Unlike contract law, however, breach of a covenant does not necessarily allow repudiation of the lease by the wronged party.

For example, if a landlord merely disturbs the tenant in his enjoyment of the lease-hold, without evicting him, the tenant cannot

treat the disturbance as grounds for rescinding the lease. Instead, he is limited to a nuisance action against the landlord in tort law. In fact, if the nuisance originates from a third source, without landlord interference, then the landlord is not liable under any law. Even though the tenant might be driven from the leasehold, his only recourse is against the third party creating the problem.

Since the covenants are the bearers of danger, it might be wise to familiarize yourself with landlord duties implied by law or firmly expressed in statute. A later comparison between a landlord's duties imposed by law and his obligations as they appear in his choicely worded lease will alert you to your rights— before you sign them away.

Covenant of Quiet Enjoyment

"The landlord hereby covenants that the tenant, upon payment of the rent and upon performance of all the covenants and conditions herein contained, shall and may peaceably and quietly have, hold and enjoy the demised premises." It is readily apparent that no tenant wishes to be disturbed in the enjoyment of his leasehold. The law recognized early that a landlord should not be in a position to be able to effect the agreement through acts intending to interfere with the tenancy. To safeguard the tenants' rights, the law therefore implies in each lease a covenant of quiet enjoyment.

In reality, the covenant is broader in scope than it may first appear to be, for not only does it protect the tenant against wrongful acts of his immediate landlord, it also extends to any successors to the landlord's interests. The landlord breaches the covenant at the outset if, in fact, he does not possess good and full title. If later, a third party appears and claims superior title, the landlord has violated his covenant to the tenant.

To invoke a cause of action for breach of the covenant of quiet enjoyment, the tenant must be forced to quit the premises. A nuisance so minor that it does not force the tenant from the leasehold may breach an expressed agreement between the parties leading to *tort* damages, but it does not give rise to an action under the implied covenant.

So, what are the tenant's remedies? The extent of the tenant's recourse against the landlord is usually contingent upon the degree of eviction. Generally the tenant may react as follows:

(a) Upon actual eviction. This action is an unequivocal invasion of the tenant's right to possession. In his defense the tenant may either treat the lease as terminated, thereby ending his duty to pay rent or, at his option, commence an action to regain possession.

(b) Upon partial actual eviction. This situation occurs when a third party, with superior title, forces the tenant from only a portion of the premises. For all practical purposes, the tenant's position is left unchanged, if the party asserting superior title wishes to continue leasing the disputed portion. Rent simply is apportioned between the holders of title. If the tenant is permanently deprived of part of the leasehold he still is liable for rent, but at a reduced amount, to compensate him for his loss.

(c) Upon constructive eviction. Sometimes, the landlord's actions which lead to eviction are negative, rather than affirmative. For example, his failure to supply heat or water to an apartment, thereby rendering the premise uninhabitable, will breach the covenant of quiet enjoyment. If after notification of substantial interference, the landlord does not act, the tenant can abandon the premises and terminate his obligations.

(d) Upon partial constructive eviction. Again, if the landlord has failed to perform his duties, but only as to a portion of the leasehold, the tenant can adjust his rent accordingly, if he has abandoned the unfit portion.

As for damages from a breach of the covenant, the tenant can request and recover all damages he incurs as a result of the eviction. This sum is inclusive of the value of the remaining, unexpired term. If the landlord's intentional act or failure of title occurs at the outset and prevents the tenant from taking his rightful possession, then damages include the full value of the leasehold as well as any expenses shouldered by the tenant in order to assume possession.

Sometimes the covenant of quiet enjoyment is an expressed provision of the lease. Although this would appear to strengthen the tenant's rights if the clause does not cover all ramifications of the implied covenant, the landlord can be absolved from certain wrongful acts. In particular, if the provision makes no mention of landlord's warranty of good title, the tenant would be precluded from obtaining relief where a third party ousts him because of superior title.

Expressed Covenants to Repair

Although the law imposes certain duties to repair on the landlord in the absence of a clause in the lease, normally all leases of premises will expressly delegate duties between the parties. The most common phrasing requires the tenant to make all repairs necessary to keep the leasehold tenantable and return it to the landlord in as good condition as received.

The tenant should be alert not to sign a lease which requires a greater duty. Some covenants state that the tenant will maintain the premises in good repair which could be construed as a duty on the tenant to put the premises in good repair if it is not already. This extra burden could prove costly and should be avoided.

By consenting to make tenantable repairs, what must the tenant do? Tenantable repairs is a phrase originating at common law. In the absence of an expressed covenant, the

17

tenant must make all reasonable repairs which will leave the property in the same condition as when he took possession. At no time is he liable for major repairs to the structure. Neither is he liable for normal wear and tear and in some states, such as New York, a tenant may terminate a lease if the premises become untenantable through ordinary wear and tear.

If the tenant does not agree expressly to tenantable repairs, but only to keep premises in repair (remember not *good* repair), then he becomes liable for major repairs and reconstruction. Many states, however, have legislated against this unfair result by both relieving the tenant of the obligation and permitting him to move out. Otherwise, under an expressed covenant to repair, the tenant is liable for all repairs, including reconstruction, regardless of their cause.

If the landlord expressly covenants to make repairs, then he is in breach if he fails to repair, after having knowledge of the defect. The tenant has a duty to notify the landlord. Thereafter, the tenant can proceed with all minor repairs and in some states deduct the cost from the rent; in some states he can demand recompense. If the extent of the repairs needed are major, the tenant has an option to either bear the immediate cost and sue for reimbursement or sue for damages based on the reduced value of the premises.

In the absence of an expressed landlord covenant to repair, the law imposes a duty upon the landlord for all leases covering multi-dwelling apartments, lofts and buildings. The landlord in this instance must keep all common areas, such as stairs, elevators and halls, in good repair.

Covenant to Pay Rent

In return for giving up possession of his land, the landlord collects rent from the lessee. Rent is the tenant's payment for use of the leasehold and does not arise from the promise to pay, but rather from the possession of the land.

Why then, do leases contain rent provisions, if the tenant is bound to make payment without it. By expressly committing himself, the tenant covenants to continue to pay rent for the entire length of the term at an agreed price. What was without the lease, privity of estate now becomes *priority of contract*, and the tenant can no longer pack up, move on and not be liable for rent that accrues for the remainder of the term.

However, the tenant also benefits. Although he cannot terminate the lease at will, he need not fear capricious actions by the landlord. Not only is the term fixed so that the length of the tenancy is assured, but the amount of rent is set and the landlord cannot whimsically increase it during the term.

Covenants on Personal Liability

Becoming legally trapped by a clause requiring you to bear the cost of repairs to the leasehold is certainly aggravating. But with today's jury awards in personal liability suits, nothing could be as odious or as financially onerous to the tenant as a clause relieving the landlord of all liability and casting it upon the tenant.

As a general rule, the tenant, as holder of the premises, is liable to third parties who are injured while rightfully on the premises. The distinguishing factor revolves upon the nature of the defect. If the defect is patent, one which the tenant could observe upon reasonable inspection of the premises, then the landlord is relieved of any obligation should injury result. On the other hand, the law does not hold the tenant liable for injury arising from defects which he could not readily observe and of which the landlord does not inform him. The landlord never warrants that the premises are free of latent defects and thus incurs no liability through privity of contract. His duty is fully discharged simply by informing the tenant of those defects of which he has knowledge. Still, should the landlord knowingly or negligently conceal a dangerous condition, he is liable in either fraud or negligence to the tenant and for injuries or damages which proximately

18

result.

The rental of a fully furnished residential premise imposes a greater duty upon the landlord. Although his liability continues for a willful or negligent failure to notify the tenant, he also is liable for patent as well as hidden dangers. In such a situation the law imposes an implied warranty by the landlord that the premises are in good repair. If the premises are not as implied, the landlord breaches the warranty and is liable for injury as a result.

In addition to the above instances where the landlord is liable for breach of warranty, certain circumstances permit the tenant to sue the landlord directly. If the landlord, after being notified of a dangerous condition by the tenant, endeavors to repair, he obligates himself to correct the condition, with reasonable care. Failure to meet this duty results in liability for any proximately-caused damage. Common areas in multiple dwellings can also lead to liability. Since the common areas, such as halls and passageways are not part of the demised premises, the landlord retains possession and incurs liability if injury results.

One other liability exception which exists in some states places the onus on a landlord who leases for a short term a building which he knows will be used by the public. If he is aware of a dangerous condition or if it can be shown that he should have known of its existence, any member of the public who is injured as a result can hold the landlord liable. Thus a tenant who is in the practice of leasing out halls or arenas for public showings is sheltered from personal liability for injuries caused by defective conditions in the building.

Additional Covenants

Parties to a lease can limit and restrict the leasehold as they see fit. Covenants, enforceable as contract rights, can be drawn to meet the particular needs of the situation. For example, in apartment leases, covenants forbidding assignment of the lease or subletting are common. Many leases also describe the use to which the premises can be put. Whatever the case, the tenant should be aware that any right which he might have as a matter of law can be extinguished by a pro-landlord lease.

Hopefully, the reader now possesses comprehension of basic lease law. Still, the purpose is not to make anyone skilled in legal theory, but to offer practical knowledge sufficient to alert the reader to possible legal entanglements. To this end, let us dissect specific lease provisions, so as to pinpoint those that should be avoided.

Typical Lease Provisions

Now that we have covered the basic knowledge concerning what is a lease and how it works, it is time to sift through the provisions of a typical lease and examine those clauses or phrases which can curtail tenants' rights and increase liabilities. Several types of leases are presented. The purpose in presenting these particular types is to acquaint the reader with the standard forms which the landlord might push across the table with a pen. Basically, the leases contain the same or nearly similar provisions, so that it is not necessary to discuss them all in detail.

As with most legal documents, the parties involved are identified in the initial provision. Few legal complications arise from this provision. However, some of the identification provisions are quite extensive. These provisions may limit the purpose for which the leasehold can be used and the number of occupants allowed to reside in it. The problems are few as long as the lessee does not bind himself to reside in a leasehold in which he initially had intended to operate some kind of enterprise—for example, a laundromat. In other words, the intended use of the premises should be stated clearly. The tenant should also be certain that the length of the tenancy and the terms of payment of the rent meet his satisfaction. Once the parties are named, the following 14 explanations cover the likely covenants which will confront the prospective tenant.

(1)   Rent is a foregone conclusion. By

holding the leasehold, the tenant has an obligation to pay rent. One advantage of the lease, as has been mentioned, is that the terms and amount of rent have been already determined. Lease forms contain the clause: "rent and any "additional rent" ... as the Landlord may designate from time to time hereafter." Regardless of the prospective tenant's bargaining position, he should demand that this clause be eliminated. When the tenant agrees to this clause, the landlord enjoys the freedom of hiking up the rent almost at whim. The tenant has lost his advantage in having the rent expressed definitively in the lease. The tenant must be cautious not to bind himself to a future occurrence which may be to his disfavor.

(2) All leases require that the tenant "take good care of the premises and fixtures." This clause can be distinguished from a covenant to maintain the premises in good repair, which places a greater burden on the tenant. Under this clause, the tenant agrees only to maintain the premises in its current condition. Generally, the provision continues by holding the tenant responsible for the cost of repairs resulting from the tenant's misuse or neglect. Such a contingency seems equitable, but the tenant should read inquisitively and ascertain that he has not committed himself to repairs other than those needed as a result of his own fault. Unless he (or a party through him) is at fault, the tenant's promise to repair should be limited to those of keeping the premises tenantable.

(3) In the chapter on realty, an explanation of *appurtenances* and *personalty* is presented. Most leases make reference to appurtenances, fixtures and personalty. The legal distinction is irrelevant. However, the tenant should note that most leases contain a clause which gives the landlord title to any improvements which the tenant makes to the premises. "All alterations or improvements made by the tenant shall be made only with the prior written consent of the landlord and at the sole expense of the tenant and shall become the property of the landlord and be surrendered with the apartment at the end of the term." What does this mean? First, the tenant must petition for approval; secondly, if granted, his improvement becomes the landlord's property. Thus, if the tenant affixes or builds anything, such as security door locks, bedloft, curtain rods, shelving, etc., he forsakes title in them in favor of the landlord.

(4) It was mentioned above that the tenant should never agree to future provisions, such as rent increases. Although most rules and regulations which landlords adopt are inconsequential, seldom obeyed, and never enforced, the landlord does have grounds for ejecting a tenant who does not comply with them—if the tenant is on notice of the restrictions at the outset and agrees to each specifically. Problems arise where the tenant also agrees to obey "such further reasonable Rules and Regulations as the Landlord may from time to time make or adopt ...". The tenant's duty may be limited to following *"reasonable* rules and regulations". However, the tenant should be aware that these provisions can be used as leverage to evict the tenant. If the landlord wishes to remove the tenant, a newly-adopted rule or regulation, whether meritorious or

20

whimsical, may create a violation and leave the tenant on the street.

(5) Inevitably, the landlord will attempt to hold the tenant liable for rent in the event of partial or total destruction of the premises. Before the enactment of statutes to the contrary, the landlord would only be reiterating the common law rule concerning premises by stating in the lease that "if the building shall be damaged by fire or other cause without the fault or neglect of the tenant, . . . the damages shall be repaired as soon as reasonably convenient by and at the expense of the landlord, and no claim for compensation shall be made by reason of inconvenience or annoyance arising from the necessity of repairing any portion of the building." However, the renting of an apartment bears different consequences. The distinction turns on whether or not the subject matter of the leasehold includes an apartment, loft, or a building and the land on which it sits. In the latter instance, the destruction of the building does not terminate the leasehold or the tenant's obligation to pay rent. Many states, such as New York, have enacted statutes to remedy this apparently inequitable result. Thus, if the premises become untenantable due to an act of nature, the tenancy is ended upon the tenant's surrender. The landlord can preclude this right of the tenant by a provision in the lease which supercedes the statute.

If the tenant has no interest whatsoever in the land, as is the case with a strict apartment lease, the law changes and terminates the lease upon total destruction of the premises rented. However in many cases, this law is circumvented by a clause to the contrary. Thus, if the lease states "if the building shall be damaged by fire or other cause without the fault or neglect of the Tenant, . . . the damages shall be repaired as soon as reasonably convenient by and at the expense of the landlord, and no claim for compensation shall be made by reason of inconvenience or annoyance . . .", then the tenant finds the lease still in effect; but during the time the building is untenantable, the rent is abated. The tenant must find suitable and temporary housing until the original leasehold is repaired, at which time, the rent obligation commences anew. Of course, the landlord agrees to repair "as soon as reasonably convenient,"; but the tenant should realize that complications could arise from such a nebulous provision.

(6) Whenever possible, people attempt to disclaim all liability, and a landlord is no different. Most disclaimer provisions refer to both personal and property damages and to all sources of possible injury (e.g., steam, electricity, gas, water, rain, ice or snow) and generally (". . . or arising from any other cause or happening whatsoever . . ."). The actual liability of the landlord has been discussed previously. The prospective tenant should understand that many leases exceed reasonable limits of disclaimers. Although some landlords accept liability resulting from personal injury or property damage caused by their own or their agent's negligence, others attempt to have the tenant indemnify them for all claims arising from the leasehold. Clauses such as "the Landlord shall not be liable for *any injury* to person or loss or damage to property . . ." are common. The important point for the tenant to

21

realize, however, is that these all-inclusive provisions are not tenable, if taken to court. Unfortunately, this method of dealing with the problem can become expensive, so that complete avoidance of these provisions is recommended.

(7) After a hard day's work, the tenant returns home only to find the landlord in the apartment. The landlord is using the tenant's apartment as a model in order to rent a similar unit to a prospective lessee. Outraged at the invasion, the tenant demands that the parties leave only to be reminded of his lease which states that "the Landlord shall be permitted to enter the apartment during reasonable hours to make such repairs . . . and to inspect or exhibit the apartment to prospective lessees or purchasers of the building. . . . If the Tenant shall not be personally present to open and permit an entry into the apartment, at any time, when for any reason an entry shall be in the judgment of the Landlord or the Landlord's agent necessary or permissible hereunder, the Landlord or the Landlord's agents may enter same by pass key or may forcibly enter the same without incurring any liability or responsibility . . ." As with the landlord's disclaimer of liability, this sweeping grant of authority to enter the apartment will normally be frowned upon by the courts. Some states, such as New York, charge the landlord with triple damages for forcible entry. However, the force must be unusual or violent and not merely the breaking of the lock. Without this provision, of course, the landlord would have no right, except in emergency situations, to invade the leasehold. His invasion would be tantamount to

trespass. The tenant should know that intrusions such as the one described are not breaches of the covenant of quiet enjoyment and therefore, do not constitute eviction, constructive or actual. If the lease has been executed and the landlord exploits this provision, remember that his rights under the clause are limited. He must act reasonably and cannot use the provision as a weapon to harrass the tenant.

(8) Several references are made to tenant's failure under the lease and the landlord's rights to terminate the leasehold and reenter the premises with or without notice. The legal entanglements that could ensue in the event that the tenant does breach the lease are manifold, complicated and beyond the scope of this book. In almost all of these situations, state or municipal laws define what procedure the landlord must follow in order to regain possession. He cannot restrict that procedure by having the tenant waive his rights. For example, in New York City, the law requires that unless the tenant fails to pay rent, the landlord must give the tenant a three-day demand notice. Until he does so, the tenant legally can have the action dismissed in court. Thereafter, a formal dispossess proceeding must be instituted which conforms to all rules and laws of procedure. The tenant must be served with all appropriate papers notifying him of the proceeding. In any event, where legal action has been commenced by the landlord, the tenant should not feel bound by the terms of the lease. The tenant has rights. An attorney should be consulted who can inform him of these rights and advocate his position.

22

(9) The tenant should always be careful not to contract to pay any of the fees of the landlord's attorney under any condition. What legal costs the landlord incurs are his financial burden and should not be assumed by the tenant. For this reason, be wary and request deletion of any clause which reads that ". . . in such event, the sum or sums so paid by the Landlord together with all interests, costs, damages, and reasonable attorney's fees shall be considered additional rent . . ." One further note—usually, additional financial obligations which might arise from covenants in a lease are labeled as "additional rent." If the tenant recalls the explanation of the independence of the covenant for rent, the reason becomes clear. If the tenant must agree to bear the landlord's financial liability, he should do so separately from his duty to pay rent.

(10) Most consumers would not buy an article without examining it, and the same holds true for letting an apartment. The tenant should always inspect the premises, note defects and make arrangements with the landlord to cure those defects. The problem is that the lease contains a provision, agreed to between the parties: "No representation or promises with respect to the apartment have been made by the Landlord . . . The assumption of the occupancy by the Tenant shall be conclusive evidence that the apartment and the building of which it is part were in good and satisfactory condition at such time." The answer to the problem is simply to include in the lease all agreements to repair or cure defects in the apartment. In this manner, the landlord will later be unable to deny his promises.

(11) "In the event the apartment is not ready for occupancy at the set time herein for commencement of the term . . ., this lease shall remain in full force and effect . . .; the Landlord shall not be liable for the failure to give possession on said date . . . As mentioned earlier, all leases contain an implied covenant to give possession at the time set for the beginning of the term. Once the tenant is unable to take possession, regardless of the cause, he is no longer bound, by the lease and can sue the landlord for breach of the covenant. By the clause above, the tenant waives this implied covenant and continues to be obligated by the terms of the lease even though occupancy is delayed.

(12) One clause to which serious consideration should be given is a renewal option at the same rental value for whatever term is agreeable to the parties. If the lease already contains a renewal clause, the tenant should consider whether he is agreeable to the terms it sets out before signing the lease. If no renewal provision exists, he should discuss with landlord the possibility of including one.

(13) Most leases contain hidden clauses against *subletting* and *assignments.* An assignment is an extension of the original lease which transfers the entirety of the tenant's interest in all or part of the premises; a sublease is a new landlord-tenant relationship carved out of part of the term of the original leasehold. In either instance, the original tenant remains liable to the landlord for all covenants agreed to in the lease.

23

The assignor-tenant is relieved, however, from liability for breach of implied covenants after the assignment. The assignee (new tenant) becomes obligated to the original landlord under all covenants in the lease, whereas the subleasee is only responsible to his landlord, the original tenant, for covenants contained in the sublease. The sample sublease form presented here incorporates all of the covenants of the original lease; room is left for amendments. Parties to either should realize that form prevails over label and, so what is in fact an assignment, cannot be made a sublease simply by naming it such. Where no restrictions exist, the tenant can either assign or sublet as he pleases. However, where he is forbidden to do either, his sublet or assignment is voidable by the landlord. Whether the landlord can re-enter and terminate the leasehold if the tenant breaches a covenant against either act, is contingent upon reservation of the right in the lease. Otherwise, the landlord is limited to suing for damages for breach of the covenant. If the tenant anticipates executing either an assignment or sublease, he should be cautious not to agree to a prohibition of such in the lease. Additionally, he should know that a restriction on subletting does not prohibit assigning and vice versa.

(14) Most leases require the tenant to secure his promise to perform according to the covenants of the lease by depositing money with the landlord. This provision is a valid demand on the landlord's part and can be for any sum which the parties concur: Many states place restrictions on the landlord's use of the money. In New York, for example, statutory law states that such money advanced as a security deposit on a contract for the lease of real property must be placed in an interest-bearing account, with the depositor or tenant retaining full possession to the money. The landlord becomes trustee of the account which cannot be commingled with his personal assets. For the tenant's concern, he should remember that the security deposit may be retained by the landlord only to the extent of the damages—the remainder must be returned. In other words, if the deposit was $300.00 and damage to the leasehold sustained by the landlord totals $100.00, the landlord could not claim that he was entitled to the entire sum because the tenant breached the lease.

Sample Leases

The remaining leases are typical ones for the renting of leaseholds other than apartments. Since all contain, with only minor variations, the same clauses and provisions which have been outlined, there is no purpose in reiterating those explanations. Each lease, however, is peculiar unto itself at times. For example, a furnished apartment lease covers not only the space but the personalty inside. In effect, the tenant is renting every chair, lamp and utensil with the apartment. Thus, he might be wise to be more cautious and take an inventory describing the condition of valuable items, so that he is not later charged with their damage. Whatever the lease, however, where confusion prevails beforehand or disputes flare up after the signing, the tenant should consult an attorney for advice on handling the matter confronting him.

"Superior" Lease of Apartment

This Lease *made the*   *day of*   *19*
BETWEEN

hereinafter referred to as the Landlord, and

hereinafter referred to as the Tenant

Witnesseth: *That the Landlord hereby leases to the Tenant and the Tenant hereby hires from the Landlord, the apartment known as Apartment   on the   floor in the building known as*

for the term of
commencing the   day of   19   and ending the   day of 19. , unless sooner terminated as hereinafter provided, at the annual rent of $

payable in equal monthly instalments in advance on the   day of each month during said term.

The parties hereto, for themselves, their heirs, executors, administrators, legal representatives, successors and assigns, hereby covenant as follows:

FIRST. The Tenant shall pay the rent as stipulated above.

SECOND. The demised premises shall be used and occupied by the Tenant and the members of the immediate family of the Tenant only, as a strictly private dwelling apartment and for no other purpose.

THIRD. The Tenant and the Tenant's heirs, executors, administrators, legal representatives, successors and assigns, shall not assign, mortgage, pledge or encumber this lease, nor sublet, or use or permit others to use the apartment or any part thereof without first obtaining the prior written consent of the Landlord in each case. Such consent may be granted upon such terms or conditions as the Landlord may impose and shall in no way operate to waive this covenant as to subsequent assignees or to dispense with the necessity for specific prior consent to each and any assignment.

FOURTH. This lease is and shall be subject and subordinate to the lien of any mortgage or mortgages which may now or hereafter affect the real property of which the demised premises are a part and to all renewals and extensions thereof. The Tenant shall on demand execute any instrument the Landlord may request in confirmation of such subordination and the Landlord is hereby authorized as the attorney in fact of the Tenant to execute any such instrument for and on behalf of the Tenant.

FIFTH. If the building or any part thereof shall be condemned for any public use or purpose, this lease shall terminate from the date when the possession of the part so taken shall be required for such purpose, and the Tenant shall not be entitled to any part of the award; however, the rent shall be apportioned accordingly.

SIXTH. The Tenant shall take good care of the apartment and fixtures therein and shall at the Tenant's own cost and expense make, when needed, all repairs and decorations therein and thereto, whenever damage or injury to the same shall have resulted from misuse or neglect by the Tenant, Tenant's family, servants, employees, agents, visitors or licensees. The Tenant shall not drill into, drive nails, or deface in any manner any part of the building or permit the same to be done. All alterations or improvements made by the Tenant shall be made only with the prior written consent of the Landlord and at the sole expense of the Tenant and shall become the property of the Landlord and be surrendered with the apartment at the end of the term.

SEVENTH. The Tenant has read the Rules and Regulations hereto sub-joined and made a part hereof, and hereby agrees to abide by and conform to the same and to such further reasonable Rules and Regulations as the Landlord may from time to time make or adopt for the care, protection and government of the building, and the general comfort and welfare of its occupants. The Landlord shall not be liable to the Tenant for the violation of any of said Rules and Regulations, or the breach of any covenants in any lease by any other tenant in the building.

EIGHTH. The Tenant shall promptly comply with any and all laws, ordinances, orders and regulations of any and all municipal, county, state and federal authorities, boards, commissions and other governmental agencies with respect to the demised premises or the use or occupation thereof; and shall not do or permit to be done, any act or thing upon said premises which might subject the Landlord to any liability or responsibility for injury to any person or persons or to any property by reason of any business or operation being conducted on said premises.

NINTH. The Tenant shall comply with all rules, regulations, orders or requirements of the New York Board of Fire Underwriters or any other similar body and shall not do or permit anything to be done in or upon the demised premises which shall increase the rate of fire insurance on the building of which the said premises form a part or on the property located therein. If by reason of the use of the premises by the Tenant the rates of insurance against loss by fire are increased, the Tenant agrees to pay as additional rent any excess premiums caused thereby, such additional rent to become due immediately upon effecting the insurance by the Landlord and payable with the next succeeding instalment of rent.

TENTH. If the building shall be damaged by fire or other cause without the fault or neglect of the Tenant, Tenant's family, servants, employees, agents, visitors or licensees, the damages shall be repaired as soon as reasonably convenient by and at the expense of the Landlord, and no claim for compensation shall be made by reason of inconvenience or annoyance arising from the necessity of repairing any portion of the building. But if the building be so damaged that the Landlord shall decide not to rebuild the same, or if the building be so damaged that the Landlord shall decide to demolish or rebuild it, then or in any of such events the Landlord may at the Landlord's option, give the Tenant a notice in writing of such decision, and the terms of this lease shall expire upon the third day after such notice is given and the Tenant shall vacate and surrender the apartment to the Landlord.

25

Leases . . . The Renter's Predicament

ELEVENTH. The Landlord shall not be liable for any injury or damage to persons or property caused by or resulting from steam, electricity, gas, water, rain, ice or snow, falling plaster, or any latent defect in the building, or from any injury or damage resulting or arising from any other cause or happening whatsoever, unless such injury or damage be caused by or be due to the negligence of the Landlord or the Landlord's agents, servants or employees; nor shall the Landlord or Landlord's agents be liable for any such damage caused by other tenants or persons in said building. The Landlord shall not be liable for loss of property by theft or otherwise. Should any windows of the demised premises become closed or darkened for any reason, the Landlord shall not be liable for any damage that the Tenant may sustain thereby, and the Tenant shall not be entitled to any compensation or abatement of rent or release from any of the obligations of this lease caused by such closing or darkening. The presence of bugs, vermin or insects, if any, shall not constitute a constructive eviction. If the Landlord shall furnish for the use of the Tenant any storeroom, laundry or any other facility in the building the same shall be furnished gratuitously and the Landlord shall not be liable for any injury to person or loss or damage to property occasioned during the use of same, whether due to the negligence of the Landlord or otherwise. The Tenant shall indemnify and save harmless the Landlord for and against any liability, or any injury to persons or property, resulting from the following acts or omissions on the part of the Tenant, the Tenant's family, employees, agents, visitors, or licensees during the term hereof; any negligence or improper conduct; any violation or non-performance of any covenant of this lease or the Rules and Regulations herein; the wrongful use of the demised premises. The Tenant shall give to the Landlord prompt notice in case of fire or accidents to or defects in, any part of the building or equipment and fixtures therein.

TWELFTH. The Landlord will furnish to the Tenant without additional charge, to the extent that the building is adapted, the following services, provided the Tenant is not in default under any of the provisions of this lease: elevator service; heat at reasonable hours during the cold season of the year; hot and cold water at all times. The interruption, curtailment, or cessation of any of such services shall not be deemed a constructive eviction, nor, unless caused by gross negligence of the Landlord, entitle the Tenant to any abatement or diminution of rent.

THIRTEENTH. If a telephone switchboard and a connection to the apartment is maintained by the Landlord, the Tenant may use such service at the same rates charged to the other tenants in the building. If electric current or gas be supplied by the Landlord, the Tenant shall purchase same at rates charged by any public service companies serving the section or locality where the premises are situated and such charges shall be computed from the Landlord's meters. All such charges shall be deemed to be and to be paid as additional rent. The Landlord may discontinue such services upon 30 days notice to the Tenant without in any way affecting the obligations of the parties hereto and the Landlord shall then permit the Tenant to be supplied with electric current and/or gas by any other person or corporation; the Landlord's wires, pipes or conduits may be used for such purposes. Refrigeration apparatus, if any, is installed solely for the Tenant's accommodation and the Landlord shall not be liable for any failure of refrigeration, leakage or damage caused by such equipment or for any reason whatsoever. Interruption, curtailment or cessation of any of such services shall not constitute a constructive eviction nor affect the obligations of the parties herein. Should any Municipal, State or Federal agency impose any tax upon the Landlord's receipts from the sale or resale of electrical energy or gas or telephone service to the Tenant, the Tenant's pro rata share of such tax shall be included in the bill of and paid by the Tenant to the Landlord.

FOURTEENTH. The Landlord shall be permitted to enter the apartment during reasonable hours to make such repairs, decorations, improvements, alterations or additions as the Landlord may consider necessary or desirable, and to inspect or exhibit the apartment to prospective lessees or purchasers of the building. For a period of four months prior to the end of the term, the Landlord shall have the right during reasonable hours to exhibit the apartment to prospective tenants. In the event that the Tenant shall have removed all or substantially all of the Tenant's property during the last month of the term, the Landlord may thereupon enter and redecorate the apartment without in any manner effecting the covenants and obligations herein contained. If the Tenant shall not be personally present to open and permit an entry into the apartment, at any time, when for any reason an entry therein shall be in the judgment of the Landlord or the Landlord's agents necessary or permissible hereunder, the Landlord or the Landlord's agents may enter same by pass key or may forcibly enter the same without incurring any liability or responsibility whatsoever for such entry or for the care of the apartment or the property of the Tenant therein.

FIFTEENTH. If, prior to the commencement of the term, the Tenant shall file a voluntary petition in bankruptcy or be adjudicated a bankrupt or make any general assignment for the benefit of creditors or otherwise, or take the benefit of any insolvency act, or if a receiver or trustee for the Tenant's property be appointed, or if this lease or the estate of the Tenant hereunder be transferred to or devolve upon any other person or corporation, by operation of law or otherwise, the Landlord may at the Landlord's option upon three days notice to the Tenant cancel this lease, and in that case neither the Tenant nor any person claiming under the Tenant shall be entitled to possession of the apartment, and the Landlord may retain as liquidated damages any instalment of rent, security, deposit or any moneys paid upon the execution of this lease.

SIXTEENTH. Upon default in the payment of any instalment of rent; or upon default in performance of, or upon the breach of, any covenant, term or condition of this lease on the Tenant's part to be observed or performed; or if the apartment shall be deserted or vacated, of which fact the Landlord's judgment shall be final; or if the apartment is occupied otherwise than by the Tenant and the Tenant's family as a strictly private dwelling apartment; or if the Landlord or the Landlord's agents or assigns shall deem objectionable or improper any conduct on the part of the Tenant or the occupants of the apartment, or shall deem the Tenant, or the Tenant's family, visitors or licensees objectionable, and the Landlord has given to the Tenant three days notice of the Landlord's intention to terminate this lease and tendered to the Tenant the rent paid on account of the unexpired term demised; or if the Tenant shall file a voluntary petition in bankruptcy, or be by any Court adjudicated insolvent or a bankrupt, or placed in liquidation; or if a temporary or permanent receiver or trustee of the Tenant's property be appointed by any Court; or if the Tenant shall make a general assignment; or any execution or attachment shall be issued against the Tenant or any of the Tenant's property, whereupon the apartment shall be taken or occupied by someone other than the Tenant; or if the Tenant shall fail to move into or take possession of the apartment within 15 days after the commencement of the term of this lease, of which fact the Landlord's judgment shall be final; then and in any of such events, the Landlord may, without notice, re-enter the apartment by summary proceedings, or by action or proceeding or by force or otherwise and dispossess the Tenant or other occupants of the apartment, and remove their effects and have, hold, repossess and enjoy the apartment, and the Tenant hereby waives the service of notice of intention to re-enter or of the institution of legal proceedings for that purpose; and/or the Landlord may at his option upon 3 days notice in writing terminate this lease and this lease and the term thereof shall automatically cease and determine at the expiration of the said three days and the Tenant shall vacate the apartment and surrender the same to the Landlord.

SEVENTEENTH. In the event of such default, re-entry, and/or expiration, the rent shall become due thereupon and be paid up to the time of such re-entry and/or expiration, together with such expenses as the Landlord may incur for legal disbursements, attorneys fees, brokerage and for putting the apartment in good order or for preparing same for re-rental; the Landlord may re-let the apartment, either in the name of the Landlord or otherwise for the balance of the term or for a longer period of time; and/or the Tenant or the Tenant's representatives shall also remain liable for and pay to the Landlord as liquidated damages for the Tenant's failure to observe and perform said Tenant's covenants herein contained, the equivalent of the amount of all the rent hereby covenanted to be paid, less the avails of re-letting, if any, collected by the Landlord during the period which would have constituted the balance of the term of this lease; such liquidated damages shall be paid by the Tenant in monthly instalments, upon statements rendered by the Landlord, and any suit brought to collect such damages shall not prejudice in any way the Landlord's rights to collect or bring suit for such damages as may be payable for any subsequent month. In case of a breach or threatened breach by the Tenant of any of the covenants hereof the Landlord shall have the right of injunction, and the right to any remedy at law or in equity, as if no provision was made herein for re-entry, summary proceedings, and other remedies and the mention herein of any particular remedy shall not preclude the Landlord from any other remedy at law or in equity. The Tenant hereby waives any and all rights of redemption granted by any present or future laws in the event of the Tenant being evicted or dispossessed for any cause or of the Landlord obtaining the premises by reason of a default by the Tenant of any of the covenants of this lease; the Tenant hereby waives the right to have any issue arising out of or under the covenants and conditions of this lease tried by a jury.

How to Handle Your Own Contracts

EIGHTEENTH. If the Landlord shall pay, or be compelled to pay a sum of money, or do any act that requires the payment of money, due to the failure of the Tenant to keep or observe or perform any or all of the covenants herein contained, to be observed and performed by the Tenant, then, and in such event, the sum or sums so paid by the Landlord, together with all interests, costs, damages, and reasonable attorney's fees, shall be considered additional rent and shall be added to the rent next becoming due in the month succeeding such payment and shall be collected at such time.

NINETEENTH. No representations or promises with respect to the apartment have been made by the Landlord or the Landlord's agents other than those contained herein. The assumption of occupancy by the Tenant shall be conclusive evidence that the apartment and the building of which it is a part were in good and satisfactory condition at such time.

TWENTIETH. In the event the apartment is not ready for occupancy at the time set herein for the commencement of the term by reason of the making of any alteration, improvement, decorations or repairs to the apartment or the building of which it is a part, or because of the holding over of any Tenant or Tenants, or if for any other reason the Landlord shall be unable to give possession to the Tenant, this lease shall remain in full force and effect but the Tenant shall not be required to pay rent until the apartment is ready for occupancy; the Landlord shall not be liable for the failure to give possession on said date and the term of this lease shall not be extended or deemed to be extended thereby.

TWENTY-FIRST. The failure of the Landlord to insist in any one or more instances upon a strict performance of any of the covenants, conditions or options in this lease, or to exercise any of the options herein conferred, shall not be construed as a waiver or relinquishment for the future of any of such covenants, conditions or options, but the same shall continue to remain in full force and effect. No provision of this lease shall be waived, modified or altered, unless it be in writing duly executed by the Landlord; the receipt by the Landlord of rent with knowledge of a breach of any covenant of this lease, or the failure of the Landlord to enforce any of the Rules and Regulations herein, or hereafter adopted against the Tenant and/or any other tenant of the building shall not be deemed a waiver of any of the covenants herein or of said Rules and Regulations. If the Landlord waives or obtains redress for any violation of the covenants herein or of any of the said Rules and Regulations, such waiver or redress shall not prevent any subsequent act from having the same force and effect as an original violation. In the event the Tenant shall at any time desire the Landlord to sublet the apartment for the Tenant's account, the Landlord having given consent, the Landlord or the Landlord's agents may accept the Tenant's keys for that purpose without affecting the Tenant's obligations under this lease, and the Landlord shall be exempt of all liability for loss of any of the Tenant's property or the occurrence of any other event in connection therewith. In no event shall the delivery of keys to any employee of the Landlord or of the Landlord's agents operate as a surrender of the apartment.

TWENTY-SECOND. The Tenant has this day deposited with the Landlord the sum of $ as security for the full and faithful performance by the Tenant of all the terms, covenants and conditions of this lease upon the Tenant's part to be performed, which said sum shall be returned to the Tenant after the time fixed as the expiration of the term herein, provided the Tenant has fully and faithfully carried out all of said terms, covenants, and conditions on Tenant's part to be performed. In the event of a bona fide sale, subject to this lease, the Landlord shall have the right to transfer the security to the vendee for the benefit of the Tenant and the Landlord shall be considered released by the Tenant from all liability for the return of such security; and the Tenant agrees to look to the new Landlord solely for the return of the said security, and it is agreed that this shall apply to every transfer or assignment made of the security to a new Landlord.

TWENTY-THIRD. The Tenant shall quit and surrender the apartment at the expiration or other termination of the term of this lease, broom clean, in good order and condition, ordinary wear excepted, and shall remove all the property of the Tenant as directed by the Landlord. The obligation of the Tenant to observe or perform this covenant shall survive the termination of the term of this lease.

TWENTY-FOURTH. This lease shall be extended and renewed by and against the parties hereto for an additional term equivalent to the original term granted herein, commencing from the expiration of the original term, at the same rental without any deduction or concession, and upon all the above terms, covenants and conditions, unless either party on or before the first day of the third month next preceding the termination of any term granted hereby, shall give notice to the other of an intention to surrender or have possession of the premises, as the case may be. This clause shall be and continue operative likewise with respect to any renewals or extensions hereof.

TWENTY-FIFTH. The Landlord hereby covenants that the Tenant, upon payment of the rent as herein reserved and upon performance of all the covenants and conditions herein contained, shall and may peaceably and quietly have, hold and enjoy the demised premises.

TWENTY-SIXTH. If the Landlord should desire, or be required to give to the Tenant any notice, bill or communication, the same shall be deemed sufficiently given or rendered, if in writing and personally delivered to the Tenant or sent by registered mail addressed to the Tenant at the demised premises. Any notice or communication by the Tenant to the Landlord may be delivered personally to the Landlord or to an officer of the Landlord, or may be sent by registered mail addressed to the Landlord at the office of the Landlord.

TWENTY-SEVENTH. This lease and all the covenants and provisions herein contained shall be binding upon the Landlord and the Tenant and their respective heirs, executors, administrators, successors and assigns.

TWENTY-EIGHTH. The Tenant agrees that he will not require, permit, suffer or allow the cleaning of any window or windows in the demised premises from the outside (within the meaning of Section 202 of the New York Labor Law) unless the equipment and safety devices required by law, ordinance, regulation or rule, including, without limitation, Section 202 of the New York Labor Law, are provided and used, and unless the rules and any supplemental rules of the Industrial Board of the State of New York are fully complied with; and the Tenant hereby agrees to indemnify and hold harmless the Landlord, Owner, Agent, Manager and/or Superintendent for all damage, loss or injury suffered or legal or other expenses incurred by said Landlord, Owner, Agent, Manager and/or Superintendent, as a result of the Tenant's requiring, permitting, suffering or allowing any window or windows in the demised premises to be cleaned from the outside in violation of the requirements of the aforesaid laws, ordinances, regulations, and/or rules.

TWENTY-NINTH. This lease and the obligation of Tenant to pay rent hereunder and perform all of the other covenants and agreements hereunder on part of Tenant to be performed shall in nowise be affected, impaired or excused because Landlord is unable to supply or is delayed in supplying any service expressly or impliedly to be supplied or is unable to make, or is delayed in making any repairs, additions, alterations or decorations or is unable to supply or is delayed in supplying any equipment or fixtures if Landlord is prevented or delayed from so doing by reason of governmental preemption in connection with the National Emergency declared by the President of the United States or in connection with any rule, order or regulation of any department or subdivision thereof of any governmental agency or by reason of the conditions of supply and demand which have been or are affected by the war.

Leases ... The Renter's Predicament

RULES AND REGULATIONS

1. Tenants, or their servants shall not make or permit any unseemly or disturbing noises, or interfere in any way with other Tenants, or those visiting them; nor throw anything out of the windows or doors, or down the dumbwaiter, passages or skylights of the building; nor mark or defile the water closets, or the walls, windows and doors of the building.

2. Supplies, goods and packages of every kind are to be delivered at the entrance provided therefor, through service elevators, or dumbwaiters, to the Tenants, and the Landlord is not responsible for the loss or damage of any such property, notwithstanding such loss or damage may occur through the carelessness or negligence of the employees of the building.

3. All garbage and refuse must be sent down to the basement in such manner and at such times as the superintendent may direct, or disposed of in the incinerator, if any.

4. Nothing shall be placed in the halls or on the staircase landings, nor shall anything be hung from the windows, or balconies, or placed upon the window sills. Neither shall any table cloths, clothing, curtains, rugs or mops be shaken or hung from any of the windows or doors. The fire escapes shall not be obstructed in any manner.

5. No Tenant shall make or permit any disturbing noises in the building by himself, his family, servants, employees, agents, visitors and licensees, nor do or permit anything by such persons that will interfere with the rights, comforts or convenience of other Tenants. No Tenant shall play upon, or suffer to be played upon, any musical instrument or operate or suffer to be operated a phonograph or radio in the demised premises between the hours of eleven o'clock P.M. and the following eight o'clock A.M. if the same shall disturb or annoy other occupants of the building. No Tenant shall conduct or permit to be conducted, vocal or instrumental practice, nor give nor permit to be given vocal or instrumental instruction.

6. No radio installation shall be made without the prior written consent of the Landlord. Any aerial erected on the roof or exterior walls of the building without the consent of the Landlord, in writing, is liable to removal without notice.

7. No animals of any kind shall be kept in the demised premises, unless the same in each instance be expressly permitted in writing by the Landlord, and such consent, if given, shall be revocable by the Landlord at any time. In no event shall any dog be permitted on any passenger elevator or in any public portion of the building unless carried or on leash.

8. The service elevators, if any, shall be used by servants, messengers and trades people, and the passenger elevators, if any, shall not be used by them, except that nurses with children may use the passenger elevators.

9. Children shall not play in the public halls, stairways, or elevators.

10. Unless automatic, the passenger and service elevators, if any, shall be operated only by employees of the Landlord, and must not in any event be interfered with by the Tenant, his family, servants, employees, agents, visitors or licensees. Elevators will be operated only during such hours as the Landlord may from time to time determine.

11. No baby carriages, velocipedes, or bicycles shall be allowed in passenger elevators, if any, or allowed to stand in the halls, passageways, areas or courts of the building, or be taken in or out of the building through the main entrance.

12. The laundry and drying apparatus, if any, and any other facilities supplied for the use of all the tenants in common shall be used in such manner and at such times as the superintendent may direct.

13. No sign, advertisement, notice or other lettering shall be exhibited, inscribed, painted or affixed by any Tenant on any part of the outside or inside of the demised premises or building without the prior written consent of the Landlord.

14. No awnings or other projections shall be attached to the outside walls of the building, and no blinds, shades, or screens shall be attached to or hung in, or used in connection with, any window or door of the demised premises, without the prior written consent of the Landlord.

15. The sidewalks, entrances, vestibules, passages, courts, elevators, stairways, corridors and halls must not be obstructed by any of the Tenants or used by them for any purpose other than ingress and egress to and from their respective apartments.

16. The Landlord may retain a pass key to all the premises. No Tenant shall alter any lock or install a new lock or a knocker on any door of the apartment without the written consent of the Landlord, or the Landlord's agent. In case such consent is given the Tenant shall provide the Landlord with an additional key for the use of the Landlord.

17. Tenants shall not send servants or employees of the Landlord out of the building at any time for any purpose.

How to Handle Your Own Contracts

Lease for Furnished House

This Lease, *made the*   *day of*   *, 19*   *, between*

hereinafter referred to as LANDLORD, and

hereinafter referred to as TENANT,

residing at

WITNESSETH, that the Landlord hereby leases to the Tenant, and the Tenant hereby hires and takes from the Landlord, all that certain lot of land with the dwelling thereon known and described as Number

excepting therefrom, such space, if any, hereby reserved by the Landlord for the storage of personal clothes and effects, such space being described as follows:

with the appurtenances for the term of
to commence at noon on the   *day of*   *, 19*   *and to end at noon on*
the   *day of*   *, 19*

     AND the Tenant hereby covenants and agrees to pay to the Landlord, the rent of

         dollars

payable as follows, viz.:   *dollars*
on signing of lease, receipt of which is hereby acknowledged

     THE TENANT HEREBY FURTHER COVENANTS that at the expiration of the said term the Tenant will quit and surrender the premises hereby demised in as good state and condition as they were in at the commencement of the term, reasonable use and wear thereof and damages by the elements excepted; the Tenant will keep all furnishings and personal property of the Landlord in good order and repair at Tenant's expense, and will replace or make good any and all damage, loss or breakage, excepting ordinary wear and tear through proper usage and damage by fire not due to Tenant's negligence and Tenant will surrender and deliver up the said personal property at the expiration of the term of this lease.

     AND the Landlord does covenant that the said Tenant on paying the said rent, and performing the covenants herein contained shall and may peaceably and quietly have, hold and enjoy the said demised premises for the term aforesaid.

     AND that if the said premises, or any part thereof, shall become vacant during the said term, the said Landlord or agents may re-enter the same, either by force or otherwise, without being liable for any prosecution thereof; and re-let said premises as the agent of the said Tenant, and receive the rent thereof, applying the same first to the payment of such expense as the Landlord will be put to in re-entering, and then to the payment of the rent due by these presents; and the balance (if any) to be paid over to said Tenant, who shall remain liable for any deficiency.

     AND the said Tenant hereby further covenants that if any default be made in the payment of said rent, or any part thereof, at the time above specified, or if any default be made in the performance of any other covenants or agreements herein contained, the said hiring, and the relation of Landlord and Tenant, at the option of said Landlord shall wholly cease and determine; and the said Landlord, shall and may re-enter said premises, and remove all persons therefrom; and the said Tenant hereby expressly waives the service of any notice in writing of intention to re-enter.

Leases . . . The Renter's Predicament

It is Understood and Agreed: *between the parties hereto—*

FIRST: That the premises hereby leased are to be completely furnished as shown, except that no bed linen, table linen, silver ware, fine china, cut glass or bric-a-brac is included, unless specified in the inventory.

SECOND: That at the request of either party to this lease, an inventory of the furnishings of the premises hereby leased will be made by the Landlord in duplicate and checked and signed by the parties before the commencement of the term of this lease—one copy will be left with the Landlord, one copy with the Tenant.

THIRD: That the Tenant shall keep, at the Tenant's expense, the furniture, furnishings and fixtures in said house or on said premises and the faucets, the furnace, the electric bells, the plumbing, range, oven, heating apparatus, electric light or gas fixtures, and all appliances, in good order and repair, it being understood that the Landlord is to have same in good order when giving possession.

FOURTH: That the Tenant will pay all charges for water, electricity, fuel, gas and telephone used during the term of this lease or any renewal thereof.

FIFTH: That the Tenant shall use the premises hereby leased exclusively for a private residence for the Tenant and Tenant's immediate family, and that the Tenant will not, without written consent of the Landlord, assign this lease, nor let or underlet the whole or any part of the said premises, nor make any alterations therein or thereupon under the penalty of forfeiture and damages, nor shall the same be permitted to remain vacant or unoccupied exceeding ten days at any one time without the like consent.

SIXTH: That the Landlord agrees that the Tenant shall have the free use of all fruit, vegetables and other products of the premises during the term of this lease, but such fruit, vegetables and products shall not be removed or disposed of without the consent of the Landlord. The Tenant agrees not to remove any tree, shrubbery or vine from the premises and further agrees to keep the grounds in neat order and condition at all times.

SEVENTH: That if the said premises or any part thereof shall, during said term or previous thereto, be slightly damaged by fire, the premises shall be promptly repaired by the Landlord and an abatement will be made for the rent corresponding with the time during which and the extent to which said premises may have been untenantable, but if the building or buildings should be so damaged that the Landlord shall decide not to rebuild, the term of this lease shall cease and the aggregate rent be paid up to the time of the fire.

EIGHTH: That in case the Tenant has the privilege of renewing this lease, the Tenant shall give notice in writing to the Landlord or Landlord's Agent of Tenant's intention to renew, at least three months prior to the expiration hereof.

NINTH: That during the last three months of this lease or any renewal thereof, the Landlord or his agent, shall have the privilege of displaying the usual "for sale" and "to let" signs on the premises and to show the property to prospective purchasers or tenants.

TENTH: That the Tenant agrees that the Landlord or the Landlord's Agent shall have the right to enter into and upon said premises, or any part thereof, at all reasonable hours for the purpose of examining the same, or making such repairs or alterations as may be necessary for the safety and preservation thereof.

ELEVENTH: That during the term of this lease the Tenant shall comply with all laws and ordinances, and all rules and orders of any governmental authority affecting the cleanliness, occupancy and preservation of the demised premises and the sidewalks connected thereto.

TWELFTH: That the Landlord agrees that the heating apparatus shall be clean and in good working condition on giving possession to the Tenant and Tenant agrees to pay for the annual servicing of the heating apparatus by a servicing company acceptable to the Landlord.

THIRTEENTH: The Tenant agrees that this lease shall be subject and subordinate to any mortgage or mortgages now on said premises or which any owner of said premises may hereafter at any time elect to place on said premises, and to all advances already made or which may be hereafter made on account of said mortgage, to the full extent of the principal sums secured thereby and interest thereon, and the Tenant agrees upon request to hereafter execute any paper or papers which the counsel for the Landlord may deem necessary to accomplish that end, in default of the Tenant so doing, the Landlord is hereby empowered to execute such paper or papers in the name of the Tenant and as the act and deed of the Tenant and this authority is hereby declared to be coupled with an interest and not revocable.

FOURTEENTH: That the Landlord agrees to deliver the premises to the Tenant in a broom clean condition, with all rubbish removed, and the Tenant agrees to leave the premises in the same condition upon the termination of this lease.

FIFTEENTH: Landlord shall not be liable for failure to give possession of the premises upon commencement date by reason of the fact that premises are not ready for occupancy, or due to a prior Tenant wrongfully holding over or any other person wrongfully in possession or for any other reason: in such event the rent shall not commence until possession is given or is available, but the term herein shall not be extended.

Lease for Offices or Lofts

This Agreement made this   day of   19   between

as Landlord

and

as Tenant

WITNESSETH: The Landlord hereby leases to Tenant and Tenant hereby hires from Landlord

in the building known as

for the term of   to commence on the   day of   19

and to end on the   day of   19   , upon the conditions and covenants following:

Rent

1st.   Tenant shall pay the annual rent of

said rent to be paid in equal monthly payments in advance on the   day of each and every month during the term aforesaid, as follows:

Occupancy

2nd.   Tenant shall use and occupy demised premises for no purpose other than

Repairs

Alterations

3rd.   Tenant shall take good care of the premises and fixtures, make good any injury or breakage done by Tenant or Tenant's agents, employees or visitors, and shall quit and surrender said premises, at the end of said term, in as good condition as the reasonable use thereof will permit; shall not make any additions, alterations or improvements in said premises, or permit any additional lock or fastening on any door, without the written consent of Landlord; and all alterations, partitions, additions, or improvements, which may be made by either of the parties hereto upon the premises, shall be the property of Landlord, and shall remain upon and be surrendered with the premises, as a part thereof, at the termination of this lease, without disturbance, molestation or injury.

Requirements of Law

4th.   Tenant shall promptly execute and comply with all statutes, ordinances, rules, orders, regulations and requirements of the Federal, State and City Government and of any and all their Departments and Bureaus applicable to said premises, for the correction, prevention, and abatement of nuisances or other grievances, in, upon, or connected with said premises during said term; and shall also promptly comply with and execute all rules, orders and regulations of the New York Board of Fire Underwriters for the prevention of fires at Tenant's own cost and expense.

Assignment

5th.   Tenant, successors, heirs, executors or administrators shall not assign this agreement, or underlet or underlease the premises, or any part thereof, without Landlord's consent in writing; or occupy, or permit or suffer the same to be occupied for any business or purpose deemed disreputable or extra-hazardous on account of fire, under the penalty of damages and forfeiture, and in the event of a breach thereof, the term herein shall immediately cease and determine at the option of Landlord as if it were the expiration of the original term.

Destruction

6th.   In case of damage, by fire or other action of the elements, to the building in which the leased premises are located, without the fault of Tenant or of Tenant's agent or employees, if the damage is so extensive as to amount practically to the total destruction of the leased premises or of the building, or if Landlord shall within a reasonable time decide not to rebuild, this lease shall cease and come to an end, and the rent shall be apportioned to the time of the damage. In all other cases where the leased premises are damaged by fire without the fault of Tenant or of Tenant's agents or employees, Landlord shall repair the damage with reasonable dispatch after notice of damage, and if the damage has rendered the premises untenantable, in whole or in part, there shall be an apportionment of the rent until the damage has been repaired. In determining what constitutes reasonable dispatch consideration shall be given to delays caused by strikes, adjustment of insurance and other causes beyond Landlord's control.

Access to Premises

7th.   Tenant agrees that Landlord and Landlord's agents and other representatives shall have the right to enter into and upon said premises, or any part thereof, at all reasonable hours for the purpose of examining the same, or for making such repairs, alterations, additions or improvements therein as may be necessary or deemed advisable by Landlord. Tenant also agrees to permit Landlord or Landlord's agents to show the premises to persons wishing to hire or purchase the same; and Tenant further agrees that during the 6 months next preceding the expiration of the term hereby granted, Landlord or Landlord's agents shall have the right to place notices on the front of said premises, or any part thereof, offering the premises "To Let" or "For Sale", and Tenant hereby agrees to permit the same to remain thereon without hindrance or molestation.

Lease Not In Effect

8th. If, before the commencement of the term, Tenant takes the benefit of any insolvent act, or if a Receiver or Trustee be appointed for Tenant's property, or if the estate of Tenant hereunder be transferred or pass to or devolve upon any other person or corporation, or if Tenant shall default in the performance of any agreement by Tenant contained in any other lease to Tenant by Landlord or by any corporation of which an officer of Landlord is a Director, this lease shall thereby, at the option of Landlord, be terminated and in that case, neither Tenant nor anybody claiming under Tenant shall be entitled to go into possession of the demised premises. If after the commencement of the term, any of the events mentioned above in this subdivision shall occur, or if Tenant

Defaults

shall make default in fulfilling any of the covenants of this lease or the rules and regulations, other than the covenants for the payment of rent or "additional rent" or if the demised premises become vacant or deserted, Landlord may give to Tenant ten days'

10 Day Notice

notice of intention to end the term of this lease, and thereupon at the expiration of said ten days' (if said condition which was the basis of said notice shall continue to exist) the term under this lease shall expire as fully and completely as if that day were the date herein definitely fixed for the expiration of the term and Tenant will then quit and surrender the demised premises to Landlord, but Tenant shall remain liable as hereinafter provided.

Remedies

If Tenant shall make default in the payment of the rent reserved hereunder, or any item of "additional rent" herein mentioned, or any part of either or in making any other payment herein provided for, or if the notice last above provided for shall have been given and if the condition which was the basis of said notice shall exist at the expiration of said ten days' period, Landlord may immediately, or at any time thereafter, re-enter the demised premises and remove all persons and all or any property therefrom, either by summary dispossess proceedings, or by any suitable action or proceeding at law, or by force or otherwise, without being liable to indictment, prosecution or damages therefor, and re-possess and enjoy said premises together with all additions, alterations and improvements. In any such case or in the event that this lease be "terminated" before the commencement of the term, as above provided, Landlord may either re-let the demised premises or any part or parts thereof for Landlord's own account, or may, at Landlord's option, re-let the demised premises or any part or parts thereof as the agent of Tenant, and receive the rents therefor,

Re-Letting

applying the same first to the payment of such expenses as Landlord may have incurred, and then to the fulfillment of the covenants of Tenant herein, and the balance, if any, at the expiration of the term first above provided for, shall be paid to Tenant. Landlord may rent the premises for a term extending beyond the term hereby granted without releasing Tenant from any liability. In the event that the term of this lease shall expire as above in this subdivision 8th provided, or terminate by summary proceedings or otherwise, and if Landlord shall not re-let the demised premises for Landlord's own account, then, whether or not the premises be re-let, Tenant shall remain liable for, and Tenant hereby agrees to pay to Landlord, until the time when this lease would have expired but for such termination or expiration, the equivalent of the amount of all of the rent and "additional rent" reserved herein, less the avails of reletting, if any, and the same shall be due and payable by Tenant to Landlord on the several rent days above specified, that is, upon each of such rent days Tenant shall pay to Landlord the amount of deficiency then existing. Tenant hereby expressly waives any and all right of redemption in case Tenant shall be dispossessed by judgment or warrant of any court or judge, and Tenant waives and will waive all right to trial by jury in any summary proceedings hereafter instituted by Landlord against Tenant in respect to the demised premises or any action to recover rent or damages hereunder. In the event of a breach or threatened breach by Tenant

Cumulative Remedies

of any of the covenants or provisions hereof, Landlord shall have the right of injunction and the right to invoke any remedy allowed at law or in equity, as if re-entry, summary proceedings and other remedies were not herein provided for. The words "re-enter" and "re-entry" as used in this lease are not restricted to their technical legal meaning.

Services

9th. As long as Tenant is not in default under any of the covenants of this lease, Landlord shall, excepting on Sundays and Holidays, provide the following services, if and insofar as the existing facilities permit: (a) furnish heat to the premises on business days from 8 A.M. to 6 P.M. when and as required by law; (b) OPERATE elevators, or permit self-operated elevators to be used, on business days from 8 A.M. to 6 P.M. except Saturdays when the hours shall be from 8 A.M. to 1 P.M.

Signs

10th. No sign, advertisement, notice or other lettering shall be exhibited, inscribed, painted or affixed by Tenant on any part of the premises or building without the prior written approval and consent of Landlord. Should Landlord deem it necessary to remove the same in order to paint, alter, or remodel any part of the building, Landlord may remove and replace same at Landlord's expense.

Cleaning

11th. Tenant shall, at Tenant's expense, keep the demised premises clean and in order to the satisfaction of Landlord. Tenant shall pay to Landlord the cost of removal of Tenant's refuse and waste, upon presentation of bills therefor and the amount of such bills shall be paid as additional rent.

Liability

12th. Landlord is exempt from any and all liability for any damage or injury to person or property caused by or resulting from steam, electricity, gas, water, rain, ice or snow, or any leak or flow from or into any part of said building or from any damage or injury resulting or arising from any other cause or happening whatsoever unless said damage or injury be caused by or be due to the negligence of Landlord.

Subordination

13th. That this instrument shall not be a lien against said premises in respect to any mortgages that are now on or that hereafter may be placed against said premises, and that the recording of such mortgage or mortgages shall have preference and precedence and be superior and prior in lien of this lease, irrespective of the date of recording and Tenant agrees to execute any such instrument without cost, which may be deemed necessary or desirable to further effect the subordination of this lease to any such mortgage or mortgages, and a refusal to execute such instrument shall entitle Landlord, or Landlord's assigns and legal representatives to the option of cancelling this lease without incurring any expense or damage and the term hereby granted is expressly limited accordingly.

Security

14th. Tenant has this day deposited with Landlord the sum of $ as security for the full and faithful performance by Tenant of all the terms, covenants and conditions of this lease upon Tenant's part to be performed, which said sum shall be returned to Tenant after the time fixed as the expiration of the term herein, provided Tenant has fully and faithfully carried out all of said terms, covenants and conditions on Tenant's part to be performed. In the event of a bona fide sale, subject to this lease, Landlord shall have the right to transfer the security to the vendee for the benefit of Tenant and Landlord shall be considered released by Tenant from all liability for the return of such security; and Tenant agrees to look to the new Landlord solely for the return of the said security, and it is agreed that this shall apply to every transfer or assignment made of the security to a new Landlord. That the security deposited under this lease shall not be mortgaged, assigned or encumbered by Tenant without the written consent of Landlord.

Sprinklers

15th. If there now is or shall be installed in the building a "sprinkler system", and such system or any of its appliances shall be damaged or injured or not in proper working order by reason of any act or omission of Tenant, Tenant's agents, servants, employees, licensees or visitors, Tenant shall forthwith restore the same to good working condition at its own expense; and if the New York Board of Fire Underwriters or the New York Fire Insurance Exchange or any bureau, department or official of the state or city government, require or recommend that any changes, modifications, alterations or additional sprinkler heads or other equipment be made or supplied by reason of Tenant's business, or the location of partitions, trade fixtures, or other contents of the demised premises, or for any other reason, or if any such changes, modifications, alterations, additional sprinkler heads or other equipment, become necessary to prevent the imposition of a penalty or charge against the full allowance for a sprinkler system in the fire insurance rate as fixed by said Exchange, or by any Fire Insurance Company, Tenant shall, at Tenant's expense, promptly make and supply such changes, modifications, alterations, additional sprinkler heads or other equipment. Tenant shall pay to Landlord as additional rent the sum of $ on the rent day of each month during the term of this lease, as Tenant's portion of the contract price for sprinkler supervisory service.

Water — 16th Tenant shall pay to Landlord the rent or charge, which may, during the demised term, be assessed or imposed for the water used or consumed in or on the said premises, whether determined by meter or otherwise, as soon as and when the same may be assessed or imposed, and will also pay the expenses for the setting of a water meter in the said premises should the latter be required.

Sewer — Tenant shall pay Tenant's proportionate part of the sewer rent or charge imposed upon the building. All such rents or charges or expenses shall be paid as additional rent and shall be added to the next month's rent thereafter to become due.

Fire Insurance — 17th. Tenant will not, nor will Tenant permit undertenants or other persons to do anything in said premises, or bring anything into said premises, or permit anything to be brought into said premises or to be kept therein, which will in any way increase the rate of fire insurance on said demised premises, nor use the demised premises or any part thereof, nor suffer or permit their use for any business or purpose which would cause an increase in the rate of fire insurance on said building, and Tenant agrees to pay on demand any such increase as additional rent.

No Waiver — 18th. The failure of Landlord to insist upon a strict performance of any of the terms, conditions and covenants herein, shall not be deemed a waiver of any rights or remedies that Landlord may have, and shall not be deemed a waiver of any subsequent breach or default in the terms, conditions and covenants herein contained. This instrument may not be changed, modified or discharged orally.

Condemnation — 19th. That should the land whereon said building stands or any part thereof be condemned for public use, then in that event, upon the taking of the same for such public use, this lease, at the option of Landlord, shall become null and void, and the term cease and come to an end upon the date when the same shall be taken and the rent shall be apportioned as of said date. No part of any award, however, shall belong to Tenant.

Fixtures — 20th. If after default in payment of rent or violation of any other provision of this lease, or upon the expiration of this lease, Tenant moves out or is dispossessed and fails to remove any trade fixtures or other property prior to such said default, removal, expiration of lease, or prior to the issuance of the final order or execution of the warrant, then and in that event, the said fixtures and property shall be deemed abandoned by Tenant and shall become the property of Landlord.

Inability To Perform — 21st. This lease and the obligation of Tenant to pay rent hereunder and perform all of the other covenants and agreements hereunder on part of Tenant to be performed shall in nowise be affected, impaired or excused because Landlord is unable to supply or is delayed in supplying any service expressly or impliedly to be supplied or is unable to make, or is delayed in making any repairs, additions, alterations or decorations or is unable to supply or is delayed in supplying any equipment or fixtures if Landlord is prevented or delayed from so doing by reason of governmental preemption in connection with any National Emergency declared by the President of the United States or in connection with any rule, order or regulation of any department or subdivision thereof of any governmental agency or by reason of the condition of supply and demand which have been or are affected by war or other emergency.

No Diminution of Rent — 22nd. No diminution or abatement of rent, or other compensation, shall be claimed or allowed for inconvenience or discomfort arising from the making of repairs or improvements to the building or to its appliances, nor for any space taken to comply with any law, ordinance or order of a governmental authority. In respect to the various "services," if any, herein expressly or impliedly agreed to be furnished by Landlord to Tenant, it is agreed that there shall be no diminution or abatement of the rent, or any other compensation, for interruption or curtailment of such "service" when such interruption or curtailment shall be due to accident, alterations or repairs desirable or necessary to be made or to inability or difficulty in securing supplies or labor for the maintenance of such "service" or to some other cause, not gross negligence on the part of Landlord. No such interruption or curtailment of any such "service" shall be deemed a constructive eviction. Landlord shall not be required to furnish, and Tenant shall not be entitled to receive, any of such "services" during any period wherein Tenant shall be in default in respect to the payment of rent. Neither shall there be any abatement or diminution of rent because of making of repairs, improvements or decorations to the demised premises after the date above fixed for the commencement of the term, it being understood that rent shall, in any event, commence to run at such date so above fixed.

Rules and Regulations — 23rd. Tenant and Tenant's employees, agents and visitors shall comply strictly with the Rules and Regulations set forth on the back of this lease, and such other and further reasonable Rules and Regulations as Landlord or Landlord's agents may from time to time adopt. Landlord shall not be liable to Tenant for violation of any of said Rules or Regulations, or the breach of any covenant or condition in any lease, by any other tenant in the building.

Window Cleaning — 24th. Tenant will not clean, nor require, permit, suffer or allow any window in the demised premises to be cleaned, from the outside in violation of Section 202 of the Labor Law or of the rules of the Board of Standards and Appeals, or of any other board or body having or asserting jurisdiction.

Possession — 25th. Landlord shall not be liable for failure to give possession of the premises upon commencement date by reason of the fact that premises are not ready for occupancy, or due to a prior Tenant wrongfully holding over or any other person wrongfully in possession or for any other reason: in such event the rent shall not commence until possession is given or is available, but the term herein shall not be extended.

Headings — The marginal headings are inserted only as a matter of convenience and in no way define the scope of this lease or the intent of any provision thereof.

Quiet Enjoyment — Landlord covenants that the said Tenant on paying the said rent, and performing all the covenants aforesaid, shall and may peacefully and quietly have, hold and enjoy the said demised premises for the term aforesaid, provided however, that this covenant shall be conditioned upon the retention of title to the premises by Landlord.

And it is mutually understood and agreed that the covenants and agreements contained in the within lease shall be binding upon the parties hereto and upon their respective successors, heirs, executors and administrators.

In Witness Whereof, Landlord and Tenant have respectively signed and sealed this lease as of the day and year first above written.

Signed, sealed and delivered

in the presence of

....L. S.

RULES AND REGULATIONS

1. The sidewalks, entrances, passages, courts, elevators, stairways, or halls shall not be obstructed by any Tenant or used for any purpose other than ingress and egress to and from the demised premises, and if said premises are situate on the ground floor the Tenant thereof shall keep the sidewalks and curbs directly in front of said premises clean and free from ice, snow, etc. Nothing shall be thrown out of windows or doors or down passages of building.

2. Movement of goods in or out of the premises and building shall only be effected through entrances and elevators designated for that purpose. No hand trucks, carts, etc. shall be used in the building unless equipped with rubber tires and side guards.

3. No awnings or other projections shall be attached to the outside walls of the building and no curtains, blinds, shades, or screens shall be used without the prior written consent of the Landlord.

4. The skylights, windows, and doors that reflect or admit light and air into the halls, or other public places in the building shall not be covered or obstructed by any Tenant, nor shall any thing be placed on the windowsills.

5. The water and wash closets and other plumbing fixtures shall not be used for any purposes other than those for which they were constructed, and no rubbish, rags, or other substances shall be thrown therein. All damages resulting from any misuse of the fixtures shall be borne by the Tenant who, or whose employees, agents, visitors or licensees, shall have caused the same.

6. No Tenant shall mark, paint, drill into, or in any way deface any part of the demised premises or the building of which they form a part. No boring, cutting or stringing of wires shall be permitted, except with the prior written consent of the Landlord, and as the Landlord may direct. No Tenant shall lay linoleum, or other similar floor covering, so that the same shall come in direct contact with the floor of the demised premises, and, if linoleum or other covering is used an interlining of builder's deadening felt shall be first affixed to the floor, by a paste or other material, soluble in water, the use of cement or other adhesive being expressly prohibited.

7. No Tenant shall make, or permit to be made, any unseemly or disturbing noises or disturb or interfere with occupants of this or neighboring premises or those having business with them whether by the use of any instrument, radio, talking machine, unmusical noise, whistling, singing, or otherwise.

8. No Tenant, nor any of Tenant's employees, agents, visitors or licensees, shall at any time bring or keep upon the demised premises any inflammable, combustible or explosive fluid, chemical or substance, or allow any unusual or objectionable odors to be produced upon the demised premises, or permit animals or birds to be brought or kept on the premises.

9. No machine may be operated on the premises without the written consent of the Landlord; machinery shall be placed in approved settings to absorb or prevent any noise or annoyance.

10. No Tenant shall place a load upon any floor of the building exceeding the floor load per square foot area which such floor was designed to carry, and all floor loads shall be evenly distributed. All removals, or the carrying in or out of any safes, freight, furniture or bulky matter of any description must take place during the hours which the Landlord or Landlord's agent may determine from time to time. The Landlord reserves the right to prescribe the weight and position of all safes, which must be placed so as to distribute the weight. The Landlord reserves the right to inspect all freight to be brought into the building and to exclude from the building all freight which violates any of these Rules and Regulations or this lease. Safes and machinery may not be put on elevators.

11. Canvassing, soliciting and peddling in the building is prohibited and each Tenant shall co-operate to prevent the same.

12. No water cooler, air conditioning unit or system or other apparatus shall be installed or used by any Tenant without the written consent of Landlord.

State of New York, County of ss.:	State of New York, County of ss.:
On this day of , 19 , before me personally came	On this day of , 19 , before me personally came to me known, who being by me duly sworn, did depose and say that he resides in that he is the of
to me known and known to me to be the individual described in and who executed the foregoing instrument and acknowledged to me that he executed the same.	the corporation described in and which executed the foregoing instrument; that he knows the seal of said corporation; that the seal affixed to said instrument is such corporate seal; that it was so affixed by order of the Board of Directors of said corporation, and that he signed his name thereto by like order.

In Consideration of the letting of the premises within mentioned to the within named Tenant and the sum of $1.00 paid to the undersigned by the within named Landlord, the undersigned hereby covenants and agrees, to and with the Landlord and the Landlord's successors and assigns, that if default shall at any time be made by the said Tenant in the payment of the rent and the performance of the covenants contained in the within lease, on the Tenant's part to be paid and performed, that the undersigned will well and truly pay the said rent, or any arrears thereof, that may remain due unto the said Landlord, and also pay all damages that may arise in consequence of the non-performance of said covenants, or either of them, without requiring notice of any such default from the said Landlord. The undersigned hereby waives all right to trial by jury in any action or proceeding hereinafter instituted by the Landlord, to which the undersigned may be a party.

In Witness Whereof, the undersigned ha   set   hand   and seal   this   day of   , 19

WITNESS

_____ L. S.

Seasonal Lease

𝕿𝖍𝖎𝖘 𝕬𝖌𝖗𝖊𝖊𝖒𝖊𝖓𝖙, made between

as Landlord and

as Tenant

𝖂𝖎𝖙𝖓𝖊𝖘𝖘𝖊𝖙𝖍 That the said Landlord has let unto the said Tenant and the said Tenant has hired from the said Landlord

situated at

for the term beginning the   day of   19   and ending the

day of   19   to be used and occupied for dwelling purposes only, for   persons and

no more; upon the conditions and covenants following:—

1st. That the Tenant shall pay the rent for said premises as follows:—

2nd. The Tenant shall pay for all gas, water, electric current and fuel consumed in Tenant's premises during the term hereof as follows:

Gas $

Water $

Electric $

Fuel $

The above charges shall be considered as additional rent and payable as rent.

3rd. The Tenant shall take good care of the premises and the furniture and chattels therein contained, and at the end or sooner termination of the term shall deliver up the demised premises and furniture and chattels in as good state and condition as they were in at the commencement of the term, reasonable use and wear thereof and damage by the elements excepted.

4th. The Tenant shall promptly execute and comply with all laws, orders, ordinances and regulations of the Federal, State, Municipal or Local Government, and of any of their Departments and Bureaus and with all rules, orders, recommendations and regulations of the local Board of Fire Underwriters or any responsible Fire Insurance Company, at Tenant's own cost and expense.

5th. The Tenant shall do no cooking in any room used for sleeping purposes, but shall have the right to use jointly with other tenants a room set aside by the Landlord for that purpose.

6th. The Tenant shall not assign this agreement, or underlet or underlease the premises, or any part thereof, or make any alterations on the premises, nor permit the same to be used at any time during the said term for any purpose other than above mentioned, without the Landlord's consent in writing.

7th. The Tenant agrees that the Landlord and Landlord's agents and other representatives, shall have the right to enter into and upon said premises, or any part thereof, at all reasonable hours for the purpose of examining the same, or making such repairs or alterations therein as may be necessary for the safety and preservation thereof.

8th. If Tenant defaults in the performance of any of the covenants or conditions herein contained other than the covenants to pay rent, or if any conduct of Tenant or Occupants of the leased premises shall be objectionable, Landlord may give to Tenant three days notice thereof, and if such default has not been cured or the objectionable conduct stopped within said three day period, then at the expiration of said three days Landlord may give three days notice of the termination of this lease and at the expiration of said three days notice the term of this lease shall expire and Tenant shall then surrender premises to Landlord but Tenant shall remain liable as hereinafter provided. In case of default by Tenant in payment of rent, or if the three days notice above provided for shall have been given and the three days period shall have elapsed without curing such default or stopping the objectionable conduct and the three day notice of termination shall have been given and the period thereof elapsed, or if the leased premises become vacant or deserted, Landlord may at any time thereafter without further notice re-enter said premises by summary proceedings, or by action or proceeding, or by force or otherwise, and dispossess Tenant or other occupants of premises and remove their effects without being liable to prosecution or damage therefor.

9th. In the event of such default, re-entry or re-possession by Landlord, Tenant shall remain liable for all rent due or to become due during the balance of the term, together with such expenses Landlord may incur in re-entering and re-possessing premises, brokerage, repairs, cleaning and decorating premises for re-rental. Landlord may re-let premises in Landlord's name or otherwise for the balance of the term or for a longer period of time and apply the proceeds of such re-letting, received for the period constituting the balance of the term of this lease, to the reduction of Tenant's obligations herein enumerated. Tenant hereby waives all right of redemption to which Tenant or any person claiming under Tenant might be entitled by any law now or hereafter in force. Tenant hereby waives the right to have any issue arising out of or under the covenants and conditions of this lease tried by a jury.

10th. The Tenant agrees not to permit any visitors to bathe from premises, nor shall the Tenant nor any one else enter any rooms hereby leased attired in a bathing suit.

11th. The Tenant hereby further agrees to reimburse the Landlord for any fine or penalty which may be imposed upon the Landlord by any court by reason of any violation upon the premises through the fault of the Tenant herein, his agents or servants.

12th. The Tenant further covenants to permit said Landlord, or his agents, to show the premises to persons desiring to rent or purchase 45 days before the expiration of this lease, and will permit the usual notice, "To Let" or "For Sale," to be placed upon the walls or doors of said premises and remain thereon without hindrance or molestation after said date.

13th. The Tenant shall, in case of fire, give immediate notice thereof to the Landlord who shall thereupon cause the damage to be repaired forthwith; but if the premises be so damaged that the Landlord shall decide to terminate this lease, then upon 10 days written notice given to the Tenant either personally or by certified mail, this lease and the term thereof shall cease and terminate at the expiration of such 10 day period and the accrued rent shall be paid up to the time of the fire.

14th. The Tenant agrees that this lease shall be subject and subordinate to any mortgage or mortgages now on said premises or which any owner of said premises may hereafter at any time elect to place on said premises, and to all advances already made or which may be hereafter made on account of said mortgage, to the full extent of the principal sums secured thereby and interest thereon, and the Tenant agrees upon request to hereafter execute any paper or papers which the counsel for the Landlord may deem necessary to accomplish that end, in default of the Tenant so doing, the Landlord is hereby empowered to execute such paper or papers in the name of the Tenant and as the act and deed of the Tenant and this authority is hereby declared to be coupled with an interest and not revocable.

15th. The Tenant has this day deposited with the Landlord the sum of $..
as security for the full and faithful performance by the Tenant of all the terms and conditions upon the Tenant's part to be performed, which said sum shall be returned to the Tenant after the time fixed as the expiration of the term herein, provided the Tenant has fully and faithfully carried out all of the terms, covenants and conditions on the Tenant's part to be performed.

16th. This instrument may not be changed, modified or discharged orally.

The Landlord hereby recognizes
as the Broker negotiating this lease and agrees to pay the commission to said Broker. The Landlord shall pay a commission upon renewal of this lease on the same or different terms, or the sale or exchange of the premises between the parties hereto. Commissions shall be paid in accordance with the established rates of

and shall be due and payable on execution and delivery of this lease, renewal of lease, contract of sale or of exchange.

And the said Landlord hereby covenants that the said Tenant on paying the said rent and performing the covenants aforesaid shall and may peaceably and quietly have, hold and enjoy the said demised premises for the term aforesaid.

And it is further understood and agreed, that the covenants and agreements herein contained are binding on the parties hereto and their legal representatives.

In Witness Whereof the parties hereto have hereunto set their hands and seals this
day of   19

Sealed and delivered in the presence of

Dwelling House Lease

PARTIES

THIS LEASE, made the   day of   , 19   , between

hereinafter referred to as LANDLORD, and

hereinafter jointly and severally referred to as TENANT.

PREMISES

WITNESSETH, that the Landlord hereby leases to the Tenant, and the Tenant hereby hires and takes from the Landlord, all that certain lot of land with the dwelling thereon known and described as Number

TERM
RENT

to be used and occupied solely as a strictly private dwelling for one family only, by the Tenant and the family of the Tenant consisting of   persons, and not otherwise, for a term to commence on the   day of   19   , and to end on the   day of   , 19   unless sooner terminated as hereinafter provided, at the annual rent of

due and payable in advance in equal monthly instalments on the first day of each and every month during the term.

THE TENANT COVENANTS:

FIRST.—The Tenant will pay the specified rent and any "additional rent" at the times and in the manner herein provided, to the Landlord at

State of New York, or at such other place as the Landlord may designate from time to time hereafter.

REPAIRS
ORDINANCES
MOVING INJURY
SURRENDER
INDEMNIFY LANDLORD

SECOND.—That, throughout said term, the Tenant will take good care of the demised premises and appurtenances, and suffer no waste or injury; make, as and when needed, all interior and exterior repairs in and about the demised premises and the fixtures and appurtenances, which repairs shall be in quality and class, equal to the original work; comply with all laws, ordinances and governmental regulations, and the regulations of the New York Board of Fire Underwriters or other similar board having jurisdiction, applicable to the demised premises, keep the sidewalk and curb free from snow and ice; throughout said term and forever afterward, indemnify and save harmless the Landlord from and against any and all liability, arising from injury during said term to person or property, occasioned wholly or in part by any act or omission of the Tenant, or of the guests, servants, assigns, under-tenants or sub-tenants of the Tenant; repair, at or before the end of the term, all injury done by the installation or removal of furniture and property so as to restore the demised premises to their original state; and, at the end of the term, to quit and surrender the demised premises in as good order and condition as they were at the beginning of the term, reasonable wear and damage by the elements excepted. If said premises be not surrendered at the end of the term, the Tenant will make good to the Landlord all of the damage which the Landlord shall suffer by reason thereof, and will indemnify the Landlord against all claims made by any succeeding tenant against the Landlord founded upon delay by the Landlord in delivering possession of the premises to said succeeding tenant, so far as such delay is occasioned by failure of the Tenant to so surrender the premises.

NEGATIVE COVENANTS

THIRD.—That the Tenant will not drive nails in, drill into, disfigure or deface any part of the building or suffer the same to be done; will not do anything, or suffer anything to be done upon the demised premises which will increase the rate of fire insurance upon said building; will not permit the accumulation of waste or refuse matter, and will not without the written consent of the Landlord first obtained in each case, either sell, assign, mortgage, pledge, encumber or transfer this lease, underlet or sublet the demised premises or any part thereof, make any alteration in the demised premises, expose any sign or advertisement thereon, or use the demised premises or any part thereof or suffer the same to be used, for any purpose other than as a private dwelling apartment, nor by anybody other than the Tenant and the above designated members of the Tenant's family. It is hereby expressly understood and agreed that the character of the occupancy of the demised premises, as above expressed, is an especial consideration and inducement for the granting of this lease by the Landlord to the Tenant, and in the event of a violation by the Tenant of the restrictions against sale, assignment, mortgaging, pledging, encumbering or transferring this lease or underletting or subletting the demised premises or any part thereof, or if the Tenant shall cease to occupy the premises or shall permit the same to be occupied by parties other than as aforesaid or allow the use of the same for any purpose not herein permitted, or violate any other restriction, condition or requirement of this lease, then this lease may, at the option of the Landlord, or the agents or assigns of the Landlord, be terminated in the manner provided in the first paragraph of Section "Sixth" hereof.

WATER CHARGES, ETC.

FOURTH.—That, throughout said term, the Tenant will pay for all water consumed on the demised premises and will pay each and every rent or charge assessed or imposed according to law against the demised premises for water consumed thereon, and will make such payments promptly as the same become due; and, if the Tenant fails to make any such payment, the Landlord may make the same and the amount so paid shall be "additional rent" due and payable by the Tenant to the Landlord on the first day of the month following such payment, or, at the option of the Landlord, on the first day of any succeeding month. The Tenant will keep the water meter on the demised premises in repair. The Tenant will pay for any and all oil, coal, electric current or gas consumed on the demised premises.

IT IS MUTUALLY COVENANTED AND AGREED THAT:

FIRE, ETC., CLAUSE

FIFTH.—If, through no fault or negligence of the Tenant, the said demised premises shall be partially damaged by fire or other casualty, repairs shall be made by the Landlord as speedily as conveniently possible; and in case the damage shall be so extensive as to render the demised premises wholly untenantable, the rent shall cease until such time as said premises shall have been put in repair; but in the event of the substantially total destruction of the demised premises by fire or otherwise, or in case the damage to the demised premises shall be so extensive that they cannot, in the opinion of the Landlord, be repaired within thirty days, or if the Landlord shall decide to remodel or reconstruct the building, then the rent shall be paid only up to the time of such destruction or damage and any rent paid for a period subsequent to that time shall be refunded by the Landlord, and all interest of the Tenant in the demised premises shall thereupon terminate, and this lease shall become void from such time, excepting that the Tenant shall be and continue liable for any such destruction or damage caused by the carelessness, negligence or improper conduct of the Tenant, his family, agents, servants, guests or visitors. In determining reasonable time for the making of repairs, allowance shall be made for all time lost in connection with the adjustment of the fire insurance loss and all time lost by reason of what are commonly known as "labor troubles."

DEFAULTS

FIVE-DAY NOTICE

SIXTH.—If the Tenant shall default in fulfilling any of the covenants or conditions of this lease, other than the covenant for the payment of rent, or if the Tenant becomes insolvent or be adjudicated a bankrupt or applies for or takes the benefit of any bankruptcy or insolvent act or any act or statutory provisions for the relief of debtors, now or hereafter enacted, or makes a general assignment for the benefit of creditors or if a Receiver or Trustee be appointed for the Tenant's property, or if this lease or the estate of the Tenant hereunder be transferred or pass to or devolve upon any other person or corporation, or if the Landlord, or the assigns of the Landlord, or the agent for the time being of the Landlord or of said assigns in respect to said demised premises, shall deem objectionable or improper any conduct on the part of the Tenant or occupants, the Landlord may give to the Tenant five days' notice of intention to end the term of this lease, and thereupon at the expiration of said five days, the term under this lease shall expire as fully and completely as if that day were the date herein definitely fixed for the expiration of the term, and the Tenant will then quit and surrender the demised premises to the Landlord, but the Tenant shall remain liable as hereinafter provided.

RIGHTS UPON DEFAULTS, RE-ENTRY

RELETTING

WAIVER BY TENANT

If the Tenant shall default in the payment of the rent reserved hereunder, or any part thereof, or if the notice last above provided for shall have been given and said five days' period shall have elapsed, or if the demised premises become vacant or deserted, the Landlord, by its agents and servants, may immediately, or at any time thereafter, re-enter the demised premises and remove all persons and property therefrom, either by summary dispossess proceedings or by any suitable action or proceeding at law, or by force or otherwise, without being liable to indictment, prosecution or damage therefor, and the Tenant, whether or not the premises be re-let as hereinafter provided, shall remain liable to the Landlord for damages equivalent in amount to all of the rent reserved hereunder to the time when this lease would have expired but for such termination, and the same shall be due and payable by the Tenant to the Landlord on the several rent days above specified, and also in case of any such re-entry the Tenant shall pay to the Landlord on demand, as additional damages, all legal and other expenses incurred in removing the Tenant, the commissions for re-letting the demised premises and collecting rent, the cost of redecorating, refinishing and repairing the demised premises and such other expenses as the Landlord may incur in connection therewith. Upon any such re-entry, the Landlord, at its option, may re-let the demised premises or any part or parts thereof, for the remainder of the demised term or any part or parts thereof or for a period extending beyond the date for the expiration of this lease and receive the rents therefor; and the rents collected for the balance of the agreed term of the Tenant on any such re-letting may be applied to pay any of the aforesaid items of "additional damages" remaining unpaid and to the fulfillment and performance of the other covenants of the Tenant hereunder, and the net avails thereof shall be applied by the Landlord on account of any rent unpaid by the Tenant for the remainder of the demised term; but the Tenant, however, shall pay to the Landlord upon each of such rent days the amount of any and all deficiencies then existing. The Tenant hereby waives all rights of redemption and the Tenant waives all rights now or hereafter existing under Real Property Law, §227; and the Tenant waives all rights to trial by jury in any summary proceeding hereafter instituted by the Landlord against the Tenant in respect to the demised premises and in any action hereafter brought to recover rent or "additional rent" becoming due hereunder and in any other proceeding or action involving the terms, covenants or conditions of this lease or the demised premises, and on any defense or counterclaim interposed by Tenant in any of such proceedings or actions. The words "re-enter" and "re-entry" as used in this lease are not restricted to their technical legal meaning. Tenant agrees that the covenants of the Tenant in this lease contained on the part of the Tenant to be performed, shall be deemed conditional limitations as well as covenants and conditions.

REMEDIES CUMULATIVE

OTHER REMEDIES

ADDITIONAL RENT

In the event of a breach or threatened breach by the Tenant of any of the terms, covenants or conditions of this lease, the Landlord shall have the right of injunction, and the right to invoke any remedy allowed at law or in equity, as if re-entry, summary proceedings and other remedies were not herein provided for. If the Tenant shall default in the performance of any covenant herein contained, the Landlord may immediately, or at any time thereafter, without notice, perform the same for the account of the Tenant. If a notice of mechanic's lien be filed against the demised premises, for, or purporting to be for, labor or material alleged to have been furnished, or to be furnished to or for the Tenant at the demised premises, and if the Tenant shall fail to take such action as shall cause such lien to be discharged within fifteen days after the filing of such notice, the Landlord may pay the amount of such lien or discharge the same by deposit or by bonding proceedings, and in the event of such deposit or bonding proceedings, the Landlord may require the lienor to prosecute an appropriate action to enforce the lienor's claim. In such case, the Landlord may pay any judgment recovered on such claim. Any amount paid or expense incurred by the Landlord, as in this section of this lease provided, and any amount other than rent as to which the Tenant shall at any time be in default for or in respect to any provision of this lease, and at any expense incurred or sum of money paid by the Landlord by reason of the failure of the Tenant to comply with any provision hereof, or in defending any such action, shall be deemed to be "additional rent" for the demised premises, and shall be due and payable by the Tenant to the Landlord on the first day of the next following month, or, at the option of the Landlord, on the first day of any succeeding month. The receipt by the Landlord of any installment of the regular stipulated rent hereunder or any of said "additional rent", shall not be a waiver of any other "additional rent" then due. For the non-payment of any "additional rent" the Landlord shall have the same rights and remedies that the Landlord has for any of the regular first above specified rent.

ALL RENT DUE

SEVENTH.—Anything herein to the contrary notwithstanding, the premises herein mentioned are demised for the whole term with the whole amount of rent herein reserved due and payable at the time of the making of this lease, and the payment of rent in installments as above provided is for the convenience of Tenant only and upon default by Tenant in the making of any installment payment of rent, then the whole of the rent reserved for the whole of the period then remaining unpaid shall, at Landlord's option, at once become due and payable without any notice or demand.

COLLECTION OF RENT FROM OTHERS

EIGHTH.—No payment by Tenant or receipt by Landlord of an amount less than the monthly rent herein stipulated, shall be deemed to be other than on account of the stipulated rent, nor shall any endorsement on any check nor any letter accompanying such payment of rent be deemed an accord and satisfaction, but Landlord may accept such payment without prejudice to Landlord's rights to collect the balance of such rent. If this lease be assigned, or if the demised premises or any part thereof be underlet, sublet or occupied by anybody other than the Tenant, the Landlord may collect rent from the assignee, undertenant, subtenant or occupant and apply the net amount collected to the rent herein reserved, and no such collection shall be deemed a waiver of the covenant herein against assignment, underletting and subletting, or as an acceptance of the assignee, undertenant, subtenant, or occupant as tenant, and in every such case the Tenant shall perform and continue to perform all of the covenants of this lease on the part of the Tenant to be performed.

AS TO WAIVERS

KEYS

NINTH.—The failure of the Landlord to insist, in any one or more instances upon a strict performance of any of the covenants of this lease, or to exercise any option herein contained, shall not be construed as a waiver or a relinquishment for the future, of such covenant or option, but the same shall continue and remain in full force and effect. The receipt by the Landlord of rent, with knowledge of the breach of any covenant or condition hereof, shall not be deemed a waiver of such breach, and no waiver by the Landlord of any provision hereof shall be deemed to have been made unless expressed in writing and signed by the Landlord. Even though the Landlord shall consent to an assignment hereof, no further assignment shall be made without express consent in writing by the Landlord. The delivery of keys of the demised premises to any officer or employee of the Landlord or to the Landlord's agent, shall not operate as a termination of this lease or as a surrender of the demised premises.

MORTGAGE SUBORDINATION

TENTH.—This lease shall be subject and subordinate at all times to the lien of any and all mortgages or extensions or renewals thereof now or at any time hereafter placed upon the demised premises or the lands of which the demised premises are a part, and to all advances made or hereafter to be made on the security thereof, irrespective of the date of recording, and the Tenant agrees to execute and deliver on demand by Landlord such further instrument or instruments evidencing such subordination of this lease to the lien of any such mortgage or mortgages or extension or renewal thereof or advances made or to be made on the security thereof, as may be necessary or requested by Landlord, and a refusal to execute such instrument or instruments shall entitle the Landlord, at its option to cancel this lease in the manner provided in the first paragraph of section "Sixth" hereof without incurring any expense or damage and the term hereby granted is expressly limited accordingly, and the Tenant hereby appoints the Landlord the attorney-in-fact of the Tenant, irrevocable to execute and deliver any such instrument or instruments evidencing such subordination for and in the name of the Tenant. In the event of the voiding or annulment of this lease by the foreclosure of any such mortgage, the Landlord shall not be liable for any damages or loss thereby caused to or suffered by the Tenant.

IMPROVEMENTS

ELEVENTH.—All improvements made by the Tenant to or upon the demised premises shall, when made, at once be deemed to be attached to the freehold, and become the property of the Landlord, and at the end or other expiration of the term, shall be surrendered to the Landlord in as good order and condition as they were when installed, reasonable wear excepted.

NOTICES

TWELFTH.—Any notice by the Landlord to the Tenant shall be deemed to be duly given only if in writing and either delivered personally to the Tenant or left upon the demised premises, or delivered to any person in charge of the demised premises, or mailed by registered letter in any general or branch post office enclosed in a postpaid envelope addressed to the Tenant at his or its above address or at the demised premises. Any notice by the Tenant to the Landlord shall be deemed to be duly given only if in writing and either delivered personally to an officer of the Landlord or to the agent (if any) of the Landlord charged with the renting and management of the demised premises, or mailed by registered letter in any general or branch post office, enclosed in a postpaid envelope addressed to the Landlord at the address hereinbefore given.

NO LIABILITY

THIRTEENTH.—The Tenant accepts the demised premises in their present condition unless otherwise herein expressly stated. The Landlord shall not be liable for any failure of water supply, electric current, mechanical refrigeration, if any, or other service. The Landlord shall not be liable for injury, loss or damage to the person or property of the Tenant caused by the elements, or by steam, gas, electricity, water, rain or snow which may leak or flow from any part of the demised premises or from the pipes, appliances or plumbing works of the same or from any other place, or by falling plaster, or by defects in the demised premises or in any improvements, alterations or repairs now or hereafter made thereto, or by any act or thing heretofore or hereafter done or omitted by the Landlord, unless caused by the negligence of the Landlord. The Tenant shall give the Landlord prompt written notice of any accident to or defects in water pipes, gas pipes, heating apparatus or other equipment or appliances in the demised premises. The Landlord shall not be liable for the presence of Croton bugs, vermin or insects, if any, in the demised premises, nor shall their presence in any way affect this lease. The Landlord shall not be liable for any latent defect in the building.

NO ABATEMENT

FOURTEENTH.—There shall not be any diminution or abatement of rent because of the making of repairs or improvements, if any be made, to the demised premises after the date above fixed for the commencement of the term, but the same are to be done with reasonable dispatch and with as little inconvenience to the Tenant as reasonably possible, it being understood that rent shall, in all events, commence to run at the date above fixed therefor. No diminution or abatement of rent, or other compensation, shall be claimed or allowed for loss, inconvenience or discomfort arising from the making of repairs or improvements to the building or to its appliances or from fumes or dirt issuing out of the heating or refrigerating equipment in the building, or from the closing or darkening of any windows of the demised premises from any cause whatever, or by reason of any space taken to comply with any law, ordinance or order of a governmental authority.

FIFTEENTH.—If the demised premises are available for occupancy before the date above specified for commencement of the term, the Tenant may then take possession of the demised premises provided and only upon condition that the Landlord consent in writing to the taking of such possession by the Tenant; and in the event that the Tenant thus takes earlier possession of the demised premises, the term of this lease shall be deemed for all purposes to commence from the time of the taking of such possession by the Tenant, but the Tenant shall not be required to pay any rental in addition to that above specified by reason of taking earlier possession of the demised premises unless otherwise provided. If the Landlord shall not be ready or able to give possession of the demised premises to the Tenant at the date above prescribed for the commencement of the term, then the date of the commencement of the term shall be postponed until the Landlord shall be ready and able so to give possession, and rent shall not run in the meantime but shall be apportioned as of the date that the Landlord shall notify the Tenant that the demised premises will be ready for occupancy; and the Landlord shall not be liable for damages, if any, sustained by the Tenant because of failure to deliver possession before the demised premises are ready for occupancy. The Landlord assumes no responsibility to the Tenant for delay in giving possession due to failure of present occupant of demised premises to vacate at termination of lease, except that the Tenant will be credited upon the rent next to accrue with an allowance equal to the daily pro rata amount of the rent multiplied by the actual number of days during which possession is withheld, and the Tenant agrees to accept the lease subject to such contingency and condition. If the Tenant shall, before the date above fixed for the commencement of the term hereof, default in the performance of any agreement by the Tenant herein or contained in any other lease or letting by the Landlord to the Tenant, then, at the option of the Landlord this lease shall not go into effect, and the Tenant shall not be entitled to possession hereunder.

SIXTEENTH.—The Tenant hereby acknowledges notice from the Landlord that no agent, manager or representative of the Landlord has the power or authority to either modify, cancel or accept a surrender of this lease, and that such power and authority is vested solely in the senior officers of the Landlord. No modification, cancellation or surrender of this lease shall be effective unless in writing signed by the Landlord by its duly authorized officers. The Landlord has made no representations or promises in respect to the demised premises except those contained herein, and those, if any, contained in some written communication to the Tenant, signed by the Landlord or the Landlord's agent authorized so to do.

SEVENTEENTH.—That during three months prior to the expiration of the term hereby granted, the Tenant will permit the Landlord to place in a conspicuous part of the exterior of the demised premises, the usual notice offering the premises "To Let" and/or "For Sale," and will permit the same to remain without hindrance or molestation, and during such time applicants shall be admitted at all reasonable hours of the day to view the premises until rented; and the Landlord and the Landlord's agents shall be permitted at any time during the term to visit and examine the premises at any reasonable hours of the day, and workmen may enter at any time, when authorized by the Landlord or the Landlord's agents, to make or facilitate improvements, alterations or repairs in any part of the building; and if the said Tenant shall not be personally present to open and permit an entry into said premises, at any time, when for any reason an entry therein shall be necessary or permissible hereunder, the Landlord or the Landlord's agents may forcibly enter the same without rendering the Landlord or such agents liable to any claim or cause of action for damages by reason thereof (if during such entry the Landlord shall accord reasonable care to the Tenant's property) and without in any manner affecting the obligations and covenants of this lease; it is, however, expressly understood that the right and authority hereby reserved, does not impose, nor does the Landlord assume, by reason thereof, any responsibility or liability whatsoever for the care or supervision of said premises, or any of the pipes, fixtures, appliances or appurtenances therein contained or therewith in any manner connected.

EIGHTEENTH.—If the Tenant shall at any time be in default hereunder, and if the Landlord shall institute an action or summary proceeding against the Tenant based upon such default, then the Tenant will reimburse the Landlord for the expense of attorney's fees, costs and disbursements thereby incurred by the Landlord, so far as the same are reasonable in amount; and the amount of such expenses, costs and disbursements shall at the option of the Landlord, be deemed to be additional rent hereunder, and shall be due from the Tenant to the Landlord on the first day of the month following the incurring of such respective expenses, or on the first day of any succeeding month.

NINETEENTH.—If the demised premises or any part thereof, be taken by virtue of eminent domain, or for any public or quasi-public improvement, this lease shall, at the option of the Landlord, expire ten days after notice to the Tenant; and in the event of the exercise of such option by the Landlord, the Tenant shall pay the rent pro rata, up to the time of the expiration of this lease and thereafter neither party hereto shall have any claim against the other by reason of such termination, and any and all awards for any such taking are assigned to and shall be made to the Landlord, and the Tenant shall not have any claim of any kind against any such award or awards.

TWENTIETH.—The Tenant has deposited with the Landlord, the sum of...Dollars, and agrees from time to time to pay to the Landlord, any sum or sums of money paid by the Landlord out of the sum so deposited, or deducted therefrom by the Landlord, pursuant to the provisions of this lease, to the end that at all times during the term of this lease there shall be continually deposited with the Landlord a sum which shall never be less than the amount originally deposited; the money so deposited shall remain with the Landlord as security for the faithful performance by the Tenant of all the terms, covenants and conditions of this lease until the date herein originally fixed for the expiration of the term, except as herein otherwise provided.

If the Landlord shall pay or be liable to pay any sum or sums of money whatsoever, or do or perform any act or thing on behalf of the Tenant, or make good any default by the Tenant hereunder, or if any penalty be assessed or imposed against the Landlord or any owner of the premises because of any default of the Tenant under this lease, any amount paid by the Landlord or such owner, or for which the Landlord or such owner may become liable together with all interest, costs, expenses, fees and damages, may be paid by the Landlord or such owner at its option out of such security or may be deducted therefrom. If the Tenant becomes insolvent or be adjudicated a bankrupt or applies for or takes the benefit of any bankruptcy or insolvent act or any act or statutory provisions for the relief of debtors, now or hereafter enacted, or makes a general assignment, or if a receiver or trustee be appointed for the Tenant's property, then in either such case said security shall be deemed to be and hereby is assigned to the Landlord; in any such event, or in case of any default by Tenant in performing the terms of this lease by reason of which this lease is terminated either by summary proceedings or by notice as herein provided, such security shall belong to the Landlord and shall be retained by the Landlord without any right thereto or to any part thereof by the Tenant, and the right to retain such security shall survive summary proceedings or other proceedings for the recovery of possession of the premises. Upon a sale or conveyance of the demised premises, the Landlord or any owner of the premises may transfer or assign such security to any new owner of said premises, and upon such transfer all liability of the transferrer or assignor of such security shall cease and come to an end.

TWENTY-FIRST.—The term "Landlord" as used in this lease means only the party who for the time being is the owner, or the assignee of rents, or the mortgagee in possession, or the owner of a lease of the land and building of which the demised premises form a part, as the case may be; and the Tenant agrees that as, if and when any Landlord hereunder sells or transfers title to or conveys or assigns such land and building or lease, or in the event its or his rights under such assignment of rents or as mortgagee in possession are terminated, or in the event of any subsequent lease of the entire building, such Landlord shall be and hereby is wholly released, discharged and relieved of and from all of the covenants and obligations of the Landlord hereunder, and thereupon and thereafter the sole and exclusive right or rights, remedy or remedies and recourse of the Tenant for any subsequent violation or breach of the covenants and obligations of the Landlord hereunder shall be against the person, firm or corporation succeeding to the rights of such Landlord, whether or not such person, firm or corporation shall assume or agree to perform or comply with such covenants and obligations of the Landlord hereunder.

THE LANDLORD COVENANTS:

That if and so long as the Tenant pays the rent reserved hereby, and performs and observes the covenants and provisions hereof, the Tenant shall quietly enjoy the demised premises, subject however, to the terms of this lease and to the mortgages above mentioned and provided for, and to any foreclosure of any such mortgages.

The marginal notes are inserted only as a matter of convenience and for reference and in no way define, limit or describe the scope or intent of this lease, and in no way affect this lease.

This lease, and every provision hereof, shall bind, apply to and run in favor of the Landlord, its successors and assigns, and of the Tenant and the heirs and personal representatives of the Tenant.

IN WITNESS WHEREOF, the Landlord and Tenant have signed and sealed this lease the day and year first above written.

Witness as to Tenant:

....(L. S.)
Landlord

....(L. S.)
Tenant

Sub-Lease

𝕿𝖍𝖎𝖘 𝕾𝖚𝖇-𝕷𝖊𝖆𝖘𝖊 *made the*   *day of*   *19*   *, between*

hereinafter referred to as Lessor, and

hereinafter referred to as Lessee

WITNESSETH, *that the Lessor hereby leases to the Lessee, and the Lessee hereby hires and takes from the Lessor, the following premises, to wit;*
in the building known as

to be used and occupied by the Lessee for

and for no other purpose, for a term to commence on the   *day of*   *19*   *, and to end on the*   *day of*   *19*   *, unless sooner terminated as hereinafter provided, at the* ANNUAL RENT *as hereinafter provided, payable in equal monthly instalments in advance on the*   *day of each and every calendar month during said term, except the first instalment, which shall be paid upon the execution hereof.*

The said premises are the same premises, or a part of the premises, referred to in a lease between

as the landlord and the Lessor herein as the tenant therein, dated the   *day of*   *19*

The Lessee represents that the Lessee has read the said lease (an exact copy thereof is attached hereto).

The terms, covenants, provisions and conditions of said lease are hereby incorporated herein and shall be binding upon both parties hereto, those applying to the landlord therein shall apply to the Lessor herein and those applying to the tenant therein shall apply to the Lessee herein with the following exceptions:

    a. *The annual rent payable hereunder shall be $*

    b. *The security, if any, to be deposited hereunder shall be $*

    c. *The following numbered paragraphs of said lease shall not apply to this sub-lease:*

The following numbered paragraphs of said lease are amended to read as follows:

IN WITNESS WHEREOF, *the parties have executed this sub-lease in duplicate the day and year first above written.*

Signed, sealed and delivered in the presence of

----

* *Strike out words within parenthesis if they do not apply.*

Extension of Lease

Landlord

EXTENSION OF LEASE

Date

Tenant(s) :	Re: LEASE
Premises:	Dated
	Expires on
	Apt. — office — etc. :

Dear Tenant(s) :

The LEASE referred to above expires shortly. If you wish to extend your LEASE the annual rent for the premises commencing on   19   will be $ payable $
monthly in advance, for an extended term of

In connection with the foregoing, additional security will be required in the amount of $
making the total security of $

If prior to the commencement of the extended term you default in any of the terms, covenants and conditions of the LEASE this agreement shall, at the option of the Landlord, be null and void.

All other terms, covenants and conditions of the LEASE shall remain in full force and effect for the duration of the extended term.

If you wish to extend the term of the LEASE please sign this agreement where indicated (X) and return two copies to the Landlord together with a check in the amount of the additional security within   days of the above date.

If you intend to vacate the premises please sign your name under the words "Tenant(s) will vacate the premises at the end of the present term" and return two copies to the Landlord.

SIGN HERE TO EXTEND LEASE

Tenant(s) : X_____

each Tenant on
original Lease   X_____
must sign

This EXTENSION AGREEMENT does not become binding until the return to you of a copy signed by the Landlord.

Tenant(s) will vacate the premises at the end of the term
_____
_____

Landlord

By_____

The Model Lease

THE PROTENANT LEASE: A SUMMARY

A Brooklyn Legal Services office has published what may be the first protenant lease for use by individual tenants and tenants groups in New York City.* From a tenant viewpoint, it represents an improvement over the "standard form" prolandlord lease in at least three important respects.

First, the protenant lease omits the onerous "boilerplate" clauses which premeate the prolandlord lease. Among the *deleted* clauses are the following:

A waiver of the constitutional right to a jury trial;

A waiver of the right to countersue when the landlord sues for nonpayment of rent—for example, to counterclaim for money the tenant has spent on necessary repairs;

The notorious "no dog" clause;

A prohibition against subletting (under the protenant lease, the landlord may not unreasonably refuse to permit it);

A clause requiring the tenant to pay the landlord's legal expenses.

Second, the protenant lease provides needed information to the tenant and seeks to resolve, before they arise, many of the most common disputes between landlords and tenants:

The landlord must tell the tenant the name and phone number of a real person who is responsible for repairs. This is essential if the landlord is a corporation.

The landlord agrees to pay interest on the tenant's security deposit, and if he sells the building, either to return the se-security deposit or to turn it over to the new owner (¶¶19, 20).

The lease specifies how the rent shall be collected (¶4) and requires the landlord to issue receipts (¶5). Many

small landlords refuse to issue receipts and have no regular procedure for payment of rent.

It is agreed that Welfare recipients may pay the monthly rent in two installments, corresponding to their receipt of assistance payments (¶3).

Third, the protenant lease redefines the rights and obligations of the parties so that their relationship conforms to widely-held conceptions of fairness and equity:

The tenant promises that he will pay the rent and that he will not commit a "nuisance," wilfully damage the apartment, or substantially disturb others in the building (¶6). The landlord has the right to enforce this promise by evicting a tenant who breaks it (¶9). (This differs from many prolandlord leases which permit the landlord to evict a tenant for violations of nit-picking rules and regulations, such as that TVs shall not be played between 10 PM and 8 AM.)

The landlord agrees to keep the apartment in good condition, and to supply essential services such as heat and hot water (¶8). The tenant has the right to enforce this agreement by effectuating a rent abatement, after giving proper notice to the landlord, for the period during which repairs are needed or essential services are not provided (¶¶10, 11). (This differs from prolandlord leases which, while they may say that the tenant is to receive heat and hot water, fail to provide any enforcement mechanism or means of compensating the tenant for the hardship suffered when such services are interrupted.)

The protenant lease may not win immediate acceptance by landlords, for in a tight real estate market few landlords will have reason to give up the "swords of Damocles" which they now hold over the heads of their tenants in the form of unconscionably one-sided leases. But like it or not, rising tenant militancy may soon

SBLS Form Lease of Apartment No. 1

How to Handle Your Own Contracts

force landlords to release tenants from their almost-feudal bonds. The SBLS protenant lease provides a basis for negotiated rental agreements, and a goal to be pursued by an increasingly aware and power tenant movement.

FOR FURTHER INFORMATION, CONTACT:
Allen R. Bentley
Staff Attorney
South Brooklyn Legal Services
152 Court Street
Brooklyn, New York 11201
855-8003

The SBLS lease is discussed in detail in this article: Bentley, "An Alternative Residential Lease," Columbia Law Review, vol. 74, p. 836 (June 1974).

THE PROTENANT LEASE:
QUESTIONS AND ANSWERS

1. How many copies should be filled out for signing?

Two copies should be sufficient—one for the tenant and one for the landlord.

2. Can you add other clauses, such as giving the tenant the option to cancel on short notice or to renew the lease at the same rent?

Yes. Add extra clauses in the space provided above the signature lines. Be sure that the added material is the same on both copies.

3. How do you find out the multiple dwelling registration number and other preliminary information?

The landlord should have this information. The registration number must be posted in the lobby of your building. The other information can, if necessary, be obtained from the Department of Buildings in your Borough.

4. Can the lease be used by an Article 7A Administrator or a Receiver?

Yes, if the Administrator or Receiver has been given authority to enter into leases by the Court. If a person who is not the owner of the building is signing the lease as Landlord, the person's authority should be indicated. For example: "Landlord, J. Smith, Article 7A Administrator"

5. Can a tenant give the lease to a subtenant?

Yes. The lease will not bind the landlord, however, unless he or she also signs it.

6. Do you need a witness?
No.

7. Do the signatures have to be notarized?
No. The lease is binding whether or not the signatures are notarized.

8. What about long term leases?

A lease for three years or less will be valid no matter what, and your landlord himself will be bound by the lease he signs no matter how long it is. However, if the lease is for longer than three years it will not be respected by a new owner (if for example the landlord sells the building) unless it has been "recorded" in the public records kept by the City Register. You should see a lawyer about having the lease recorded.

9. What about other questions?

For further advice or information on other questions, you should contact a lawyer. If you cannot afford a private attorney and are a New York City resident, you may be able to obtain free legal help from a neighborhood office of Community Action for Legal Services (CALS). Call CALS (966-6600) for the location of the office nearest you.

10. Can the lease be used outside of New York City?

Yes. It should be noted that not all of the preliminary information (such as multiple dwelling registration) will be applicable.

11. Can the lease be used outside of New York State?

Yes. It is important to note that the answers to the above questions are based on New York law and the answers may be different under the laws of other states. Check with a lawyer in the state where you are using the lease if you have any questions.

Form Lease of Apartment

1. Landlord hereby leases to Tenant the premises described above for a term of ___ years, beginning _____ and ending _____, at a rental rate of _____ per month, making a total rental amount payable under this lease of _____ .

2. Tenant agrees to pay the rent as herein provided subject to the terms and conditions set forth herein.

3. Rent shall be payable in equal monthly installments to be paid in advance on the _____ day of each month, provided, that if Tenant is or shall become dependent upon any governmental agency for support, income supplementation, home relief, or other benefits, rent hereunder may, at the option of Tenant, be payable in equal semi-monthly installments to be paid in advance on the 2nd and 17th of each month.

4. Rent shall be paid in the following manner:
(Specify above if payments are to be made by mail, and if so, to what address; if payments are to be made to Landlord or his agent in person, state the place where and person to whom payments are to be made.)

5. Upon each payment of rent, Landlord agrees to issue a receipt stating clearly Tenant's name, a description of the premises, the amount of rent paid, and the period for which said rent is paid.

6. Tenant covenants that he shall not commit or permit a nuisance in the premises, that he shall not maliciously or by reason of gross negligence substantially damage the premises, and that he shall not engage in conduct such as to interfere substantially with the comfort and safety of Landlord or of other tenants or occupants of the same or another adjacent building or structure.

7. Landlord agrees that Tenant and Tenant's family shall have, hold, and enjoy the leased premises for the term set forth herein subject to the terms and conditions set forth herein.

8. Landlord covenants that the leased premises are safe, sound, and healthful and that said premises shall be kept in said condition at all times during the term of this lease and any extension, renewal, or continuation thereof. Landlord covenants that all essential services are now provided and shall be provided at all times during the term of this lease and any extension, renewal, or continuation thereof. "Essential services" hereunder are defined as heat, hot and cold running water, a properly functioning toilet, electricity, and if a gas stove is provided, gas. Landlord covenants that there exists in the leased premises no violation of any applicable housing code, law, or regulation, and that no such violation will be permitted to exist at any time during the term of this lease and any extension, renewal, or continuation thereof. Nothing in this lease shall be construed as an admission by Tenant concerning the condition of the leased premises at the time of Tenant's taking possession thereof or at any other time or as a waiver by Tenant of any right or remedy which he may have, now or at any future time, with respect to any condition in the leased premises, whether arising before or after the commencement of this lease.

9. In the event of any breach by Tenant of paragraphs "6" or "17" herein, Landlord may give Tenant five days' notice to cure said breach, setting forth in detail the manner in which said paragraph or paragraphs has or have been breached. If said breach is not cured within said five-day period, or reasonable steps to effectuate said cure are not commenced and diligently pursued within said five-day period and thereafter until said breach has been cured, Landlord may terminate this lease upon five days' additional notice to Tenant. Said termination shall be ineffective if Tenant cures said breach, or commences and diligently pursues reasonable steps to effectuate such cure, at any time prior to the expiration of said five-day notice of termination. Upon terminating this lease as provided herein, Landlord may commence summary proceedings against Tenant for his removal as provided by law.

10. In the event of any breach by Landlord of paragraphs "7" or "8" herein, Tenant may give Landlord ten days' notice to cure said breach, setting forth in detail the manner in which said paragraph or paragraphs has or have been breached. If said breach is not cured within said ten-day period, or reasonable steps to effectuate said cure are not commenced and diligently pursued within said ten-day period and thereafter until said breach has been cured, rent hereunder shall be fully abated from the time at which said ten days' notice expired until such time as Landlord has fully cured the breach set forth in the notice provided for in this paragraph. In no case shall any abatement of rent hereunder be effected where the condition set forth in the notice provided for herein was created by the intentional or negligent act of Tenant, but Landlord shall have the burden of proving that a rent abatement may not be effected for the foregoing reason.

11. In the event of any interruption, discontinuance, or termination of any essential service or services hereunder, the provisions of paragraph "10" herein shall apply; however, rent hereunder shall in such event be fully abated from the time that notice is given to Landlord until the time that the essential service or services is or are fully restored.

12. The remedies provided in paragraphs "9," "10," and "11" herein are not exclusive. Nothing in this lease shall be construed as a waiver by either party of such additional legal, equitable, or administrative remedies as are now, or may in the future be, available to him.

13. Tenant shall give prompt notice to Landlord of any dangerous, defective, unsafe or emergency condition in the leased premises, and said notice may be given by any suitable means, paragraph "22" herein notwithstanding. Landlord shall repair and correct said conditions immediately upon receiving notice thereof from Tenant.

14. Paragraphs "2," "6" and "17" herein shall comprise Tenant's substantial obligations under this lease.

15. Tenant shall pay for gas, electricity, and telephone service, if any, except to the extent otherwise set forth herein. Landlord covenants that consumption of electricity for the public halls and other common areas and uses and the consumption of gas for heat and hot water are recorded on separate meters, and that said electricity and gas are and will at all times be billed to and paid for by Landlord.

16. Tenant shall at reasonable times give access to Landlord or his agents for any reasonable and lawful purpose. Except in situations of compelling emergency, Landlord shall give Tenant at least 24 hours' notice of intention to seek access, the date and time at which access will be sought, and the reason therefor. Landlord covenants that Tenant shall have access at all times to the fuse-box or circuit-breakers which govern the flow of electricity to the leased premises.

17. Tenant shall not assign this lease or underlet the leased premises or any part thereof without Landlord's written consent, which consent Landlord agrees not to withhold unreasonably.

18. Landlord agrees to deliver possession of the leased premises at the beginning of the term provided for herein. In the event of the Landlord's failure to deliver possession at the beginning of said term, Tenant shall have the right to rescind this lease and to recover any consideration paid, which right shall not be deemed inconsistent with any right of action Tenant may have to recover damages.

19. Tenant agrees to make a security deposit with Landlord in the amount of one month's rent, to be used by Landlord at the termination of this lease for the cost of repairing damage, if any, to the premises caused by the intentional or negligent acts of Tenant, as well as for rent, if any, owed by Tenant. Landlord agrees, within ten days of receiving said security money, to deposit same in an interest-bearing account in a banking organization, which account shall earn interest at a rate which shall be the prevailing rate earned by other such deposits made with banking organizations in such area. Landlord agrees, within ten days of making said deposit, to notify Tenant of the name and address of the banking organization in which the deposit of security money has been made, and the amount of such deposit. Landlord shall be entitled to receive, as administration expenses, a sum equivalent to one per cent per annum upon the security money so deposited, which shall be in lieu of all other administrative and custodial expenses. The balance of the interest paid by the banking organization shall be the money of Tenant and shall be paid to Tenant on each anniversary of this lease or any extension, renewal, or continuation thereof. Landlord agrees to return said security deposit to Tenant upon Tenant's vacating the leased premises subject to the terms and conditions set forth herein.

20. In the event that Landlord conveys title to the leased premises he shall, at the time of delivery of the deed or within five days thereafter, (a) turn over the security deposit hereunder to his grantee and notify Tenant of such turning over and of the name and address of such grantee, or (b) return the security deposit hereunder to Tenant.

21. Landlord shall, within five days of any change in the preliminary information heretofore set forth herein, notify Tenant thereof.

22. Any notice required or authorized hereunder shall be given in writing, one copy of said notice mailed via U.S. certified mail, and one copy of said notice mailed via U.S. first class mail. Notice to Tenant shall be mailed to him at the leased premises. Notice to Landlord shall be mailed to him or to the registered managing agent at their respective addresses as heretofore set forth herein, or at such new address as to which Tenant has been duly notified.

23. This lease constitutes the entire agreement of the parties hereto. No changes shall be made herein except by writing, signed by each party, and dated. The failure to enforce any right or remedy hereunder and the payment or acceptance of rent hereunder shall not be deemed a waiver by either party of such right or remedy in the absence of a writing as provided for herein.

24. CAUTION TO THE PARTIES: This lease, when filled out and signed, is a binding legal obligation. Do not sign it if there are any blank spaces. Cross out all blanks before signing.

CHAPTER 3

Land Purchase Contracts & Deeds

Introduction

Like landlord-tenant law, the law of conveyances and deeds has roots which run far back into the centuries and across the Atlantic to England. Fortunately, unlike landlord-tenant law, early common law does not hold such close reins. Statutory law in most states has liberalized the law, removing archaic technicalities that in the past impeded land conveyances without purpose.

Of course, the major distinction between deeds and leases is that the former is a complete transferral of land rather than a limited estate. Because of this difference, the taker or grantee need not commit himself to oppressive covenants such as a lessee must do in order to obtain possession. Since the bargaining position between the grantor and grantee is more equal, one does not have to sign away his rights in order to realize his objective. This situation is a result of a more balanced land sales and purchase market.

Although fewer complications are encountered than with the conveyance of a less than freehold estate, the conveyance of title to property is a legal transaction and is bound by both common and statutory law. It would be helpful to understand your position as either grantor or grantee in the execution of a deed, and explanation of the document, its legal history, its current statutory status, and its requirements.

Initially, a deed was not a necessary instrument to a transfer of title of land. As long as the grantor physically presented the land to the grantee, title passed and the exchange of a deed later on was a formality—a written description of the occurrence which defined the extent of the estate. The deed, however, was essential in order to create or transfer incorporeal rights in land such as easements and estates which were to commence in the future or revert to the grantor at some later date. These less-than-freehold interests had to be granted and evidenced by a written deed since an actual physical delivery was an impossibility. As the law evolved, physical delivery known as *livery*, became extinct and was succeeded by *delivery of the deed* as an equally competent and less troublesome method of conveyance.

The law changing this tradition was the Statute of Uses which promoted what was previously known as a use, or an interest in land to commence in future, into an immediate legal estate on land. Any conveyance which fell within the purview of the statute vested the grantee with legal title at that time and eliminated the need for physical delivery on the date when the interest was to take effect. Since deeds, then, could convey all estates in land, their prominence increased as livery became outdated.

The Deed of Today

Evolving out of this overly-technical ancestry, the modern deed may now be the instrument of conveyance for all land interests, regardless of whether they are incorporeal rights, complete title, or are to commence now or in the future. All ancient deed forms now operate

33

as complete statutory deeds in transferring title between grantor and grantee, although differences still exist as to the extent of the grantor's warranties. Thus, title passes under a *statutory warranty* deed, quitclaim deed, deed of bargain and sale, deed of lease, or lease, coupled with release and surrender.

Even though title passes by any of these deeds, each has its own peculiarities. Since each still exists, at least in name, it would be worthwhile to discuss the purpose of the separate deeds.

The *warranty deed* offers the grantee the best protection of all the deeds. The covenants which it contains are similar to lease covenants as lesser contractual agreements within the deed itself. As with a lease, a warranty deed creates both privity of estate and privity of contract between the parties and, in most instances, between successors on interests as well. Although the covenants extend as far as the promises made in each, they do not have any impact on the actual conveyance. In that sense the deed and the covenants are separate operative provisions. The statutory form of a warranty deed can be seen to pass title to the property described "together with the appurtenances and all estate and rights of the part of the first part (grantor) in and to said premises." The sentence, for its purpose is fine, but the purchaser of title would be well advised to ascertain the scope of the seller's interest in the land. Under the provision, the grantee-purchaser (and his assigns) takes only that interest which the seller possesses, no more, no less. In order to protect himself and have viable causes of action against the seller, if in fact he believes himself to be buying a full-fee interest, the purchaser must obtain the covenants which follow. These will be discussed later on.

The *quitclaim deed*, on the other hand, provides the grantee with little protection against future problems. In essence, the grantor guarantees nothing except that as between himself and the grantor, the grantee prevails. In other words, the seller of the property grants to the buyer only those rights on the land that the grantor possessed. Thus, if the grantor was not

fully seized of the property, but had only a life estate, the grantee takes title of this lesser than estate in fee. At the end of the grantor's estate, i.e., at his death, the grantee is not protected from seizure of the land by the remainderman, who now has legal title to the property. Although a thorough title search should be executed before any property purchase, it is particularly important where a quitclaim deed is the instrument of conveyance. No one wants to be cast in a position of believing that he is seized of land in fee having paid consideration in anticipation of a fee and being dispossessed later on by a remainderman with paramount title. Solace is the grantee's only remedy. As the reader will note after examining the typical quitclaim deed, it is word-for-word the mirror of the full warranty deed, without the covenants.

Since no covenants are implied in the sale of land, the grantee must demand and receive covenants in the deed for any assurance of protection. This is of utmost importance since the purchaser of realty is not entitled as a matter of law to warranty deed of title. In fact, once the contract of purchase is agreed to by both parties and no express commitment is made by the grantor to supply a full warranty deed, the grantee must settle for delivery of a quitclaim deed unless defects in the grantor's title—not excepted to in the purchase agreement—become apparent. The grantee then has the option of continuing through with the sale or retracting before completion.

A deed of *bargain and sale* is like a quitclaim deed and the remaining deeds to be discussed in that no covenants pass to the grantee along with title. The bargain and sale deed is merely a description of the land being sold and the consideration being paid for it. Before the Statute of Uses, the delivery of a bargain and sale deed usually created only a use interest in land which the statute converted into a legal estate. Today, the deed simply transfers to the grantee title in whatever land it purports to convey.

Two deeds of bargain and sale are presented here—one with, and one without a covenant against the grantor. Disregarding the fact that the grantor in one instance is a corporation, it can be readily evidenced that though the deed attempts to protect the grantee, it does so only for encumbrances which he himself may have created. The assurance is limited and as will be seen in the discussion of covenants, protects the grantee in a few specific circumstances.

The remaining deeds are best left swathed in the cobwebs of history. Each provided a procedure for conveying title in specific situations. A *deed of release* was the method by which a landlord gave his tenant outright title. Since the tenant was already in possession, no livery needed to be made. The *deed of lease and release* was a method of evading English law which placed certain requirements on deeds of bargain and sale. As the name implies, the deed created first, a term lease for years and secondly, by release, a full legal estate in the tenant. Since modern deed law eliminates these technicalities, such devices have fallen into disuse.

A *surrender* is a deed only in the sense that it is an acceleration title to a later estate. Quitclaim deeds, for the most part, have taken the place of surrenders, since all that is necessary is a transfer of rights between the present and preceeding estate holders. The only requirement which a surrender must meet is that the estate must be synonymous in size. Today the term is more commonly associated with landlord-tenant law.

Deed Requirements

Unlike a multipage lease which explicitly defines the rights and liabilities of the parties, a deed by statute can be relatively free of verbiage. As long as a base statutory prescription is met, the deed accomplishes its function of conveying realty between the grantor and grantee.

Statutes may vary to a minor extent, but certain essentials are present in the laws of every state. The following requisites may be found in all deeds: (a) a description of the premises with boundaries outlined, including all buildings and fixtures; (b) names and residence of parties to the conveyance; (c) date; (d) amount and type of consideration; (e) words of conveyance expressing intent; (f) encumbrances against the premises of the habendum clause (the traditional name given to the second part of a deed) delimiting the estate which the grantee takes; (g) reservations of easements or profits by the grantor; (h) covenants warranting title on a warranty deed; (i) closing declarations, signatures and seal. (No seal is required in New York State.)

The description of the premises should be specific without being detailed. Modern technology and surveying equipment allow for an accurate description in metes and bounds. Older deeds frequently used cultural monuments or geographical features, such as rivers, streams or lakes as boundaries or as boundary markers. In most cases, certain rules of constructions prevail in resolving conflicts created by ambiguities in either the intent of the parties or because of the boundary markers used. The most important concern should be to describe the premise so as to avoid any need for calling these rules of play. Thus, always measure as precisely as possible where distances are included; cultural monuments or geographical landmarks should never be used. They are susceptible to removal or change.

Relatively few problems arise as a result of the names of the parties. As long as identities can be ascertained, misspellings are unimportant. This law even extends to deeds which fail to include the name of the grantee. Although a deed is void by law in the absence of the grantor's name, delivery of a deed without the grantee's name can be valid. In this case, the grantee's name can be added by an agent, with or without written authority.

The *granting* and *habendum* clauses are similar but not identical. Where the former expresses the grantor's intent to grant or give the estate to another, the latter further defines and limits the extent of the ownership in the land granted. In all cases, it may enlarge, explain, or qualify the estate as land so long as it is not totally contradictory. Generally, the habendum clause cannot lessen an estate created by the granting clause, although under modern law,

35

the only determination is whether the habendum clause restricts the estate to a less-than-fee
one.

Both parties should always remain cognizant of the fact that a deed is not a contract.
Consideration, even though expressed in the
deed, is not essential for the deed to be valid.
Consideration should be set out to protect creditors and the grantee, in the event that any
question develops under recording acts.

Signatures and seals are requirements
which, in the case of the granting clauses, may
be conditional, and in the case of the habendum clauses, may be eliminated in many states.
Again, contingent upon the situs (position or
site) of the property, statutes might mandate
subscription of the parties' signatures at the end
of the form. As for seals, most states have dis-
pensed with the requirement, but where doubt
exists, a seal should be impressed on the document.

Covenants of Warranty

A deed does not carry with it any implied covenants to protect the grantee from
possible disturbances because of title. To guar-
antee protection under these covenants, which
under modern law all "run with the land," the
grantee must obtain an expressed warranty
deed. As with leases, deed covenants are binding promises and are the grantee's only assurances against third party interference. The deed
does not offer this protection, because it is
strictly a conveyance of land interests.

The covenants of seizen (right of possession) and *right to convey* are identical, for all
practical purposes. Each is a warranty that the
grantor is in a position to make the conveyance.
Should the grantor not be in possession of the
premises, buildings or fixtures, he is in breach
of the lease at the time of conveyance and is
liable for damages.

A full warranty deed also provides that
no mortgages, liens or other encumbrances exist
against the premises. In many cases, where
parties are alerted to minor encumbrances,
these can be excepted from the deed and do

not effect the warranty. Similar to the two previous covenants, the conveyance against encumbrances is breached at the time of conveyance.

The covenant for quiet enjoyment mirrors the same covenant under a lease, although
in a deed, it must be explicit. The grantor is
liable if the grantee is dispossessed by the grant-
or, by any *successor-in-interest* or by anyone
holding superior title. The covenant does not
extend to wrongful third parties who disturb
the grantee's enjoyment and use of the land.

Another covenant which is broken only
upon the eviction of the grantee, is the covenant of the warranty. The grantor promises to
compensate the grantee for any damages or loss
incurred upon the assertion of superior title by
a third party. The covenant has also been interpreted to require that the grantor defend his
title in such conflicts.

The Modern Realty Transaction

Introduction

Although the deed is a necessary instrument in the conveyance of real property, today
a seller or buyer will find himself executing
legal documents in addition to the deed. The
reason for this increase in legal papers is the
interjection of the broker in the dealings between the parties. Although not a recent inclusion in real estate law, *brokerage contracts*, for-
malized *purchase options* and *purchase offers*
are not very complicated and do not trace their
roots back to ancient English real property law.
Instead, contract law prevails, but with a few
common law and statutory peculiarities.

Without tradition and entanglements
with real property law, there is no purpose to
discussing the background of the contracts
which initiate a realty transaction. Instead, we
turn to various contracts explaining, and where
necessary, elaborating on provisions.

Contract Between Owner and Broker

The initial two paragraphs identify the

36

This Indenture,

Made the   *day of*   *nineteen hundred*

and

Between

a corporation organized under the laws of

party of the first part,

and

part   *of the second part,*

Witnesseth, *that the party of the first part, in consideration of*

Dollars, lawful money of the United States,

paid by the part   *of the second part, does hereby grant and release unto the part*   *of the*

second part,   *and assigns forever.*

All

Together *with the appurtenances and all the estate and rights of the party of the first part in and*

to said premises.

37

To have and to hold *the premises herein granted unto the part*   *of the second part,*

and assigns forever,

And *the said part*   *of the first part covenant*   *as follows:*

    First. *—That the part*   *of the first part*   *seized of the said premises in fee simple,*

and ha   *good right to convey the same,*

    Second. *—That the part*   *of the second part shall quietly enjoy the said premises;*

    Third. *—That the said premises are free from incumbrances;*

    Fourth. *—That the part*   *of the first part will execute or procure any further necessary assur-*

ance of the title to said premises;

    Fifth. *—That the part*   *of the first part will forever warrant the title to said premises.*

    Sixth. *—That the grantor, in compliance with Section 13 of the Lien Law, covenants that the*

grantor will receive the consideration for this conveyance and will hold the right to receive such consid-

eration as a trust fund to be applied first for the purpose of paying the cost of the improvement and that

the grantor will apply the same first to the payment of the cost of the improvement before using any part

of the total of the same for any other purpose.

parties and the subject matter. In most cases the seller employs the broker; however, where the circumstances dictate, a buyer in search of land in a particular area may work through a broker to obtain speedier results. Whatever the case, be it buyer or seller-owner who is under contract to the broker, the party must watch for fees which may come due to the broker, even without a sale of the premises.

With that in mind, the third paragraph should be scrutinized. Subparagraph (a) states that no commissions shall be earned by the broker unless each of three requirements are satisfied:

(1)   that the sale is complete and that it is completed on the owner's terms or terms to which he acquiesces.

(2)   that the sale shall have been consummated through the broker who is party to the contract. The terms "negotiated and consummated," if read restrictively might even free the seller who initiates the transaction, arranges the details, and, in all senses, "negotiates" the sale, even though the broker obtains the finalizing assent by the purchaser. More realistically, the terms are read together. If the broker is involved on any step of the transaction, he will be due his commission.

(3)   that the deed and purchase price actually exchange hands.

Paragraphs (b) and (c) further delimit the conditions which must be met in order for the owner-seller to become liable. Under (b), the discovery on the property of a last-minute encumbrance which cannot be promptly removed may defeat the sale, but does not bind the seller to payment of brokerage fees. Under (c) the seller incurs no obligation to pay, regardless of default by either party to the sale, unless the seller's default is willful. Additionally, the wording frees the seller from costly litigation against a defaulting purchaser in order to satisfy the broker's commission claim.

Collectively, these paragraphs relieve the seller of one of the hidden dangers to realty brokerage contracts. Unknown to most people, a broker in many states earns his commission upon the presentation of a ready, willing, and able buyer, whether or not the sale is consummated. As long as the buyer accepts the seller's conditions and stands in a position to complete the deal (i.e., has the cash or has opened the channels to obtain a loan), the seller as of that moment is obligated to the broker for commissions. The broker need not even require a down payment. If the broker balks at releasing this pre-established right, the seller should at least demand that the contract mandate the payment of a portion down, equal to or in excess of the brokerage fee. By so doing, the seller does not risk the possibility of expenses without a sale.

Paragraph (d) extends the seller's protected status. The right to terminate the agreement orally is self-explanatory. The major benefits offered by the paragraph is the unequivocal language that the agreement "in no event be deemed to be an exclusive listing ... and the owner may hire and retain other and additional brokers to sell the premises ..." Under an exclusive listing contract, the broker who is party to the contract becomes entitled to the commissions due upon the consummation of the contract. Thus, if the owner through his own efforts completes the sale, or if another broker finalizes the deal, the initial broker with the exclusive listing contract still collects his fee. This can be particularly expensive to the seller who has committed himself to the second broker. Instead of being indebted on one contract, the seller will find that he suddenly owes double commissions.

The remainder of the paragraph further limits the owner's liability. Should he decide to increase the asking price after the premises have been on the market for some time, he may do so at will without altering his contractual obligation with the broker. This provision is highly important in these times of inflation and recession. Since buyers might have difficulties procuring mortgages, the seller would not want to be locked into a fixed price as land values escalate.

Contract Between Owner and Broker

KNOW ALL MEN BY THESE PRESENTS, that the undersigned, having a principal place of business at the address hereinbelow indicated, does hereby certify and agree:

1. That the undersigned is duly licensed as a real estate broker under the laws of the State of

----

2. That the undersigned is hereby employed as such real estate broker by..

...., *hereinafter called "Owner"*

in connection with the sale of premises known as..

----

3. That the terms and conditions of the contract of brokerage between the undersigned and the said Owner in connection with the premises above referred to are and have at all times been:

(a) That no commissions should be deemed earned on the part of the undersigned until;

1) a contract of sale has been executed by the Owner and the Purchaser upon the terms and conditions acceptable to the Owner in its sole and absolute judgment

2) such Contract of Sale shall have been negotiated and consummated solely through the efforts of the undersigned as broker

3) the deed conveying title be delivered pursuant to the terms, covenants and conditions of the said Contract of Sale and the full purchase price be paid

(b) That in the event the Owner shall fail to have a good title to said premises so as to be able to convey the same in accordance with the Contract of Sale, no commission shall be deemed earned on the part of the undersigned.

(c) If after the Owner has entered into the Contract of Sale with the Purchaser, title does not close whether due to the fault or default of the Owner or Purchaser or for any other reason whatsoever except Owner's wilful default in the performance of said Contract of Sale, no commission shall be deemed earned on the part of the undersigned, and in the event title does not close because of the Purchaser's default, the Owner shall not be obligated or required to resort to any legal remedy for the enforcement of the Purchaser's obligations under the said Contract of Sale and the Owner shall not be obligated to the broker for the payment of any commission.

(d) That in any event, this Agreement may be terminated by the Owner at any time by either oral or written notice to the undersigned; that this hiring and the listing of the premises with the undersigned shall in no event be deemed to be an exclusive listing thereof with the undersigned, and the Owner may hire and retain other and additional brokers to sell the premises; that the premises may be withdrawn from sale by the Owner at any time, upon either oral or written notice, without liability of any kind on the part of the Owner to the undersigned, and that the purchase price at which the premises were listed with the undersigned may be changed at any time by the Owner without liability of any kind to the undersigned, and that the Owner shall in no event be liable or responsible to the undersigned for any expenses, fees or disbursements paid or incurred by the undersigned in connection with its endeavors to sell the premises.

(e) That the commission payable to the undersigned, if earned pursuant to the provisions hereof, shall be paid upon the delivery of the deed and the payment of the purchase price, and such commission shall be the sum of $......................*at the rate prescribed by*..

That this contains all the terms of such employment and shall not be varied, changed or amended except by a written agreement signed by both the Owner and the broker.

IN WITNESS WHEREOF, the undersigned has caused this instrument to be duly executed this ....*day of*..., *19*........

....*(Seal)*

....
(Address)

Land Purchase Contracts & Deeds

Additionally, the owner should not bind himself to pay for expenses that the broker might accumulate in exorbitant efforts to sell the premises.

The final paragraph recites an ultimate concern for the seller. The seller should never place himself in a position to be liable for commissions before the sale is completed. This paragraph ties the payment of the commissions to the delivery of the deed and the receipt of the full purchase price. The clause requires that the commissions be merited only upon compliance with all other provisions. Although the broker may balk at signing such a contract, it is ideal from the seller's perspective and he should bargain to include as many of these provisions as possible.

Purchase Option

Any purchase option, whether for personal or real property, is purely a contractual agreement. All of the elements of a contract which were discussed earlier apply. Basically, an option allows a prospective buyer to consider the purchase over a period of time without fear of losing out to an intervening sale. The bilateral agreement consists of a promise by the seller not to sell to another buyer during that period, in return for the purchaser's promise to buy the premises for a preset amount and under the conditions of the option, if he so elects. In consideration for the option, the purchaser pays the seller a sum of money to which he relinquishes all rights.

As in all realty documents, the option should state the property covered by its terms. The boundaries should be clearly expressed as explained under the section on deeds. The first clause of importance which is unique to an option is the one by which the seller promises to apply the consideration for the option in reducing the already agreed upon price. A purchaser should be steadfast in his insistence to include this provision in the option. Without it, the consideration is lost, whether or not the option is exercised. The provision dictates the manner in which the full purchase price is to be rendered. The purchaser should pay close attention. If he intends to pay through installments over a period of time, he should prearrange the schedule before risking the option value. The seller, in such a situation, should consider the possibility of keeping the initial cash payment under thirty percent (30%) of the total selling price in order to qualify for an installment sale and enjoy the tax benefits.

Normally, however, the contents of this section, as with the contract for sale, include the different means by which the purchaser intends to convey the full price. Thus, the amount of down payment and the medium of exchange, i.e., check, cash, etc., the current mortgage and amount and manner of payment of the balance should all be defined clearly.

The third paragraph is not complicated although care should be taken by both parties to set a consideration and a time period commensurate with the realities of the transaction. The accompanying payment, along with the option price paid by the purchaser, can equal the down payment in order to simplify the transaction.

The remaining paragraphs contain sale contract provisions. These will be discussed below, but it should be stated now that no less concern should be given these provisions in an option than in a contract for sale. Depending on the option agreement, the purchaser is extending a sum of money which can be best secured by smoothing out the difficulties now.

Offer to Purchase

Little explanation is needed for the purchase offer. As covered in the introduction, the offer is not elevated into a binding contract until accepted, but once signed by the seller, the offer acts as effectively as the contract for sale (to be discussed).

The document is sketchy. Although its brevity leaves little to be explained, it can create latent dangers. Since acceptance of the offer binds the parties, both should examine the instrument in order to ascertain whether all matters are expressly covered. The purchaser

Option for Purchase of Property

AGREEMENT *made this*   *day of*   19   *between*

hereinafter described as the Seller, and

hereinafter described as the Purchaser.

WITNESSETH, *that for and in consideration of the sum of*
Dollars ($ *), paid by the Purchaser, the receipt of which is*
hereby acknowledged by the Seller, the Seller hereby gives and grants to the Purchaser the exclusive
option, right and privilege of purchasing,

ALL THAT TRACT OR PARCEL OF LAND *with the buildings and improvements thereon,*
situate in the   *of*   *County of*
State of   *briefly described as follows:*

for the sum of   *Dollars*
($ *) payable as follows: $*   *upon the execution and delivery of this option*
as hereinbefore provided, which amount Seller agrees to apply on the purchase price if Purchaser elects
to exercise the option; $ *upon the acceptance of this option by the Purchaser as here-*
inafter provided; and the balance of the purchase price, to wit, $ *, in the following*
manner:

Notice of election to purchase hereunder shall be given by the Purchaser in writing by registered
mail, addressed to the Seller, at
on or before   19   *, which said notice shall be accompanied by the payment*
of $ *hereinbefore specified, and title shall close and the deed shall be delivered at the*
office of
at   *o'clock*   *. M. on*   19   *, following the giving of such notice,*
or at such time and upon such other date as shall be mutually agreed upon by the parties hereto.

Seller shall convey said premises to Purchaser in fee simple, free and clear of all liens, rights of
dower or other encumbrances (unless herein otherwise specified), by a good and sufficient deed of con-
veyance, in the usual form of a warranty deed, except that if Seller conveys as executor, trustee, admin-
istrator or guardian, or in any trust capacity, the usual deed given in such cases shall be accepted. Said
conveyance shall also be made subject to all restrictions, easements and conditions of record, if any.

If Purchaser gives a mortgage on the herein referred to premises, to secure to Seller any of the
purchase money therefor, it shall be designated therein as being given for that purpose; it shall be
accompanied by the usual bond; both shall contain the usual statutory interest, insurance, tax, assess-
ment and receivership clauses, if Seller so requires. The mortgage recording tax, recording fee for the
mortgage and the revenue stamps on the bond accompanying the same, shall be paid by the Purchaser
as part of the consideration of the said purchase.

Purchaser is to have possession of the premises on the day of transfer of title, except

All rentals, insurance premiums, interest and all other matters affecting the property herein re-
ferred to, not herein otherwise provided for, shall be adjusted pro rata to the day of the transfer of
title.

The transfer is to include, without further consideration and unless herein otherwise stated, all
fixtures and appurtenances now in said premises, including the heating plant and all appliances connected
therewith, ranges, service hot water heaters, gas and electric chandeliers and fixtures (excepting portable
lamps), bathroom fixtures attached, outside shades, screens, awnings, storm sash and storm doors.

Purchase Offer

OFFER TO PURCHASE

TO THE OWNER OR PERSON EMPOWERED TO SELL THE PROPERTY DESCRIBED BELOW:

Property

I (We) agree to purchase the following property situated in the................of................

County of................, State of................ known as................

being a................

....

For a more particular description of said premises reference is hereby made to the deed thereof.

Together with all lighting, heating and plumbing fixtures, window shades, screen and storm doors and windows, if any, water heater, water meter and all fixtures and fittings appurtenant to or used in the operation of the premises and owned by you.

Price

AT THE PRICE OF................$................
Dollars, payable as follows:

Deposit

$................ cash deposited with................to be held until this offer is accepted, at which time it shall become part of the purchase price, or returned if not accepted.

Balance

$................ cash on or before................on passing of deed.

Searches

You are to deliver to me, or my attorney, at least five (5) days before closing, a forty year abstract of title and ten year search or tax receipts showing the property free and clear of all liens and encumbrances except as herein set forth, and except building and use restrictions, pole and wire easements of record, and subject to zoning ordinance and to any taxes for local improvements not now completed.

Deed

Transfer is to be completed at the office of................

....

on or before................or as soon thereafter as abstracts can be brought to date, at which time you are to convey to me by................deed, good title to the property free of all liens and encumbrances, except as hereinabove set forth, subject to rights of tenants, if any.

Adjustments

Interest, insurance premiums, rents, and taxes to be pro-rated and adjusted as of................, 19......

City, State and County Taxes shall be adjusted and apportioned on a calendar year beginning Jan. 1, and ending Dec. 31. School Taxes outside the city shall be adjusted and apportioned for the fiscal year beginning July 1st and ending the following June 30th, and Village Taxes shall be adjusted and apportioned for the fiscal year beginning June 1st and ending the last day of May following or as otherwise prescribed or authorized by law.

Possession

Possession of premises shall be delivered on or before................on passing of deed

Upon any purchase money mortgage given, I (We) agree to pay the usual mortgage tax and recording fee and Revenue stamps on bond where required.

This offer may be assigned to an individual or corporation for the purpose of holding title thereto, except that the undersigned shall remain responsible for the faithful performance of the contract.

The risk of loss or damage to said premises by fire or other causes until the delivery of the deed is assumed by you.

I (We) represent that................is the broker in this transaction and that no other real estate broker or agent has been instrumental in bringing about this sale.

This offer, when accepted shall constitute a binding contract of purchase and sale and it shall bind and inure to the benefit of the parties hereto and their respective executors, administrators, distributees, successors and assigns.

Dated................, 19...... (Signed)................(L. S.)

Witness................ (Signed)................(L. S.)

How to Handle Your Own Contracts

should be sure that the premises on which he submits an offer is identical to the one with which seller intends to part. The offer should describe not only the premises, but it should also detail the fixtures and appurtenances that accompany the property. As for the actual payment, the contract should not refer to "cash" as the medium of exchange for the balance, if the buyer intends to secure payment with a mortgage.

The remaining provisions will be discussed under the contract for sale. It is imperative that both parties are cognizant that the purchase offer, once it has been signed, binds them to its terms. Clauses that seem to be ambiguous and do not fully outline the duties of the parties should be negotiated to the satisfaction of the parties before acceptance.

Contract for the Sale of Property

Contracts for the sale of realty can take many forms, but an examination of each form will reveal that certain provisions are always included. Four different contracts have been included in the text in order to demonstrate this, and to apprise the reader of examples which may be encountered. The contract provisions will be dissected in order to illuminate frequent problems.

The identity clause, naming the parties initiates each contract. The clause is merely descriptive unless default occurs and not all parties are named. The trouble lies in the buyer's inability to sue for specific performance under the contract and to have the judgment operate against all those having an interest in the property. Both parties should be concerned that each has authority to execute the sale and conveyance. In particular, one should be alerted to inquire into this authority when dealing with anyone who holds himself out as an agent of a primary party.

The clause immediately following that clause describes the premises to be transferred. This topic has been covered under the discussion of deeds. It is sufficient to say that as long as the agreement makes the property readily

identifiable and distinguishable, the purpose of the clause has been satisfied. Additionally, many sales contracts provide on the back of the document a map on which to plot the boundaries in metes and bounds or to list the block and lot number. Even though this information may seem technical at the time, it protects the parties if later discrepancies arise.

The improved contract for the sale of realty is more explicit than the others. Being a hybrid, suitable for New York City, it makes direct reference to interests and rights to abutting property. These rights and interests include *easements* (the right to make use of land belonging to someone else for some definite and limited purpose) and succession to awards resulting from the taking or damaging of the seller's fee. Since these interests are often capitalized on the value of the property and passed on to the purchaser, he should be cautious to succeed to these interests so as not to pay for a right which the seller retains.

The seller should also include in the contract all encumbrances of which the buyer has notice and to which he takes subject. Usually the contract provides for the seller to "convey said premises to the vendee in fee simply free and clear from all liens, rights of dower or other encumbrance (unless herein after specified)." Thus, to extricate himself from any conflict that might arise over whether the purchaser had notice of any particular encumbrance, lien or easement, the existence of each and acceptance by the purchaser should be noted in all cases.

We now turn to the means and manner of payment. Much of this has been explained in the discussion on the purchase option and need not be elaborated any further. Normally, the total payment is separated into: (1) the down payment at the signing of the contract; (2) the amount of cash in currency or certified check; (3) the amount of any mortgage or lien which the purchaser takes subject to or assumes (see chapter on mortgages); and (4) the execution of a note or bond secured by a purchase money mortgage. As has been impressed before, the payment schedule and medium should be as unequivocal as possible.

43

Contracts for Property

This sale includes all right, title and interest, if any, of the seller in and to any land lying in the bed of any street, road or avenue opened or proposed, in front of or adjoining said premises, to the center line thereof, and all right, title and interest of the seller in and to any award made or to be made in lieu thereof and in and to any unpaid award for damage to said premises by reason of change of grade of any street; and the seller will execute and deliver to the purchaser, on closing of title, or thereafter, on demand, all proper instruments for the conveyance of such title and the assignment and collection of any such award.

The price is

Dollars, payable as follows:

Dollars,

on the signing of this contract, by check subject to collection, the receipt of which is hereby acknowledged;

Dollars,

in cash or good certified check on the delivery of the deed as hereinafter provided;

Dollars,

by taking title subject to a mortgage now a lien on said premises in that amount, bearing interest at the rate of per cent per annum, the principal being due and payable

Dollars,

by the purchaser or assigns executing, acknowledging and delivering to the seller a bond or note satisfactory to the seller secured by a purchase money mortgage on the above premises, in that amount, payable

together with interest at the rate of per cent per annum payable

Any bond or note and mortgage to be given hereunder shall contain the clauses usually employed by Title Companies in New York City in such instruments for mortgages of like lien; and shall be drawn by the attorney for the seller at the expense of the purchaser, who shall also pay the mortgage recording tax and recording fees and pay for and affix to such instruments any and all revenue stamps that may be necessary.

If such purchase money mortgage is to be a subordinate mortgage on the premises it shall provide that it shall be subject and subordinate to the lien of the existing mortgage of $, any extensions thereof and to any mortgage or consolidated mortgage which may be placed on the premises in lieu thereof, and to any extensions thereof provided (a) that the interest rate thereof shall not be greater than per cent per annum and (b) that, if the principal amount thereof shall exceed the amount of principal owing and unpaid on said existing mortgage at the time of placing such new mortgage or consolidated mortgage, the excess be paid to the holder of such purchase money mortgage in reduction of the principal thereof. Such purchase money mortgage shall also provide that such payment to the holder thereof shall not alter or affect the regular installments, if any, of principal payable thereunder and shall further provide that the holder thereof will, on demand and without charge therefor, execute, acknowledge and deliver any agreement or agreements further to effectuate such subordination.

If this sale is subject to the Real Property Transfer Tax imposed by Title I of Chapter 46 of the Administrative Code of the City of New York, at the closing of the title the seller shall deliver to the purchaser a certified check to the order of the City Treasurer for the amount so imposed and will also deliver to the purchaser the return required by the said statute and the regulations issued pursuant to the authority thereof, duly signed and sworn to by the seller; the purchaser agrees to sign and swear to the said return and to cause the said check and the said return to be delivered to the City Register promptly after the closing of the title.

Said premises are sold and are to be conveyed subject to:

1. Zoning regulations and ordinances of the city, town or village in which the premises lie which are not violated by existing structures.

2. Consents by the seller or any former owner of premises for the erection of any structure or structures on, under or above any street or streets on which said premises may abut.

3. Encroachments of stoops, areas, cellar steps, trim and cornices, if any, upon any street or highway.

If there be a mortgage on the premises the seller agrees to deliver to the purchaser at the time of delivery of the deed a proper certificate executed and acknowledged by the holder of such mortgage and in form for recording, certifying as to the amount of the unpaid principal and interest thereon, date of maturity thereof and rate of interest thereon, and the seller shall pay the fees for recording such certificate.

All notes or notices of violations of law or municipal ordinances, orders or requirements noted in or issued by the Departments of Housing and Buildings, Fire, Labor, Health, or other State or Municipal Department having jurisdiction against or affecting the premises at the date hereof, shall be complied with by the seller and the premises shall be conveyed free of the same, and this provision of this contract shall survive delivery of the deed hereunder. The seller shall furnish the purchaser with an authorization to make the necessary searches therefor.

If, at the time of the delivery of the deed, the premises or any part thereof shall be or shall have been affected by an assessment or assessments which are or may become payable in annual installments, of which the first installment is then a charge or lien, or has been paid, then for the purposes of this contract all the unpaid installments of any such assessment, including those which are to become due and payable after the delivery of the deed, shall be deemed to be due and payable and to be liens upon the premises affected thereby and shall be paid and discharged by the seller, upon the delivery of the deed. Westchester County Sewer System Taxes shall be excluded from the provisions of this paragraph and the installments thereof not due and payable at the time of the delivery of the deed hereunder shall be assumed by the purchaser without abatement of the purchase price.

The following are to be apportioned:

(1) Rents as and when collected. (2) Interest on mortgages. (3) Premiums on existing transferable insurance policies or renewals of those expiring prior to the closing. (4) Taxes and sewer rents, if any, on the basis of the fiscal year for which assessed. (5) Water charges on the basis of the calendar year. (6) Fuel, if any.

If the closing of the title shall occur before the tax rate is fixed, the apportionment of taxes shall be upon the basis of the tax rate for the next preceding year applied to the latest assessed valuation.

If there be a water meter on the premises, the seller shall furnish a reading to date not more than thirty days prior to the time herein set for closing title, and the unfixed meter charge and the unfixed sewer rent, if any, based thereon for the intervening time shall be apportioned on the basis of such last reading.

The deed shall be the usual

deed in proper statutory short form for record and shall be duly executed, acknowledged, and have revenue stamps in the proper amount affixed thereto by the seller, at the seller's expense, so as to convey to the purchaser the fee simple of the said premises, free of all encumbrances, except as herein stated, and shall also contain the covenant required by subdivision 5 of Section 13 of the Lien Law.

The seller shall give and the purchaser shall accept a title such as

will approve and insure.

All sums paid on account of this contract, and the reasonable expenses of the examination of the title to said premises and of the survey, if any, made in connection therewith are hereby made liens thereon, but such liens shall not continue after default by the purchaser under this contract.

All fixtures and articles of personal property attached or appurtenant to or used in connection with said premises are represented to be owned by the seller, free from all liens and encumbrances except as herein stated, and are included in this sale; without limiting the generality of the foregoing, such fixtures and articles of personal property include plumbing, heating, lighting and cooking fixtures, air conditioning fixtures and units, ranges, refrigerators, radio and television aerials, bathroom and kitchen cabinets, mantels, door mirrors, venetian blinds, shades, screens, awnings, storm windows, window boxes, storm doors, mail boxes, weather vanes, flagpoles, pumps, shrubbery and outdoor statuary.

The amount of any unpaid taxes, assessments, water charges and sewer rents which the seller is obligated to pay and discharge, with the interest and penalties thereon to a date not less than two business days after the date of closing title, may at the option of the seller be allowed to the purchaser out of the balance of the purchase price, provided official bills therefor with interest and penalties thereon figured to said date are furnished by the seller at the closing. If at the date of closing title there may be any other liens or encumbrances which the seller is obligated to pay and discharge, the seller may use any portion of the balance of the purchase price to satisfy the same, provided the seller shall have delivered to the purchaser at the closing of title instruments in recordable form and sufficient to satisfy such liens and encumbrances of record, together with the cost of recording or filing said instruments. The purchaser, if request is made within a reasonable time prior to the date of closing of title, agrees to provide at the closing separate certified checks as requested, aggregating the amount of the balance of the purchase price, to facilitate the satisfaction of any such liens or encumbrances. The existence of any such taxes or other liens and encumbrances shall not be deemed objections to title if the seller shall comply with the foregoing requirements.

If a search of the title discloses judgments, bankruptcies or other returns against other persons having names the same as or similar to that of the seller, the seller will on request deliver to the purchaser an affidavit showing that such judgments, bankruptcies or other returns are not against the seller.

In the event that the seller is unable to convey title in accordance with the terms of this contract, the sole liability of the seller will be to refund to the purchaser the amount paid on account of the purchase price and to pay the net cost of examining the title and the net cost of any survey made in connection therewith incurred by the purchaser, and upon such refund and payment being made this contract shall be considered canceled.

The deed shall be delivered upon the receipt of said payments at the office of

at   o'clock on   19   .

The parties agree that

brought about this sale and the seller agrees to pay the commission at the rates established or adopted by the Board of Real Estate Brokers in the locality where the property is situated.

It is understood and agreed that all understandings and agreements heretofore had between the parties hereto are merged in this contract, which alone fully and completely expresses their agreement, and that the same is entered into after full investigation, neither party relying upon any statement or representation, not embodied in this contract, made by the other. The purchaser has inspected the buildings standing on said premises and is thoroughly acquainted with their condition.

This agreement may not be changed or terminated orally. The stipulations aforesaid are to apply to and bind the heirs, executors, administrators, successors and assigns of the respective parties.

If two or more persons constitute either the seller or the purchaser, the word "seller" or the word "purchaser" shall be construed as if it read "sellers" or "purchasers" whenever the sense of this agreement so requires.

IN WITNESS WHEREOF, this agreement has been duly executed by the parties hereto.

In presence of:

Before considering other sections, the purchaser should be aware of the recording statute at this time. Prior to purchase, a full title search should always be conducted and an acquaintance with the recordation of realty transactions and liens should be made by the purchaser. He should consider the importance of recording his interest in the property from the moment of the down payment. The recording of a memorandum or the executed contract, prevents the seller from conveying the property to a third party. The purchaser's status as an equitable liener is recorded which secures his down payment against the property should the seller default. The complete consequences of the recording statutes are far beyond the scope of this book, but the recording act can be used to advantage even before the sale is consummated by delivery of the deed.

All of the contracts have special provisions dealing in detail with mortgages. (See chapter on mortgages). Further discussion here would only confuse rather than inform. Moreover because of the complexity of mortgages the parties should seek legal advice.

We are next confronted with the clause describing the time and place of delivery of the deed, and the type of deed. The purchaser should attach great importance to this provision. Normally, time is not of the essence in realty transactions and the law does not impose a time requirement. If the purchaser or even the seller requires the property or proceeds on a particular day, the contract should expressly make time of the essence. If, at the closing, minor encumbrances lie against the property, the seller cannot postpone the delivery for a short time in order to discharge the liens. The seller is immediately in default and the purchaser is relieved of performance. The clause can make time of the essence bilateral, which releases the seller, if the purchaser defaults by failing to tender the necessary cash payment or mortgage.

The purchaser should be wary of the type of deed. Since the purchaser is entitled only to a quitclaim deed (see discussion of deeds) unless the contract provides otherwise, he should be certain that reference is made to a full warranty deed. Without it, the purchaser does not have the assurances of title, etc., from the seller.

All of the contracts make expressed references to the inclusion of personal property, i.e., "heating, cooking and lighting fixtures, air conditioning fixtures and units, ranges, refrigerators, radio and television antennas ... mailboxes, weather vanes, flagpoles, pumps, shrubbery and outdoor statuary," in the sale. Both parties should be alerted to the provision on personal property and determine if it meets the needs of the situation. Case law has concluded that these terms are not deemed part of the sale of real property unless expressly provided for, yet the purchase price may reflect their value. A further distinction is made as to appurtenances and personal property. The former pass automatically with the conveyance of property, while the latter become the purchaser's possessions only if the sale contract so expresses.

The better practice is to request a bill of sale from the seller for the personal property in conjunction with the contract of sale for the realty. This procedure protects the purchaser by giving him a warranty of title to the personalty which he does not receive under the realty contract. The seller should be cautious not to include items which he either does not own or has encumbered as the result of a chattel mortgage. In order to avoid later legal consequences, the seller should qualify the clause, passing only those items of personalty which he owns and earmarking in the contract those items subject to liens and mortgages.

In most cities, contracts make reference to the existence of municipal zoning laws, earlier structures and possible encroachments. Although the first provision which subjects the property to zoning regulations and ordinances of the city, town or village in which the premises are located, which are not violated by existing structures, "in effect" assures the purchaser that no current violations exist, this clause and the other remaining two do not justify rejection of the deed by the purchaser. Obviously, the seller should avoid this clause if possible, whereas the purchaser should avoid the latter two which releases the seller from liability for former grants of authority to encroach upon the property and for his own encroachments upon public property.

Several clauses mention the burden of paying specific costs relating to the property. These clauses are of particular importance to the purchaser, since by obtaining the seller's acquiescence, he relieves himself of expenses for which he becomes liable upon ownership. The first are the installment assessments. Again the purchaser must realize that improvements to the property are usually capitalized in its value. Assessments are municipal charges for local public improvements which the owner can elect to pay over a period of time. Since the seller most likely increases the price of the property because of the improvement, the purchaser should be certain to hold the seller liable for the complete discharge of the cost by contracting that the unpaid assessments become liens against the property at the time of the delivery of the deed.

The other provisions require the prorata distribution of profits and expenses arising from the property. Specifically, "one such" clause refers to rents, mortgage interests, taxes, sewer rents and fuel costs, all of which are apportioned according to the percentage of time owned by each party. Another separate provision mandates the allocation of water costs based upon a last reading of the meter 30 days before the closing. All of these provisions accomplish the same purchase—to charge each party his equitable share.

Minor encumbrances associated with these exchanges can be alleviated by the contract. Generally, the agreement creates liens against the property for costs attributable to the seller. Since liens can render the title unmarketable, the contract should allow for a reduction of the selling price by the amount of the cost in discharge of the liens. Such provision can protect the seller by not giving the purchaser opportunity to claim default on the seller's part and back out of the agreement, if time is of the essence. Additionally, the seller can further safeguard against default by allowing himself to use any portion of the purchase

price to satisfy other minor encumbrances.

Another occurrence which all of the contracts provide for is the danger of destruction of the premise while the contract is executory. If strict attention is paid, it will be noticed that in all but one instance, the seller is responsible for insuring the premises. Under common law, the majority of states placed the risk of loss for destruction or injury to the property on the purchaser. Because the purchaser held equitable title after execution of the contract, courts believed that it was his duty to procure insurance or suffer the loss. Thus purchasers began to contract for the seller to assume the obligation. The problem was that the usual provision, as can be noted on two of the contracts, only requires that the seller maintain fire insurance and thereby the purchaser risked loss resulting from any other catastrophe.

In attempts to solve the dilemma, many states adopted laws, such as New York's Uniform Vender and Purchaser Risk Act, which supposedly spells out rights and liabilities. Similar to the earlier court decrees and unsophisticated contract attempts to cure the ill, the act proved to be somewhat ineffective to the extent that it did not define liabilities in all situations. The result is that the act solves some but not all problems. Since the act is deemed part of contract, the safest course for both parties is to reduce to writing the rights and liabilities of each under all circumstances, covering all foreseeable happenings such as "fire or the elements or by any cause beyond either party's control or ... by eminent domain." The provision should also state to whom the insurance proceeds are payable and what time in the transaction one or both parties may cancel without repercussions. If the question of loss revolves around "materiality" or the degree of destruction necessary to trigger any clause in the provision, another clause should express some procedure such as arbitration to equitably and quickly resolve the issue.

The other provisions which appear in some of the contracts deserve comment. First, both parties should consent to a provision precluding oral changes or terminations. Any claims by either party that an oral agreement modified the contract would be dismissed, thus deterring fraudulent attempts to back out of the sale. Also the purchaser should be aware that under the law, the contract for sale is merged with deed upon its delivery. Although a merger clause stating that the contract completely encompasses the agreement is not detrimental to the parties, if they have fully investigated the ramifications of the sale, such provisions in the deed could be potentially harmful to the purchaser. By so agreeing, he no longer has any course of action under any covenant or the contract which is expressed on the deed.

The purchaser should demand a provision which reaffirms and adopts in the deed all earlier agreements.

Finally, the contract may make mention of brokerage fees for which the seller is liable. To safeguard his position the seller should clarify this provision so as not to become bound to pay a broker with whom the purchaser dealt. Since, more likely than not, the seller is under contract to his own broker, he should be cautious not to assume the cost of the purchaser's broker as well.

How to Handle Your Own Contracts

CHAPTER 4

Realty Mortgages

Introduction

A mortgage is any conveyance of land which is intended by the parties at the time of making to be a security for the payment of money or the doing of some prescribed act. In essence, it is a security for a debt. The mortgagor has the right to possession and title in the land, while the mortgagee (e.g., a bank) has a lien upon the land (in some states such as New York, but not in all states).

The objective in this section is to familarize the reader with commonly used mortgage documents. However, a few introductory notes are helpful in acquiring an understanding of the purpose and functions of a mortgage and how it might affect the legal transaction to which the person is a party.

Any transferable interest in real property may be mortgaged. The mortgage covers all real property described within the document, including fixtures on the property. The most common fixture that would be the object of a mortgage would be a house located on the property described in the mortgage. All accessions to mortgaged real property are subject to the mortgage. An *accession* is a legal principle by which the owner of property becomes entitled to all which the property produces, and to all that is added or united to it, either naturally or artifically, (that is, by labor or skill of another) even where such addition extends to a change of form or materials. The possessor of property becomes entitled to it as against the original owner.

Rights of the Parties

What are the rights of the parties involved in the transaction? The legal names of the parties are mortgagor and mortgagee. The mortgagor has, until foreclosure, the title and right to possession. He has a duty to maintain the property value and must not commit any affirmative acts of waste or other acts that would impair the value of the property. As stated earlier, the mortgagee merely has a lien. (Some states, like New York, follow this construction for mortgages which gives the mortgagee an equitable interest in the property while the mortgagor holds legal title. However, one should consult the interpretation of his own locality in the event that his particular state has a different rule of construction whereby the mortgagor might be deemed to have equitable title and the mortgagee legal title until the debt is paid, at which time the legal title passes to the mortgagor.)

Let us pause here and define our basic terms—such as mortgagor, mortgagee, lien, and others. The *mortgagor* is one who, having all or some part of title to property, by written instrument, pledges that property for some particular purpose, such as security for debt. The classic example is where one purchases a home and borrows money from a bank to purchase the property. To secure the loan of the purchaser, the bank gets a mortgage on the property which is the security on the loan. In the event the purchaser defaults on a repayment installment of the loan, the bank holds the

49

Mortgage Statutory Form

THIS MORTGAGE, made the   day of   , nineteen hundred and

BETWEEN

herein referred to as the mortgagor,

and

herein referred to as the mortgagee,

WITNESSETH, that to secure the payment of an indebtedness in the sum of

dollars,

lawful money of the United States, to be paid

with interest thereon to be computed from   day of   , 19   , at
the rate of   per centum per annum, and to be paid

according to a certain bond, note or obligation bearing even date herewith, the mortgagor hereby mortgages to
the mortgagee, **ALL**

How to Handle Your Own Contracts

TOGETHER with all right, title and interest, if any, of the mortgagor of, in and to any streets and roads abutting the above-described premises to the center lines thereof.

TOGETHER with all fixtures and articles of personal property now or hereafter attached to, or contained in and used in connection with, said premises, including but not limited to all apparatus, machinery, plumbing, heating, lighting and cooking fixtures, fittings, gas ranges, bathroom and kitchen cabinets, ice boxes, refrigerators, food freezers, air-conditioning fixtures, pumps, awnings, shades, screens, storm sashes, aerials, plants and shrubbery.

TOGETHER with any and all awards heretofore and hereafter made to the present and all subsequent owners of the mortgaged premises by any governmental or other lawful authorities for taking by eminent domain the whole or any part of said premises or any easement therein, including any awards for any changes of grade of streets, which said awards are hereby assigned to the holder of this mortgage, who is hereby authorized to collect and receive the proceeds of any such awards from such authorities and to give proper receipts and acquittances therefor, and to apply the same toward the payment of the amount owing on account of this mortgage and its accompanying bond or note, notwithstanding the fact that the amount owing thereon may not then be due and payable; and the said mortgagor hereby covenants and agrees, upon request, to make, execute and deliver any and all assignments and other instruments sufficient for the purpose of assigning the aforesaid awards to the holder of this mortgage, free, clear and discharged of any and all encumbrances of any kind or nature whatsoever.

AND the mortgagor covenants with the mortgagee as follows:

1. That the mortgagor will pay the indebtedness as hereinbefore provided.

2. That the mortgagor will keep the buildings on the premises insured against loss by fire for the benefit of the mortgagee; that he will assign and deliver the policies to the mortgagee; and that he will reimburse the mortgagee for any premiums paid for insurance made by the mortgagee on the mortgagor's default in so insuring the buildings or in so assigning and delivering the policies.

3. That no building on the premises shall be removed or demolished without the consent of the mortgagee.

4. That the whole of said principal sum and interest shall become due at the option of the mortgagee: after default in the payment of any instalment of principal or of interest for twenty days; or after default in the payment of any tax, water rate, sewer rent or assessment for thirty days after notice and demand; or after default after notice and demand either in assigning and delivering the policies insuring the buildings against loss by fire or in reimbursing the mortgagee for premiums paid on such insurance, as hereinbefore provided; or after default upon request in furnishing a statement of the amount due on the mortgage and whether any offsets or defenses exist against the mortgage debt, as hereinafter provided.

5. That the holder of this mortgage, in any action to foreclose it, shall be entitled to the appointment of a receiver.

6. That the mortgagor will pay all taxes, assessments, sewer rents or water rates, and in default thereof, the mortgagee may pay the same.

7. That the mortgagor within six days upon request in person or within fifteen days upon request by mail will furnish a written statement duly acknowledged of the amount due on this mortgage and whether any offsets or defenses exist against the mortgage debt.

8. That notice and demand or request may be in writing and may be served in person or by mail.

9. That the mortgagor warrants the title to the premises.

10. That the mortgagor will, in compliance with Section 13 of the Lien Law, receive the advances secured hereby and will hold the right to receive such advances as a trust fund to be applied first for the purpose of paying the cost of the improvement and will apply the same first to the payment of the cost of the improvement before using any part of the total of the same for any other purpose.

11. That fire insurance policies which are required by paragraph No. 2 above shall contain the usual extended coverage endorsement; in addition thereto the mortgagor, within thirty days after notice and demand, will keep the buildings on the premises insured against loss by other insurable hazards including war damage for the benefit of the mortgagee, as may reasonably be required by the mortgagee; that he will assign and deliver the policies to the mortgagee; and that he will reimburse the mortgagee for any premiums paid for insurance made by the mortgagee on the mortgagor's default in so insuring or in so assigning and delivering the policies. The provisions of subdivision 4, of Section 254 of the Real Property Law, with reference to the construction of the fire insurance clause, shall govern the construction of this clause so far as applicable.

12. That in case of a sale, said premises, or so much thereof as may be affected by this mortgage, may be sold in one parcel.

13.   That in the event of any default in the performance of any of the terms, covenants or agreements herein contained, it is agreed that the then owner of the mortgaged premises, if he is the occupant of said premises or any part thereof, shall immediately surrender possession of the premises so occupied to the holder of this mortgage, and if such occupant is permitted to remain in possession, the possession shall be as tenant of the holder of this mortgage and such occupant shall, on demand, pay monthly in advance to the holder of this mortgage a reasonable rental for the space so occupied and in default thereof, such occupant may be dispossessed by the usual summary proceedings. In case of foreclosure and the appointment of a receiver of rents, the covenants herein contained may be enforced by such receiver.

14.   That the whole of said principal sum shall become due at the option of the mortgagee after default for thirty days after notice and demand, in the payment of any instalment of any assessment for local improvements heretofore or hereafter laid, which is or may become payable in annual instalments and which has affected, now affects or hereafter may affect the said premises, notwithstanding that such instalment be not due and payable at the time of such notice and demand, or upon the failure to exhibit to the mortgagee, within thirty days after demand, receipts showing payment of all taxes, assessments, water rates, sewer rents and any other charges which may have become a prior lien on the mortgaged premises.

15.   That the whole of said principal sum shall become due at the option of the mortgagee, if the buildings on said premises are not maintained in reasonably good repair, or upon the actual or threatened alteration, removal or demolition of any building on said premises or of any building to be erected upon the mortgaged premises, or upon the failure of any owner of said premises to comply with the requirement of any governmental department claiming jurisdiction within three months after an order making such requirement has been issued by any such department.

16.   That in the event of the passage after the date of this mortgage of any law of the State of New York, deducting from the value of land for the purposes of taxation any lien thereon, or changing in any way the laws for the taxation of mortgages or debts secured by mortgage for state or local purposes, or the manner of the collection of any such taxes, so as to affect this mortgage, the holder of this mortgage and of the debt which it secures, shall have the right to give thirty days' written notice to the owner of the mortgaged premises requiring the payment of the mortgage debt. If such notice be given the said debt shall become due, payable and collectible at the expiration of said thirty days.

17.   That the whole of said principal sum shall immediately become due at the option of the mortgagee, if the mortgagor shall assign the rents or any part of the rents of the mortgaged premises without first obtaining the written consent of the mortgagee to such assignment.

18.   That if any action or proceeding be commenced (except an action to foreclose this mortgage or to collect the debt secured thereby), to which action or proceeding the holder of this mortgage is made a party, or in which it becomes necessary to defend or uphold the lien of this mortgage, all sums paid by the holder of this mortgage for the expense of any litigation to prosecute or defend the rights and lien created by this mortgage (including reasonable counsel fees), shall be paid by the mortgagor, together with interest thereon at the rate of six per cent. per annum, and any such sum and the interest thereon shall be a lien on said premises, prior to any right, or title to, interest in or claim upon said premises attaching or accruing subsequent to the lien of this mortgage, and shall be deemed to be secured by this mortgage and by the bond or note which it secures. In any action or proceeding to foreclose this mortgage, or to recover or collect the debt secured thereby, the provisions of law respecting the recovering of costs, disbursements and allowances shall prevail unaffected by this covenant.

19.   That the whole of said principal sum shall immediately become due at the option of the mortgagee upon any default in keeping the buildings on said premises insured as required by paragraph No. 2 or paragraph No. 11 hereof, or if after application by any holder of this mortgage to two or more fire insurance companies lawfully doing business in the State of New York and issuing policies of fire insurance upon buildings situate in the place where the mortgaged premises are situate, the companies to which such application has been made shall refuse to issue such policies, or upon default in complying with the provisions of paragraph No. 11 hereof, or upon default, for five days after notice and demand, either in assigning and delivering to the mortgagee the policies of fire insurance or in reimbursing the mortgagee for premiums paid on such fire insurance as hereinbefore provided in paragraph No. 2 hereof.

If more than one person joins in the execution of this mortgage, and if any be of the feminine sex, or if this mortgage is executed by a corporation, the relative words herein shall be read as if written in the plural, or in the feminine or neuter gender, as the case may be, and the words "mortgagor" and "mortgagee" where used herein shall be construed to include their and each of their heirs, executors, administrators, successors and assigns.

This mortgage may not be changed orally.

IN WITNESS WHEREOF, this mortgage has been duly executed by the mortgagor.

IN PRESENCE OF:

mortgage which allows it certain legal remedies and rights on the property. The bank in this example is the *mortgagee*. A mortgagee is simply the one who takes or receives a mortgage. A mortgagee does not have to be a bank. A *lien* is simply a claim on property for payment of some debt, obligation, or duty. In the above example, if the mortgagor breached the duty to repay the bank the money loaned to the purchaser, the bank could assert a lien (claim) on the property. A mortgage standing alone is void. It must serve a legal obligation. Without a legal obligation, there can be no mortgage.

Assuming and Taking Subject To

In the above example there is an implied assumption that the purchaser was buying property not subject to any previous mortgage. However, in many instances the buyer will be confronted with situations in which the property to be purchased is subject to a pre-existing mortgage previously executed by the seller. The purchaser must find out if the premises are to be sold merely *subject* to existing mortgages, or if the purchaser is required to *assume* the payment of existing mortgages. The purchaser should avoid the assumption of payment of existing mortgages. Simply stated, when a purchaser assumes this obligation, the purchaser becomes personally liable for the payment of the debt, and the seller of the property (original mortgagor) becomes a *surety*, as opposed to an *obligor* on the debt. (A surety promises to pay money or to do any other act in event that his principal fails to do so). In essence, what happens is that the purchaser has become primarily liable on the debt. Also, any material modification of the mortgage without the seller's consent will discharge him from responsibility.

If mortgaged property is transferred subject to the mortgage, the property becomes the primary source for the payment of the debt; the original mortgagor becomes a surety and continues to be liable on the note (debt). However, the difference is that if the mortgagee and the transferee modify the mortgage obligation, without the original mortgagor's consent, the original mortgagor (seller) is discharged from his suretyship, but only to the extent of the value of the land at the time of the mortgage-transferee agreement.

So far, we have discussed what the mortgage document represents; who are the mortgagor and mortgagee; and what obligations result if a purchaser takes subject to, or assumes a pre-existing mortgage. Hopefully, the reader has an understanding of the legal implications of a mortgage and of the roles of the particular parties to the mortgage.

Other Important Elements

The mortgage subject to which the property is being sold, should be identified and described as fully as possible. This is accomplished by attaching copies of the bond (notes) and mortgage to the bill of sale. This allows the purchaser to examine the documents fully and removes the possibility of error. The purchaser should insist upon a summary of the terms of the mortgage. This will allow him the opportunity to determine the accuracy of the information given to him. The purchaser should know the rate of interest, the date of maturity, the name of holder and whether or not the mortgage contains any unusual provisions which might render it unjust.

Termination of the mortgage can happen in a few ways. Payment of the mortgage debt terminates the mortgage. The recording officer marks the record of a mortgage "discharged" when presented with a certificate signed and acknowledged by the mortgagee, specifying that the mortgage has been paid. A mortgage may also be terminated by acquisition by the same person of both the property described and the mortgage. If the mortgagor makes an appropriate offer of money in payment of the debt secured by the mortgagee, and the offer is refused, the mortgage is terminated (but this does not terminate the underlying debt). A statute of limitations can also terminate a mortgage.

MORTGAGE NOTE

$ New York, 19

FOR VALUE RECEIVED,

promise   to pay to the order of

at

or at such other place as may be designated in writing by the holder of this note, the principal sum of

Dollars

with interest thereon to be computed from the   day of   19   , at the rate of   per centum per annum and to be paid

IT IS HEREBY EXPRESSLY AGREED, that the said principal sum secured by this note shall become due at the option of the holder thereof on the happening of any default or event by which, under the terms of the mortgage securing this note, said principal sum may or shall become due and payable; also, that all of the covenants, conditions and agreements contained in said mortgage are hereby made part of this instrument to the same extent and with the same effect as if fully set forth herein.

The makers and all others who may become liable for the payment of all or any part of this obligation do hereby severally waive presentment for payment, protest and notice of protest and non-payment.

This note is secured by a mortgage made by the maker   to the payee   of even date herewith, on property situate in the

This note may not be changed orally, but only by an agreement in writing and signed by the party against whom enforcement of any waiver, change, modification or discharge is sought.

Know all Men by these Presents,

THAT

*

DO   HEREBY CERTIFY *that the following Mortgage*   IS PAID, *and do*   *hereby consent*
that the same be discharged of record.

Mortgage dated the   *day of*   *, 19*   *, made by*

to

in the principal sum of $ *and recorded on the*   *day of*   *19*   *,*
in Liber   *of Section*   *of Mortgages, page*   *, in the office*
of the   *of the*

which mortgage   *has not been* †   *assigned of record.*

Dated the   *day of*   *, 19*

IN PRESENCE OF:

Realty Mortgages

Foreclosure

When the mortgage debt is due and is unpaid, the mortgagee may either sue on the debt or foreclose the mortgage. The foreclosure action is the action brought by the mortgagee to foreclose the exercise of what is otherwise the equitable right of the mortgagor—to redeem the property from the mortgagee by offering payment. The foreclosure action may be brought upon any default on the payment of the debt which the mortgage secures. It is the sale which extinguishes all interests of persons included as party defendants in the foreclosure proceedings. In short, the foreclosure decree orders the sale of the mortgaged premises and the proceeds obtained from the sale are applied to satisfy the debt. The foreclosure sale is the actual sale of the mortgaged property. Its purpose is to obtain satisfaction of the mortgage debt out of the proceeds. The sale may be authorized by a decree of the court or by a power of sale contained in the mortgage.

Mortgages are extremely intricate legal instruments. It would be unfair to the reader to imply that he should undertake negotiation of a mortgage instrument without the aid of an attorney. This discussion of mortgages does not even scratch the surface of the subject. But, a discussion of basic concepts of mortgage instruments will not hurt. Many people get involved in mortgage transactions and regret it later. The dream purchase today could be tomorrow's nightmare. Hopefully, this chapter will alert the reader to some of the problems that await a purchaser. Investment in property has many serious legal ramifications and the extra expenditure on legal counsel would be well spent.

Acceleration of Payment in New York State

A clause that can trigger the acceleration of payment on the balance of the debt can place the mortgagor in a precarious predicament. These acceleration clauses, which the reader will notice in the individual mortgage documents that follow, are very powerful, and are binding.

An acceleration clause (or clauses) is part of a fair and legal contract which the parties had a right to enter into. It should not be regarded as a forfeiture or penalty clause. It merely accelerates the time when a legal obligation must be performed. The repayment of the debt is a legal obligation to be performed by the mortgagor. Acceleration of the time period, in which it is to be fully repaid, is simply an immediate demand for that legal obligation. The legal obligation has not been altered; only the time to perform has been changed. As in the case of the mortgage contracts contained in this section, acceleration clauses must be clear and certain and will not be explained by inference. As long as the mortgagee has not acted in an unconscionable manner, he is entitled to the benefit of the acceleration clause.

An acceleration clause takes effect after a default in the payment of installment of an interest or principal occurs and must be evidenced by an unequivocal act of the mortgagee in conjunction with an election to declare the full amount of real estate mortgage due. A demand is unnecessary to enable the mortgagee to exercise his election to declare the full amount of the mortgage due.

The mortgagee, however, cannot make his demand simply because a payment was missed. Some unequivocal act by the mortgagee must demonstrate the election. Generally, notice to the mortgagor of the mortgagee's election to demand full payment is sufficient; directing a foreclosure search would not be deemed sufficient.

The mortgagor should not be in despair if he is late on an installment payment of interest or principal. He might be in trouble, but the mortgagor has up to the time that the mortgagee makes an effective election to declare the entire principal due to tender the amount of that installment. It is not recommended that the mortgagor engage in this type of conduct, but if the situation occurs, always attempt to tender payment before an effective election is made. If the mortgagee has not made an effective election to declare the entire principal of mortgage due, the mortgagor has the right to pay installments past due with interest. In

MORTGAGE LOAN DISCLOSURE STATEMENT

The statements herein contained are for disclosure only and do not in any way change, modify or vary the terms and conditions of any note, security instrument or other document relative to this loan:

Borrower(s):   Lender:

Loan No..

Date...19..........

....

....

street address (residence)   street address

city & state   zip   telephone   city & state   zip   telephone

IDENTIFICATION OF TRANSACTION

☐ Purchase money first lien mortgage loan (you may omit item A(5))

☐ Non-purchase money mortgage loan or loan transaction extending, modifying or refinancing an outstanding mortgage loan

A. BASIC TERMS OF LOAN CONTRACT

(1) Loan Proceeds .... $.........................

(2) Prepaid Finance Charge:

   a) VA funding fee ....

   b) ....

(3) Amount Financed   (1) minus (2)................ $.........................

(4) **FINANCE CHARGE:**

   a) prepaid finance charge   item (2) ....

   b) interest ....

   c) FHA mortgage insurance premium ....

   d) ....

(5) Total of Payments   (1) + (4) ....

(6) **ANNUAL PERCENTAGE RATE** .... **%**

C. The **FINANCE CHARGE** begins to accrue on ....19..............

D. Terms of payment

(1) $....................on....................19......., ...payments of $.........................each on same day of each succeeding

month; and $.........................on.........................19.......**BALLOON PAYMENT of $**.........................is payable on

.........................19........**and no provision is made for refinancing the same.**

(2) Prepayment penalty charge: Prepayment penalty charge, as hereafter computed, shall be due and payable if the mortgage loan is prepaid:

(3) Default charge: If any payment is overdue in excess of 15 days borrower shall pay a default charge equal to.........................cents for each dollar so overdue.

E. SECURITY INTEREST A mortgage lien upon real estate described in the mortgage to be made in connection with the underlying transaction shall secure the interest of the lender. The mortgage lien will cover after-acquired property. The real estate is located at ....

F. INSURANCE

(1) Property insurance in the minimum amount of $......................... is required under the terms of the loan, and may be obtained through any duly licensed agent or broker of borrower's choice, subject to lenders right to refuse to accept any insurer for reasonable cause.

*(2) CREDIT LIFE INSURANCE IS *NOT* REQUIRED. Cost of credit life insurance per month $.........................

☐ I desire credit life insurance	☐ I do not desire credit life insurance
Party, covered	
............date............signature	............date............signature

Undersigned borrower(s) hereby acknowledges receipt of this disclosure statement prior to the consummation of the underlying transaction described herein.

Dated...19.........

....

Borrower   **Borrower**

* If credit life insurance is required, stike out *not*, complete line F.(2) and enter amount in line A.(4)d) also.

B. OTHER CHARGES:

(1) Fees

   a) title examination .... $.................... ....

   b) title insurance ....

   c) survey ....

   d) legal, preparation of documents.. ....

   e) appraisal ....

   f) credit report ....

   g) recording mortgage ....

   h) recording deed ....

   i) mortgage recording tax ....

   j) ....

   k) ....

(2) Escrow: **annual**   **monthly**

real estate tax .... $.................... $....................

water & sewer rent ....

insurance premium ....

Total monthly payment .... $....................

Escrow payment at closing .... $....................

Realty Mortgages

general, until an effective election is made by the mortgagee, the mortgagor has the right to pay and thus prevent acceleration.

There is no provision under Section 254 of the Real Property Law of New York that makes notice to the mortgagor a prerequisite to the mortgagee's election to deem the mortgage accelerated. However, a provision for written notice of default and election to accelerate the payment of principal is permissible in the mortgage contract; although not mandatory. This is an element that a mortgagor should attempt to insert in the contract.

Acceleration of payment of interest and principal does not result only from default of an installment payment due and owing. As evidenced by the mortgage contract illustrated in this chapter, the mortgagor's default in the performance of any covenant or agreement contained in a mortgage can operate as an acceleration, if the clause stipulates such. Another word of caution: The mortgagor should know what clauses in a mortgage contract have stipulated acceleration of payment. The reader must remember that in any contractual transaction, it is prudent to ask questions first and sign later. Failure to do this will lead to many problems in the future.

T-139 Mortgage Loan Disclosure Statement

This form is included to give the reader an opportunity to see what a typical disclosure statement looks like. Since it is not particularly complicated, not much will be said about it. Notice the statement at the top of the form, which states in bold print: "The statements herein contained are for disclosure only and do not in any way change, modify or vary the terms and conditions of any note, security instrument or other document relative to this loan:"

This is a disclosure statement—not the mortgage loan instrument. Make sure (1) that when this form is filled out, it is understood that it is a disclosure statement of a mortgage loan and not an actual mortgage document, and (2) that any of the terms in the disclosure state-ment are not different from the terms of the mortgage loan. Even though that statement is placed at the top of the form, it is much wiser to make sure that the terms coincide with the terms and conditions of any note, security instrument, or other document relating to the loan. It is a very good practice not to execute conflicting documents, regardless of statements which direct the document that will control. It is a minor point, but one that can save problems later on.

A-283 Mortgage Statutory Long Form

Form #1 is a mortgage statutory long form with special clauses. It can be used by either an individual or corporation.

Page 1 sets forth the essential elements of the contract. On this page the names of the mortgagee and mortgagor, the amount of the debt, the manner and time of payment(s), the interest rate to be charged, and any other information that is relevant to payment (e.g., where the payments are to be made), can be located. The second half of page 1 is the description of the property to which the mortgage applies. This is a very important feature since the mortgage applies only to the property described on the face of the document. The mortgagee wants to make certain that the property is accurately described and defined as to location, boundaries, fixtures, and other property that is includable in the mortgage. Page 1 should be drawn up clearly, so that the mortgagor understands his obligation, the amount and time of payments, interest due thereon and a full description of the property that is subject to the mortgage.

Page 2 begins the formal clauses of the contract. The first three clauses, beginning with the word "TOGETHER" are read in conjunction with page 1, and in particular with the mortgaged property described on the front page. The contract reads, beginning midway on page 1, "according to an urban bond, note or obligation bearing even date herewith, the mortgagor hereby mortgages to the mortgagee, ALL described property." After the property has been described, the TOGETHER clauses are read in relation to the described property. The first TOGETHER clause is self-explanatory. The second TOGETHER clause gives the mortgagee rights in the fixtures and personal property on the property now or whether currently attached or to become affixed in the future. This is a standard clause which means that if the mortgagor gives a mortgage on his property where his house is located, and after execution of the mortgage, he puts an addition on his house, that addition would be subject to the terms of the mortgage. The third TOGETHER clause simply states that any awards (money) made to the owners of the mortgaged property by a governmental or other lawful authority for any taking for whatever reason, are automatically to be given to the mortgagee to be applied to the note due (debt) in reduction of the note (debt). The clause does not place the mortgagor at a disadvantage. Mortgagor also agrees to execute any instrument to effectuate the assignment to the mortgagor.

Beginning with "AND the mortgagor covenants with the mortgagee as follows:", the contract enters into specifics. Only those clauses which need some explanation or which could be detrimental to the mortgagor will be discussed. Clauses that are favorable to mortgagor will not be discussed. We do not mean by this that such clauses are unimportant. Each and every clause is important, but some do not require explanation.

Special Clauses

Clauses 2, 11, and 19: These clauses simply state that the mortgagor is responsible for maintaining fire insurance policies which cover the mortgaged property. The mortgagor agrees to assign and deliver the policies to the mortgagee and the mortgagor is liable to the mortgagee for any premiums the mortgagee is required to pay by virtue of the fact that the mortgagor defaults on the premium payment.

Clause 11 states that the mortgagee is only covered by the fire insurance policy to the extent of the mortgage debt. This rule is based on the theory that an insurance policy insuring property is a contract of indemnity; hence, the insured is not entitled to recover more than his loss. This is the law in New York and is generally accepted in most states. However, the reader should consult the state laws to ascertain whether his state has the same policy. When both interests—that of mortgagor and mortgagee—are covered in the mortgagor's policy (as is often the case), the mortgagee is paid first up to the amount of the mortgage debt which is reduced as of that moment. The mortgagor recovers the remainder up to the amount of the loss. Naturally, all the above could vary with different types of clauses in the particular insurance policies. This is meant to be just a quick view of the standard fire insurance coverage expected by a mortgagee. It is a standard clause—one that every mortgagee will insist upon. Section 254 of the Real Property Law, subdivision 4, states in statutory language what has been covered in Clauses 2, 11, and 19. The section is attached hereto if the reader is interested in reading the statutory language applicable to this particular clause (11 in the mortgage instrument).

Clause 19 is the third part of the trilogy of clauses relating to fire insurance coverage. It has a little more bite to it. It is highly unlikely that the mortgagor will be able to negotiate any of the terms of the clause, but it is important that the mortgagor understands the penalty for failing to fulfill his requirements. The main thrust of this clause is that the mortgagee has the option to demand payment in full for the debt secured by the mortgage, if the mortgagor defaults on keeping the buildings on the property insured as required by clause 2 and 11. This is a serious penalty imposed upon the mortgagor and one of which the mortgagor should be aware. This provision, which will effectuate an acceleration of payment of the debt, will take effect if the mortgagor fails to assign and deliver to the mortgagee the policies of fire insurance or reimburse the mortgagee for premiums paid on such fire insurance (as provided in clause 2).

57

Clause 10 refers to a statute that is applicable if the mortgage is executed on property located within the state of New York. Section 13 of Lien Law states that a subsequently recorded mortgage will have priority over previously recorded mechanics liens to the extent of advances of the mortgage made prior to the mechanics lien, provided that the mortgage includes a provision that payments under it are subject to the trust fund provisions of section 13 of the Lien Law. This clause is protection for the mortgagee against other parties (i.e., materialmen) who might have other liens against the property. The mortgagor does not have to concern himself with the mechanics of Section 13 of the Lien Law and should not worry about its application.

Clauses 4, 14, 15, 16, and 17: These are grouped together because they can be classified in one large category entitled acceleration clauses. They primarily concern themselves with the right of the mortgagee to demand payment of the debt (this is termed *acceleration of payment*). This acceleration is triggered by the mortgagor's failure to perform an obligation called for under the contract. Specifically, he has failed to perform an obligation arising out of one of these particular clauses. In that sense, the clauses are similar in the penalty imposed for failure to perform the duties they require. Each clause has a distinct breach which could result in the acceleration of payment. Of course, failure to make payment of the debt due gives the mortgagee the right to foreclose.

The mortgagor of property must be able to fulfill his duties or he is in serious danger. The mortgagee might require him to tender full payment of the balance of the debt due and owing. Another remedy afforded the mortgagee would be to foreclose on the mortgaged property. Neither situation is a desirable one and the mortgagor should realize that these potential problems will become unfortunate realities upon a failure to perform as required. It is imperative that the mortgagor has the ability to live up to the obligations called for under the mortgage agreement. Failure to perform these obligations could result in loss of property.

Clause 13 allows the mortgagee the additional right to possession in the event of default on the part of the mortgagor in performing any of the terms, covenants, or agreements. If the mortgagor is allowed to remain on the premises, the mortgagee is allowed to charge him rent; if he defaults on these payments, the mortgagee may dispossess him by summary proceedings. Foreclosure once again, is a remedy afforded the mortgagee.

It is emphasized that if a mortgagor defaults on any of the obligations contained within a mortgage contract, he will find himself at the mercy of the mortgagee. It is not automatic that the mortgagee would bring an action to accelerate payment of the debt, nor is it automatic that the mortgagee would bring an action to foreclose or repossess on account of mortgagor's default of an obligation contained within the mortgage instrument. But it is very unlikely that the mortgagee would not proceed legally against the mortgagor. This is the purpose of the mortgage. It is a security instrument executed just for the purpose of providing remedies to the mortgagee in the event of some default on the part of the mortgagor. The mortgagee is interested in repayment of the debt. If the mortgagee cannot get the money, acquiring the property is probably just as good, if not better. In most instances, the property is worth more than the debt and the mortgagee stands to benefit by acquiring title to the property.

Form 27—Mortgage Note, Individual or Corporation

The mortgage note is another document, which on its face does not have much content, but is capable of much impact. It is simply the short form of a mortgage note. The parties to the contract have the same rights, liabilities and remedies that have been discussed before. Any obligations or duties provided on this form, or in any other form which is executed in conjunction, are enforceable. A reference on this form to the other document would probably be present. If none is made, ask that all documents be referred to specifically on this form. Despite its brevity, this note will cause the mortgagor many problems if he does not fulfill his obligations.

There is only one clause to be especially noted. It applies to all mortgage instruments. It is the last clause on the document, which states: "This note may not be changed *orally*, but only by an agreement in *writing* and signed by the party against whom enforcement of any waiver, change, modification or discharge is sought."

This clause is very important; perhaps an illustration of the legalities involved is appropriate: Peter Propertyholder is the mortgagor and XYZ Bank is the mortgagee. Peter's payments on the note (debt) are due monthly to the bank and if he defaults, the bank has the option to accelerate payment of the debt to make him pay within 20 days. If he fails to make total payment within that time, the bank can foreclose on the property. This is a very serious and real consequence. Peter's best friend is the president of XYZ Bank. In fact, it is his signature in the capacity as president of the bank, that is alongside Peter's signature at the bottom of the mortgage note. The president is the highest ranking officer in the bank. One day, while playing tennis together, Peter informs him that money is scarce and that he is having a hard time making ends meet. The bank president then informs Peter that he can skip the next payment of his mortgage loan and make it up when things are going well. Peter believes him. He is Peter's best friend and president of XYZ Bank. So, Peter skips a payment. The bank brings an action against Peter to accelerate payments or foreclosure. He claims as a definse that his friend, president of XYZ Bank, had waived that right by authorizing him to skip a payment. He relied on the statement, and it is now going to work to his detriment. What was the result? Peter loses the case and along with it his property. Moral of the story: Any other agreements, regardless of their content, in relation to the mortgage note, must be in writing and signed by the parties.

Form 124—Satisfaction of Mortgage

This instrument is the mortgagor's release from bondage. When this instrument has been executed between the mortgagor and mortgagee, the property is no longer encumbered by a mortgage. The mortgagor has clear title to the property (provided there are no other liens on the property).

In essence, all this instrument states is that the mortgagee has fulfilled his obligations under the mortgage agreement, and as of this date forward, the mortgage does not exist. This generally means that the debt in which the mortgage was security has been paid in full. Remember what was mentioned in the introduction. The mortgage instrument follows the note (debt). If there is no debt, no legal obligation, then there is no mortgage. This instrument is the proof and when the mortgagor has this document in his hands signed by the mortgagee, he should go out and celebrate.

Appendix To Mortgages
New York Real Property Law, Article 8,
§ 254, (2), (3), (4), (5), (6), (8).

59

Two. Covenant that whole sum shall become due. A covenant "that the whole of the said principal sum and interest shall become due at the option of the mortgagee: after default in the payment of any installment of principal or of interest for . . . . . . days; or after default in the payment of any tax, water rate or assessment for . . . . . . days after notice and demand; or after default after notice and demand either in assigning and delivering the policies insuring the buildings against loss by fire or in reimbursing the mortgagee for premiums paid on such insurance, as hereinbefore provided; or after default upon request in furnishing a statement of the amount due on the mortgage and whether any offsets or defenses exist against the mortgage debt as hereinafter provided," must be construed as meaning that should any default be made in the payment of any installment of principal or of any part thereof, or in the payment of the said interest, or any part thereof, on any day whereon the same is made payable, or should any tax, water rate or assessment, and/or any installment of any assessment which has been divided into annual installments pursuant to provision of law in such cases made and provided which now is or may be hereafter imposed upon the premises hereinafter described, become due or payable, and should the said installment of principal or interest remain unpaid and in arrear for the space of ...... days, or such tax, water rate or assessment or annual installment remain unpaid and in arrear for ...... days after written notice by the mortgagee or obligee, his executors, administrators, successors or assigns, that such tax or assessment and/or annual installment is unpaid and demand for the payment thereof, or should any default be made after notice and demand either in assigning and delivering the policies insuring the buildings against loss by fire or in reimbursing the mortgagee for premiums paid on such insurance, as hereinafter provided, or upon failure to furnish such statement of the amount due on the mortgage and whether any offsets or defenses exist against the mortgage debt, as hereinafter provided, after the expiration of ...... days in case the request is made personally, or after the expiration of ...... days after the mailing of such request in case the request is made by mail, then and from thenceforth, that is to say, after the lapse of either one of said periods, as the case may be, the aforesaid principal sum, with all arrearage of interest thereon, shall at the option of the said mortgagee or obligee, his executors, administrators, successors or assigns, become and be due and payable immediately thereafter, although the period above limited for the payment thereof may not then have expired, anything thereinbefore contained to the contrary thereof in any wise notwithstanding.

Three. Covenant to pay indebtedness. In default of payment, mortgagee to have power to sell. A covenant "that the mortgagor will pay the indebtedness, as hereinbefore provided," must be construed as meaning that the mortgag-

or for himself, his heirs, executors and administrators or successors, doth covenant and agree to pay to the mortgagee, his executors, administrators, successors and assigns, the principal sum of money secured by said mortgage, and also the interest thereon as provided by said mortgage. And if default shall be made in the payment of the principal sum or the interest that may grow due thereon, or of any part thereof, or in the case of any other default, that then and from thenceforth it shall be lawful for the mortgagee, his executors, administrators or successors to enter into and upon all and singular the premises granted, or intended so to be, and to sell and dispose of the same, and all benefit and equity of redemption of the said mortgagor, his heirs, executors, administrators, successors or assigns therein, at public auction, and out of the money arising from such sale, to retain the principal and interest which shall then be due, together with the costs and charges of advertisement and sale of the said premises, rendering the overplus of the purchase-money, if any there shall be, unto the mortgagor, ...

Four. Mortgagor to keep buildings insured. A covenant "that the mortgagor will keep the buildings on the premises insured against loss by fire for the benefit of the mortgagee; that he will assign and deliver the policies to the mortgagee; and that he will reimburse the mortgagee for any premiums paid for insurance made by the mortgagee on the mortgagor's default in so insuring the buildings or in so assigning and delivering the policies," shall be construed as meaning that the mortgagor, his heirs, successors and assigns will, during all the time until the money secured by the mortgage shall be fully paid and satisfied, keep the buildings erected on the premises insured against loss or damage by fire, to an amount to be approved by the mortgagee not exceeding in the aggregate one hundred per centum of their full insurable value and in a company or companies to be approved by the mortgagee, and will assign and deliver the policy or policies of such insurance to the mortgagee, his executors, administrators, successors or assigns, which policy or policies shall have endorsed thereon the standard New York mortgagee clause in the name of the mortgagee, so and in such manner and form that he and they shall at all time and times, until the full payment of said moneys, have and hold the said policy or policies as a collateral and further security for the payment of said moneys, and in default of so doing, that the mortgagee or his executors, administrators, successors or assigns, may make such insurance from year to year, in an amount in the aggregate not exceeding one hundred per centum of the full insurable value of said buildings erected on the mortgaged premises for the purposes aforesaid, and pay the premium or premiums therefor, and that the mortgagor will pay to the mortgagee, his executors, administrators, successors or assigns, such premium or premiums so paid, with interest from the time of payment, on demand, and that the same shall be deemed to be secured by the mortgage, and shall be collectible thereupon and thereby in like manner as the principal moneys, and that should the mortgagee by reason of such insurance against loss by fire receive any sum or sums of money for damage by fire, and should the mortgagee retain such insurance money instead of paying it over to the mortgagor, the mortgagee's right to retain the same and his duty to apply it in payment of or on account of the sum secured by the mortgage and in satisfaction or reduction of the lien . . . Any excess of said insurance money over the amount so payable to the mortgagor shall be applied in reduction of the principal of the mortgage. Provided, however, that if and so long as there exists any default by the mortgagor in the performance of any of the terms or provisions of the mortgage on his part to be performed the mortgagee shall not be obligated to pay over any of said insurance money received by him. If the mortgagor shall fail to comply with any of the foregoing provisions within the time or times hereinabove limited, . . . or if the entire principal of the mortgage

shall have become payable by reason of default or maturity, the mortgagee shall apply said insurance money in satisfaction or reduction of the principal of the mortgage; and any excess of said insurance money over the amount required to satisfy the mortgage shall be paid to the mortgagor. . . .

Five. Mortgagor to warrant title. A covenant "that the mortgagor warrants the title to the premises," must be construed as meaning that the mortgagor warrants that he has good title to said premises and has a right to mortgage the same and that the mortgagor shall and will make, execute, acknowledge and deliver in due form of law, all such further or other deeds or assurances as may at any time hereafter be reasonably desired or required for the more fully and effectually conveying the premises by the mortgage described, . . .

Six. Mortgagor to pay all taxes, assessments or water rates. A covenant "that the mortgagor will pay all taxes, assessments or water rates and in default thereof, the mortgagee may pay the same" must be construed as meaning that until the amount hereby secured is paid, the mortgagor will pay all taxes, assessments and water rates which may be assessed or become liens on said premises, and in default thereof the holder of this mortgage may pay the same, and the mortgagor will repay the same with interest, and the same shall be liens on said premises and secured by the mortgage.

Eight. Notice and demand. A covenant "that notice and demand or request may be made in writing and may be served in person or by mail" must be construed as meaning that every provision for notice and demand or request shall be deemed fulfilled by written notice and demand or request personally served on one or more of the persons who shall at the time hold the record title to the premises, or on their heirs or successors, or mailed by depositing it in any post-office station or letter-box, . . .

61

62

How to Handle Your Own Contracts

CHAPTER 5

Partnership

Introduction

In this chapter only two contracts will be examined. One is an article of co-partnership and the other is a certificate of conducting business as partners. The latter is much less detailed and shorter in length. The contents of this chapter will be based totally on New York law, whether it be the Uniform Partnership Act or case law.

Obviously, the rules and principles which apply to partnerships within New York do not apply outside the state. However, whether for reasons dealing with local law or general partnership law, legal counsel should be sought.

Many friendships have ended because two friends became partners in some operation and in the end, each claimed that the other owed him money. The situation is aggravated when other people (non-partners) also claim that both of these friends held themselves out to be partners and owe them money for debts incurred while operating this "partnership." Not only were friendships lost, but also a lot of money. The problems might have been avoided, if the parties had possessed some knowledge of the implications of their acts before the commencement of the venture. They might have proceeded anyway, but with a little more caution, had they known the consequences.

Formation

A partnership may be defined as an association of two or more competent persons to carry on a business as co-owners for profit. A partnership is not a corporation, although it does have some similar elements. For example, a partnership may hold title to property in the partnership's name and it may be sued and bring suit.

One of the key aspects of a partnership is that the debts of the partnership are the debts of the individual partners. In addition, one partner may be held liable for the partnership's entire indebtedness. These are a couple of reasons why some people are wary of entering into partnerships. Not only are they afraid of losing a good friendship, but their money also is at stake.

A partnership is a contract (agreement), and is governed by the general rules of contract law (and agency, which when applicable, will be explained). Any person can enter into a partnership if he is capable of entering into a legal contract. However, if a party enters into a partnership with another party who lacks capacity, no liability extends to the incompetent party except to the extent of his contribution of capital to the partnership.

Thus, for example: X and Y form a partnership. X contributes $100.00 and Y contributes $100.000. X is 15 years old. The partnership incurs debts of $130.00 to Z. Z can collect out of the $100.00 contributed by X. However, if the partnership had incurred debts of $230.00, X would be liable for only $100.00. Y would be liable for the remaining $130.00.

How is a partnership formed? Two forms have been provided at the end of this chapter, but they are not absolutely necessary to the

63

Partnership

formation of a partnership. In fact, there are no particular set of formalities to be followed. One statutory requirement is that in certain situations a partnership agreement must conform with the Statute of Fraud. This means, for example, that a partnership agreement must be in writing where it cannot be performed within one year of its inception. If there is no statute relating to partnership or its formation, it may be formed simply by the conduct of the parties, without a formal agreement.

If two people represent themselves to the public as partners, and their conduct would lead a third party to believe that they are in fact partners, the law will imply a partnership, and both will be held liable under partnership law. If another person desires to enter into a pre-existing partnership, there must be consent, either expressed or implied, by the other partners.

What are the determining factors which establish the existence of a partnership if there is no express agreement? Certain types of evidence tend to prove the existence of a partnership, but they are by no means conclusive. Title to property in a partnership name and the designation of the entity as a partnership might be indicative of intent. If the parties agree to share in the profits of a business, this is considered *prima facie* evidence that they are partners in the business. If there is evidence that indicates the parties did not intend to share losses, this evidence supports the presumption that there was not a partnership.

One must be wary of his conduct with another person in his representations to the public. When one person, in conjunction with another, represents himself, either privately or publicly, to be a partner with that person, he is liable to third parties who extended credit to the actual or apparent partnership. If a person permits another to represent him as a partner, he will be liable to third persons who extend credit to the partnership (even though it does not actually exist). A person who consents to being held out publicly as a partner is liable to any third party who extends credit, regardless of whether the third party knows of the repre-

sentation. If a person consents only to being privately held out, he is only liable to third persons if they in fact relied on that representation.

In any of these situations, the result can be disastrous, since a party is held liable for debts incurred by his partner. Under no circumstances should one allow himself (or his name) to be held out as a partner, unless he is one in fact.

General and Limited Partnerships

There are two fundamental forms of partnerships—the general and limited partnerships. Discussion throughout the chapter is geared to the general partnership situation; however, mention should be made about the characteristics of a limited partnership, in order to cover the scope of the subject.

In a general partnership, each partner devotes his time, money, and efforts to the furtherance of the firm's business. As mentioned, subject to the terms of the agreement, each partner has complete authority to act within the scope of the partnership and is equally as completely liable for partnership obligations.

On the other hand, the limited partnership, which is created in accordance with state law, is comprised of partners who are both active and inactive. The latter or limited partners perform no managerial functions and their liability is limited to their monetary contribution.

A limited partner does become personally liable where his actions exceed statutory restrictions. This does not mean that the limited partner bears the risk of loss without possessing certain corresponding rights. Specifically, the limited partner has the right to a full appraisal of partnership affairs and activities and a right to an accounting. He likewise has the right to his allocable share of the profits and priority over all funds upon dissolution. However, these rights only apply between the limited and general partners and do not extend to actual business conduct with the public. In fact, the limited partner's name may not appear in the partnership name except for certain statutorily defined purposes. In essence, the limited partner is a silent partner.

Rights

Assuming that a partnership has been formed, what are the rights and liabilities between partners and third parties? What is partnership property? What is an individual partner's property? In other words, what happens once Joe and Lou open that motorcycle shop as a partnership?

Partnership capital is the property or money contributed by each of the partners, intended to be used for carrying on the firm's business. Partnership property generally consists of everything that the firm owns. Property acquired with partnership funds is usually partnership property. The term "generally" is used, since, if the partners have a different intent, their intent will govern. Common sense factors are considered by the court in determining the intention of the parties and need not be discussed.

The rights of partners in partnership property are straightforward. Each partner has a specific partnership property right which is termed a *tenancy in partnership*. This ownership entitles each partner to an equal right to possess the property with his co-partners; a partner needs the consent of the co-partners to possess it for any other reason. Upon the death of a partner, his interest passes and vests in the remaining partners.

A partner has an interest in the firm. He has an interest in his share of the profits and any surplus of the partnership which is treated as personal property. Assignment of this interest, which is allowable since it is a personalty, does not dissolve the partnership.

All partners are deemed to have equal rights in the running of the partnership business regardless of their individual percentage of profits. The simple rule is that one man is entitled to one vote. Profits made in the course of the

partnership belong to the firm and one partner will not be allowed to profit personally at the expense of the firm. If a partner makes payments or incurs liabilities in the furtherance of business, the partnership must indemnify that partner for those expenditures. This would also apply if the partner makes a capital outlay to preserve the property of the partnership. Along the same lines, if a partner pays a partnership debt, he is entitled to contribution from the other partners for their proportionate shares. Each and every partner has a right to inspect the partnership books which are to be kept at the partnership's place of business.

Authority to Act

As a general rule, a partner may not sue or be sued by the partnership, because he is personally liable for all debts and obligations of the partnership, and the effect of the suit would be a suit against himself.

Each and every partner, when dealing with third parties, is considered an agent of the partnership, if his course of conduct is in the furtherance of the partnership business. This theory is based upon the law of agency. The acts of the partners bind the partnership as long as their acts are within the scope of the partnership. Liability may be in contract, tort, or breach of trust.

Authorization is the term that is used to determine if a particular partner was acting within his authority. If authority was granted him in the Article of Partnership, then the partnership will be bound by his act. If the partner was not authorized to do the particular act by the agreement, then a majority vote of the partners is needed to ratify his actions.

The partnership agreement governs the partnership. However, if the agreement fails to provide certain authorizations, then a unanimous vote is required to authorize a partner to perform certain acts which will effectively bind the partnership. The situations requiring this measure are matters involving arbitration, assignment for benefit of creditors, confession

Article of Co-Partnership

WITNESSETH: *The said parties above named have agreed to become co-partners and by these presents form a partnership under the trade name and style of*

for the purpose of buying, selling, vending and manufacturing

and all other goods, wares and merchandise belonging to the said business and to occupy the following premises:

their co-partnership to commence on the   day of   19 and to continue

and to that end and purpose the said

to be used and employed in common between them for the support and management of the said business, to their mutual benefit and advantage. AND it is agreed by and between the parties to these presents, that at all times during the continuance of their co-partnership, they and each of them will give their attendance, and do their and each of their best endeavors, and to the utmost of their skill and power, exert themselves for their joint interest, profit, benefit and advantage, and truly employ, buy, sell and merchandise with their joint stock, and the increase thereof, in the business aforesaid. AND ALSO, that they shall and will at all times during the said co-partnership, bear, pay and discharge equally between them, all rents and other expenses that may be required for the support and management of the said business; and that all gains, profit and increase, that shall come,

grow or arise from or by means of their said business shall be divided between them, as follows:

and all loss that shall happen to their said joint business by ill-commodities, bad debts or otherwise shall be borne and paid between them, as follows:

AND it is agreed by and between the said parties, that there shall be had and kept at all times during the continuance of their co-partnership, perfect, just, and true books of account, wherein each of the said co-partners shall enter and set down, as well all money by them or either of them received, paid, laid out and expended in and about the said business, as also all goods, wares, commodities and merchandise, by them or either of them, bought or sold, by reason or on account of the said business, and all other matters and things whatsoever, to the said business and the management thereof in anywise belonging; which said book shall be used in common between the said co-partners, so that either of them may have access thereto, without any interruption or hindrance of the other. AND ALSO, the said co-partners, once in

How to Handle Your Own Contracts

or oftener if necessary, shall make, yield and render, each to the other, a true, just and perfect inventory and account of all profits and increase by them or either of them, made, and of all losses by them or either of them, sustained; and also all payments, receipts, disbursements and all other things by them made, received, disbursed, acted, done, or suffered in this said co-partnership and business; and the same account so made, shall and will clear, adjust, pay and deliver, each to the other, at the time, their just share of the profits so made as aforesaid.

AND the said parties hereby mutually covenant and agree, to and with each other, that during the continuance of the said co-partnership,   of them shall nor will endorse any note, or otherwise become surety for any person or persons whomsoever, nor will sell, assign, transfer, mortgage or otherwise dispose of the business of the co-partnership, nor each of   share, title and interest therein without the written consent of the parties hereto. And at the end or other sooner termination of their co-partnership the said co-partners each to the other, shall and will make a true, just and final account of all things relating to their said business, and in all things truly adjust the same; and all and every the stock and stocks, as well as the gains and increase thereof, which shall appear to be remaining, either in money, goods, wares, fixtures, debts or otherwise, shall be divided between them as follows:

after the payment of the co-partnership liabilities; and should said co-partners be unable to ascertain the value of any of the assets belonging to the co-partnership at the termination of their co-partnership, the said assets shall then be sold either at private or public sale to be agreed upon by the parties hereto and a division of the proceeds of said sale shall be made as herein provided.

IT IS FURTHER AGREED that during the continuance of the co-partnership herein, all notes, drafts or money received for and in behalf of the said co-partnership by the parties hereto shall be deposited in a bank to be agreed upon by the parties hereto and the moneys credited to said co-partnership shall only be withdrawn by check signed by

who shall also receive said notes, drafts or moneys or other orders for payment of moneys of the said co-partnership for the purpose of making said deposits.

IT IS FURTHER AGREED that during the continuance of said co-partnership the parties hereto shall mutually agree in writing, upon a weekly allowance, to be paid to each of the parties hereto for services to be rendered, and said allowance shall be charged as an item of expense of the co-partnership business, or if otherwise agreed upon in writing may be charged against their personal interest in said business.

IN THE EVENT of the death of a party hereto, the surviving co-partner   shall within a period of   weeks, make and give, to the legal representative of the deceased co-partner, a true, just and final account of all things relating to the co-partnership business, and within a period of   months, in all things truly adjust the same with the legal representative of the deceased co-partner. The surviving co-partner   shall have the privilege of purchasing the interest of the deceased co-partner from his legal representative, upon a true and proper valuation of the interest of the deceased co-partner; and until the purchase of said interest by the surviving co-partner , or a division as herein agreed upon, the legal representative of the deceased co-partner during reasonable business hours shall have access to the books of the co-partnership and examine same personally or with the aid of other persons and make copies thereof or any portion thereof without any interruption or hindrance, and the said legal representative of said deceased co-partner shall have equal and joint control of the said co-partnership with the surviving partner or partners.

Business Certificate for Partners

The undersigned do hereby certify that they are conducting or transacting business as members of a partnership under the name or designation of

at

in the County of   , State of New York, and do further certify that the full names of all the persons conducting or transacting such partnership including the full names of all the partners with the residence address of each such person, and the age of any who may be infants, are as follows:

NAME *Specify which are infants and state ages.*   RESIDENCE

....

....

....

....

....

....

WE DO FURTHER CERTIFY that we are the successors in interest to

the person or persons heretofore using such name or names to carry on or conduct or transact business.

In Witness Whereof, We have this   day of   19   made and signed this certificate.

....

....

....

....

....

....

State of New York, County of   ss.:   INDIVIDUAL ACKNOWLEDGMENT

On this   day of   19   , before me personally appeared

to me known and known to me to be the individual   described in, and who executed the foregoing certificate, and   he   thereupon   duly acknowledged to me that   he   executed the same.

How to Handle Your Own Contracts

of judgment, and the disposition of the good will of the firm.

If a partner does not have actual authority, he may be deemed to have apparent authority. Generally, a person is not responsible for the acts of another who assumes to represent him. However, partners are not assuming to represent the other partners when business is conducted. That is the purpose of the partnership and each partner actually does represent the partnership. So, when a partner holds himself out to a third party as having authority and that party reasonably believes that the authority exists, the partner has the apparent authority to act, even though the partnership agreement has not granted it to him, and the partners have not actually consented to his act. This theory is grounded in agency law to provide protection for innocent third parties in dealing with partners. Example: **X** and **Y** are partners in the **XY Co. XY Co.** owns an apartment building in which **Z** has leased an apartment. The rent is due on the fifth of the month. **Z** sees **X** on the fifth of the month and explains that he will not be able to pay for two weeks due to some illness in the family and a shortage of funds. **X** tells **Z** that late payment is permissible and not to worry about it. **XY Co.** will accept the rent late. Even though **X** might not have had the actual authority to extend the due date of the rental payment, he had the apparent authority, and the partnership will be bound by his extension. **Z** relied on **X**'s apparent authority to extend the payment date and would have a valid defense for non-payment.

Liabilities

The partnership is liable for any wrongful act by a partner if committed while the partner was conducting business within the scope of the partnership or with the other partner's consent. Where a partner, acting within the scope of business, defrauds a third party, the partnership will be held liable. If a partner defrauds the partnership in alliance with a third party, the partnership is not liable to the third party.

Whenever a partner acts outside the scope of the partnership, it will not be held liable. If a partner breaches a trust, such as misapplication of money from a third person given to him within the scope of his apparent (or actual) authority, the partnership is liable.

One of the major reasons why there are so many small, closed corporations instead of partnerships is that the liability of partners is rather far reaching. Partners are liable on contracts executed by the firm in the scope of business and on any other contracts expressly authorized by the partnership. Partners are also liable for torts committed by the other partners (or employees), if committed within the course and scope of the firm's business. Again, in general, partners are jointly liable for civil liability and jointly and severally liable in tort actions.

This is the key point to note. Each partner is personally and individually liable for the entire amount of all partnership obligations, whether resulting from contract or tort; and to relate to an earlier part of this chapter, if one partner pays more than his share, he is then entitled to indemnification from the partnership and may also get a *pro rata* contribution from the partners if the partnership is unable to pay. Personal liability should make one think carefully with whom he desires to form a partnership. If liabilities are incurred and the partnership cannot pay, the creditor has the right to satisfy the debt from a partner's personal assets.

An incoming (new) partner to the firm is liable for all pre-existing debts incurred by the partnership before he enters. It is as if he had been one of the partners at the time the obligations were incurred. His liability, however, is limited only to the partnership property; he is not held personally liable, although he may become personally liable, if he promises to pay the existing debts that extend beyond his interest in the partnership property. A partner who is leaving the firm is liable on all debts incurred by the firm up to the time of departure. Partners are not responsible for criminal acts performed by another partner, even if committed within the scope of partnership business, unless the other partners participated in the commission of the crime.

69

Concluding Remarks

Under no circumstances should a partnership be dissolved without the consultation of an attorney. Dissolution of a partnership can be a complex process, but does not necessarily involve a court proceeding. In most instances, the partnership is dissolved effectively without court interference. However, the "wrapping up" of partnership business does involve settling all matters that relate to the partnership and an attorney should be consulted in order to assure each and every partner that all matters relating to the partnership have been terminated property.

Article of Co-Partnership

This is a model of a formal partnership agreement. If two parties enter into this signed agreement, a formal partnership exists. The Article of Co-Partnership is a good model, since it defines the scope of the partnership and details basic rights and duties of the partners.

On page 1 of the agreement, the parties are identified and a partnership is in formation. The partnership name is indicated and the nature of business is declared. This is very important, since, as previously pointed out, action by one partner conducted outside the scope of the partnership business does not hold the partnership liable.

It is on the first page of the agreement that the parties should definitely outline the scope and nature of the business to be undertaken. This page is the most important one and has to be constructed carefully by the parties. The language does not have to be lengthy or complicated. In fact, the opposite effect is desired. Simple and straightforward language which accurately describes what business is to be conducted by the partnership is advantageous. If well constructed (whenever possible, always consult an attorney), this agreement might prevent future problems.

The latter part of the first page deals with duties and obligations touched upon in this chapter. The language is not particularly obtuse and should be readily understood. In essence, it states that the partners will work in furtherance of partnership business and their primary objective is to promote the best interests of the firm. They agree to share profits, losses, and expenses incurred in the course of conducting partnership business.

The top of page 2 allows for the parties to divide profits at various percentage rates, in the event they do not want to share them equally. In addition, the clause following allows the parties to distribute losses at variable percentage levels, if they desire. Note: The rule of one man, one vote still applies, regardless of the fact that profits and losses are allocated in various percentages.

Clause (A) simply states that the books of the partnership's records will be kept in order to record the transactions of the partnership business. Each and every partner has the right to inspect the books at any time. Clause (A) allows a partner to determine the specific time and place where the books may be examined regularly.

Clause (B) states that the parties are prohibited to engage in certain transactions, such as assignments, transfers, mortgages, etc.,— basically it prohibits a partner from tampering with partnership property. For these transactions to be authorized, the consent of the partners is required. The language of the clause is straightforward and self-explanatory.

The second part of Clause (B) provides a method of distribution in the event of the dissolution of the partnership. The parties can determine the division of the assets that the partnership retains after dissolution. However, as stated previously, this is a very intricate procedure and an attorney should be consulted. If there is enough left in the kitty to require a distribution, there is enough to pay for an attorney who will distribute it properly.

Clause (C) designates the bank of the partnership account. The important element of this clause is the designation of the partner(s) whose signature must appear on any negotiable instrument negotiated by the partnership. The party who is authorized to sign the partnership's negotiable instruments could be considered the treasurer. If the partnership consists of only two parties, a requirement for both parties' signature would be wise.

Clause (D) limits the expense account of each partner. Each partner relishes the thought of having an unlimited expense account, but this tends to be abused. Reasonable expenses should be estimated and allocated appropriately. Remember, as a partner, a person is spending his own money.

Clause (E) is concerned with the procedure of final accounting when a partner dies. Since this is another form of dissolution (partial), an attorney is recommended.

The partnership form entitled "Business Certificate for Partners" is a short form of an agreement of partnership. All rules of partnership law are applicable to persons signing this agreement, just as if they had signed a lengthier one. The short form does not spell out the rights and obligations of the parties in detail, but many of them still apply.

Dissolution

Unless the partnership agreement provides to the contrary, a partnership necessarily must dissolve and terminate upon the death of any one partner. The actual practice of dissolution and the final cleaning up of business affairs is one fraught with legal complexities and financial entanglements. In order to avoid incurring further liabilities, surviving partners would be best advised to seek legal counsel. Still, a person should be aware of the ramifications of his continuing business activities after dissolution is in order.

Dissolution occurs from a change in the relationship of the partners, whether it be through election or death. Any partner withdrawing from the agreed purpose of the firm's existence forces termination of the partnership, since all parties' original position is altered if only to a minor extent. The law similarly mandates dissolution in the event of partnership bankruptcy, illegality of business activities or incapacity or misconduct of a partner.

Upon dissolution, the surviving partners are obliged to wind up partnership affairs. Generally, this duty entails the finishing if incomplete business transactions, the collection of unpaid accounts, the payment of business debts, the liquidation of partnership assets and distribution to all involved parties, partners or representatives, of net amounts owed as a result of capital contributions or respective shares in profits and surplus. In fulfilling these obligations, the surviving partners become liquidating trustees and are liable for indiscretions or breaches of their fiduciary responsibilities. They must make a full accounting and disclosure of partnership assets and liabilities and distribute accordingly.

Dissolution and "winding up," then, are different concepts. Once dissolution is called for, the authority of all partners to act is terminated except that necessary to wind up the business. Thus, the partners can conclude old business, but any new business places sole liability upon the acting partners. Yet even though dissolution gives each partner the right to have the partnership liquidated and to receive his share in cash, the remaining partners can carry on in certain situations. If a partner is expelled in accordance with the agreement, if the dissolution contravenes the agreement or if the agreement provides for continuation, then after satisfying the withdrawing partner's share in the business, the remaining partners may proceed with partnership activities. Still in order to avoid unnecessary personal liability, a partner should consult an attorney, so that all prior business is properly terminated.

How to Handle Your Own Contracts

CHAPTER 6

Wills

Not A Contract

This chapter will concern itself with New York State law titled "Estates, Powera and Trusts Law." From a legal standpoint, a discussion of wills should not appear in a book on contracts, since a will is not a contract. However, since wills are an important part of everyone's life, a short summary of what to be on the lookout for when having a will drawn should prove helpful.

A will is a revocable instrument which is executed with all the formalities of law. Through a will a person makes a disposition of his property, exercises powers of appointment, and provides for the administration of his estate after death. The laws governing testamentary dispositions vary from state to state. Perhaps no other legal document requires greater formalities in order to become effective. For this reason, it is sound advice to avoid "homemade" wills; the prudent conduct is to consult an attorney in the formal drafting of a will. This summary is only intended as a check list by which you can comprehend and appreciate the legal implications involved in the execution of a will, and can be assured that your property will be properly disposed of after death.

An illustration of the formal nature of wills might be useful. Let us suppose that a person wishes to give his spouse 100 shares of his IBM stock upon his death. Let us also assume that upon death the person no longer has the 100 shares of IBM stock that he possessed when the will was executed. The executor reads the will and, among other things, it states: "I give my spouse my 100 shares of IBM

Stock." Since he no longer has these shares his wife gets nothing. However, if the will had said "I give my spouse 100 shares of IBM stock," the executor would be required, if possible, to buy 100 shares of IBM with other proceeds of the estate and distribute the shares to the spouse. This illustrates how the inclusion or deletion of a two letter word can drastically alter the distribution of an estate. Since technicalities of this type abound in the law of wills, an attorney should always be consulted so as to insure that the estate is distributed according to the decedent's wishes. This chapter can help the reader, however, in selecting prudent methods for distributing his or her assets.

Contents of Wills

Purpose

The primary purpose of a will is to dispose of one's assets in the manner deemed most appropriate. Not only is it personally important to whom the estate is left, but as shall be seen later, the manner in which the estate is divided can have a great influence on the percentage of the estate that will be absorbed by state and Federal estate taxes and other settlement costs. To begin, let's examine the common ways in which assets can be conveyed by will.

Specific Bequests

When a person wishes to convey a specific piece of personal property, real estate or a

73

designated amount of cash, he must make a specific bequest. The above example giving "my 100 shares of IBM stock to my spouse" is such a bequest. This type of distribution of property is especially desirable when the person has valuable personal effects such as heirlooms or jewelry which he wishes to pass on to a specific person. Specific bequests of cash, especially to charitable institutions, are also common. Such sums can be passed on by either naming a designated amount in the will or by setting aside a specific proportion of the estate for such purposes. Specific bequests of valuable real estate are also desirable, since centralized control is usually essential in maintaining the value of that real estate.

Frequently, business interests are disposed of by specific bequest in a will, whether they be in corporations (by means of bequeathing controlling interests in stock), interests in partnerships or sole proprietorships. Such dispositions often require the approval of other stockholders or partners, and such approval should be reduced to writing prior to the execution of a will. This written agreement should be recognized and referred to in the subsequent will. Basically, all specific bequests may be set up in one of two ways: either to individuals, or in custody to someone to dispose of as he sees fit.

General Bequests

When a person wishes to split his estate among various people, and does not care what form these bequests take, i.e., in cash, personal property, real estate, or any combination of these, then a general bequest is the appropriate method of distribution. These bequests are easily accomplished by instructing the executor to give a designated percentage of the estate a set cash value to a particular person. In this instance the executor has discretion in selecting the form of the bequest.

Trusts

A trust is a legal arrangement whereby a

right in property, real or personal, is transferred by one person (the creator) to another (the trustee) for the benefit of a third party (the beneficiary). Trusts may be created while the creator is still alive, or in his will, to take effect upon his death. Trusts are created in wills for basically two reasons. First, they may offer substantial estate tax savings to the creator and certain beneficiaries. This factor will be discussed later in some detail. Second, trusts assure that large sums of money which are left to people unaccustomed to handling such sums, are properly cared for. In creating a trust, always make sure that special consideration is given to the selection of a trustee who is a shrewd businessman, or business institution, such as a bank. Otherwise, the primary purpose of the trust, which involves wise management of large bequests for the benefit of the beneficiary, is defeated. Trusts are expensive to administer (trustees do not manage trust out of the goodness of their hearts!). Therefore, trusts of small monetary value usually are not advisable. Unless the creator has a rather large amount of money (or property) to devise by will, the trust device is not for him. It should be left in a specific bequest and hope that the recipient has the good sense not to waste it away.

Residuary Estate

After all specific bequests, general bequests, trusts and taxes are satisfied, the remainder of the estate is called the *residuary*. The residuary estate may be disposed of in several ways. If large enough, it may be placed in one or more trusts for the benefit of specific individuals; or it may be distributed outright to specific individuals along prescribed guidelines.

Revising Wills

The properly drafted and executed will should dispose of property in accordance with the testator's wishes. However, the testator may live for many years after execution of his will. During these years his family needs most likely will change; he should consider periodic revisions of his will.

There are two basic ways to revise a will: the old one may be destroyed and a new will executed; or the old one may be revised by adding to it. These additions are *codicils* and must be executed in the same formal manner as wills. Codicils are frequently used when the revision is not a drastic one. However, where a person wishes to change the entire distributive scheme of his estate, it is in his best interests to execute an entirely new will. He then should destroy all copies of the old will immediately.

Since an individual's personal estate is constantly changing, it is advisable to revise a will periodically (about every six months) to make sure it meets all needs. The particular situation will dictate when a revision is necessary. One problem that is overlooked frequently when considering revision is *estate liquidity*. Estate liquidity simply means the amount tied up in assets that can or cannot be converted to ready cash (such as real estate or business interests). Upon death, the executor will be required to pay estate taxes, probabe costs and other claims against the estate, and enough cash or cash-convertible assets should be available to cover these settlement costs. If the bulk of the estate is tied up in non-liquidated assets, which are not easily converted to cash, the executor may be required to sell real estate at a distressed price or convert some other valuable asset at less than market value in order to pay these costs. This "liquidity problem" should be kept in mind when a will is drawn or revised.

Tax Considerations

The primary purpose of a will is to distribute the testator's assets upon death according to his desires. There are many different ways to accomplish this purpose. In drawing up a will, a person should never lose sight of his primary purpose, but at the same time, he should distribute his assets in a manner that will make his estate liable for the least amount of estate taxes. Tax law is a very specialized and complex field and many devices can be employed that could legitimately reduce an estate's tax burden. The following list is by no means conclusive, but it does illustrate a few of the common devices which might be considered when drawing up a will.

Lifetime Gifts

The amount of estate taxes which an executor must pay is dependent upon the value of the estate at the time of death. In order to reduce the value of his estate, a person may wish to make periodic gifts of certain assets to persons who would receive these assets under the will. If these gifts are made more than three years prior to death, their value will not be included in the estate and will not be subject to estate taxes. Gift taxes might be assessed on these transfers, but the gift tax rate is less than the estate tax rate. By means of a lifetime $30,000 gift tax exemption and an annual ($3,000) gift tax exclusion per donee, property may be gifted to future beneficiaries of the will without incurring tax consequences.

Most people are unaware that the value of an insurance policy upon a person's life is includable in his estate and hence is subject to estate taxes, even though the estate is not the beneficiary of the policy. As long as the decedent retains the right to change the beneficiary of the policy or the right to borrow against the policy, its value will be included in his estate. If any incident of ownership is possessed by the decedent at time of death, the policy's value is includable in his estate. However, if he transfers these rights by making a gift of the policy to the beneficiary, the policy's value will not be includable in his estate. He could still pay the premiums, if so desired, since the payment could be deemed an annual gift, and probably be lower than the allowable gift tax exclusion of $3,000 annually per donee. A gift made within three years of death is deemed to be a transfer made in contemplation of death, and is includable in decedent's estate.

75

Charitable Contributions

A generous person can greatly reduce his estate tax burden. All bequests to charity, whether given outright or in trust, are estate tax deductible and avoid estate taxes. Therefore, where the entire estate is left to charity, no federal estate taxes are incurred. However, in certain states, such as New York, charitable bequests of greater than one half the estate may be contested by the decedent's parents or issue (children, grandchildren, great-grandchildren, etc.); if successful the charitable bequest may be reduced to one-half of the estate.

Marital Deduction

This is probably the most common device for reducing estate taxes in non-community property states (such as New York). If a person is married, he may leave up to one-half of the adjusted gross estate (the value of the estate at death, diminished by funeral and administrative expenses, debts and claims) to the spouse, free of estate tax. There are, however, some requirements on how this property is devised to the spouse. The primary requirement is that no strings be attached to the property; it must be given to the spouse outright so that he or she can do whatever they wish with it. If restrictions are placed on the enjoyment of the property, it will be considered terminable interest and will not qualify for the marital deduction. It will be taxed with all other non-qualifying property in the estate.

Husbands often take advantage of the marital deduction because they generally own the bulk of the assets in the family and are likely to die sooner than their wives. However, there is nothing prohibiting the wife from using this deduction also if she predeceases the husband.

In the most common situation, where the husband is taking full advantage of the marital deduction, it is imperative that the wife have a will that disposes of the property that she will receive from her husband through the marital deduction. If the wife dies intestate (without a will), her property and property inherited from her husband will be distributed by the inflexible laws of "intestate succession." Her husband's primary purpose may be frustrated if the wife does not have a properly drawn will also.

Another problem arises in the event that husband and wife perish simultaneously in a common disaster (e.g., an air crash, automobile accident, etc.). Generally, the laws in most states presume that each spouse predeceased the other. Unless the executor can submit medical evidence that indicates the spouse who wishes to take advantage of the marital deduction predeceased the other, the tax advantages of the marital deduction will be lost. To guard against this possibility, a provision should be inserted in both spouses' wills stating that the spouse using the marital deduction is presumed to have predeceased his or her mate.

The best method to take full advantage of the marital deduction is to distribute property under a two-part will as opposed to a simple one. A simple will satisfies all statutory requirements of due execution, but fails to take full advantage of the marital deduction. The difference results in the tax liability incurred in the estate of the second spouse to die. Basically, a simple will leaves the decedent's net estate to his wife. Although taxes may not be excessive since the marital deduction is effective to pass half of the adjusted gross estate tax free, the ultimate result is a second taxation of these assets upon the death of the surviving spouse. However, a two-part will does not result in overqualification. By limiting the surviving spouse's share to the maximum allowable federal marital deduction and passing the remainder to children or other devisees (hence a two-part will) the spouse's estate is not saddled with additional taxation of the same assets. In short, a large portion of a person's estate can bypass a generation and escape estate taxes. Tax laws are even lenient enough to permit the surviving spouse to have an income interest in that part of the estate passing to the children (e.g., it passes in trust). A two-part will gives the surviving spouse all property and income necessary to

76

meet personal needs and simultaneously wards off significant tax costs.

Examples of a simple and a two-part will are presented here. Both meet the formal requirements that have been discussed throughout this chapter. For example in New York, these requirements are:

(1) Declaration or publication of will—"...do make publish and declare this to be my last Will and Testament..."

(2) Signature of testator (or a person in his presence and at his direction).

(3) Signature at end of will.

(4) Two attesting witnesses who sign in his presence.

In addition, these examples have an attestation clause, which is evidence of due execution where witnesses are no longer available to testify during probate.

Concluding Remarks

There has been much left unsaid about wills but this chapter is only meant as an introduction to the topic. The important thing to consider is how should your assets be distributed upon your death. Tax considerations are an important element of estate planning; take advantage of the tax considerations that do not alter the distributive plan. Thereafter, the will should be revised as frequently as is necessary so that it continues to satisfy testamentary objectives. With these thoughts in mind and a qualified attorney supplying his expertise, a person can rest assured that his estate will meet his family needs or his charitable spirit.

Will

𝕴, ...

being of sound and disposing mind and memory, and considering the uncertainty of this life, do

make, publish and declare this to be my last **Will** *and* **Testament** *as follows, hereby*

revoking all other former Wills by me at any time made.

First, after my lawful debts are paid, I give ....

I hereby appoint ....

....*to be Execut*..............*of*

this my last Will and Testament.

In Witness Whereof, *I have hereunto subscribed my name, and affixed my seal,*

the ....*day of* ....*in the year one thousand nine*

hundred and ....*.*

Last Will and Testament

I, _____ of the

of _____ in the County of _____

and State of _____ being of sound mind and memory, do make,

publish and declare this my last Will and Testament, in manner following that is

to say:

First. I direct that all of my just debts and funeral expenses be paid as soon

after my death as may be practicable.

Second: I bequeath all my personal and household effects, including all automobiles, to my wife, _____, if she survives me, otherwise to my children who survive me, in equal shares.

Third: I bequeath to my wife, _____, an amount equal to one-half of my "adjusted gross estate" as defined in the Internal Revenue Code, less the value of all other interests in property which are included in my gross estate for federal estate tax purposes and which pass or have passed from me to my wife either under any other provision of this will or otherwise in any manner outside of this will including those passing by operation of law, but only if such interests in property pass or have passed in such a manner as to qualify for the marital deduction under the federal estate tax law. It is my intention to bequeath outright to my wife the maximum value in property, but no more, that may be deducted from my estate as a marital deduction under the federal estate tax law.

In the preparation of the estate tax returns for my estate and the tentative determination by my executors of the amount of the legacy given and bequeathed by this Article, if my Executors in good faith deem it uncertain whether any particular property or interest in property should be included in my gross estate for estate tax purposes, the value of such property shall be excluded from my gross estate, and if my Executors in good faith entertain a doubt as to the value of any property or interest in property included in my gross estate, my Executors shall place thereon such value as my Executors shall deem fair, and my Executors shall not be liable to my wife or any other beneficiary under this Will by reason of any such exclusion or valuation. However, such tentative determinations shall be adjusted to conform with the final determinations, whether by agreement, litigation or otherwise, in the United States estate tax proceeding in my estate and such final determinations shall be used in computing:

(a) the amount of all property and interests in property which qualify for said marital deduction and which pass or have passed from me to my wife under any other provisions of this Will, and

(b) the amount of the legacy given and bequeathed by this Article. Such legacy may be satisfied by distribution in cash or in kind or partly in cash and partly in kind. Each item of

property or interest in property so distributed in kind shall
be valued at the date or dates of such distribution or at the
value determined therefor in the United States estate tax proceeding in my estate, whichever value shall be lower, provided
however, that such legacy shall not be satisfied by the distribution of

      (i) any property or interest in property which
does not qualify for said marital deduction or the
proceeds of the sale or other disposition of any
such property, or

      (ii) any property or interest in property
located outside the United States of America
(including securities issued by or other evidences
of interests in corporations organized outside
the United States of America) or the proceeds of
the sale or other disposition of such property or
interests in property, or

      (iii) any property or interest in property
(including any right to receive income) which shall
be eligible in any way for a tax credit or deduction because it shall be subject to both the
income tax and the estate tax under the provisions
of the Internal Revenue Code applicable to my
estate.

However, property described in clauses (ii) and (iii) may
be used to the extent that my other property or interests in
property which do qualify for said marital deduction shall be
insufficient to satisfy said legacy.

Subject to the preceding provisions of this Article, the
decision of my Executors as to which assets shall be distributed
in satisfaction of such legacy shall be binding and conclusive
on all persons, it being my intention that my Executors shall
have absolute discretion in this respect.

In the event that my wife should predecease me, I bequeath
all my property to the family trust provided in the succeeding
section of this Will.

Fourth: I bequeath and devise the residue of my estate of
every nature and wherever situate to my trustees or their successors
in a family trust for the following purposes:

A. Income to or for wife for life. To pay over to or apply
for the benefit of my wife in convenient installments, as nearly
equal as practicable and at least quarter-annually, all the net
income from this trust;

B. Use of principal for wife. In addition to the net
income, to pay over to or apply for the benefit of my wife so
much of the principal of this trust as my trustees, in the exercise
of their uncontrolled discretion, shall deem needful or desirable
for her support and maintenance, including medical, surgical,
hospital, or other institutional care, having in mind both the
standard of living to which she has been accustomed and the income
or principal that may be available to or for her from other
sources;

C. Separate trust for each child. After the death of my wife,
to divide the property in this trust, including any property
bequeathed or given to this trust from any other source, into as

many equal shares as I then shall have children living and dead with issue surviving, and to set up a separate trust (except as to the share of a child then thirty (30) years of age) for each child then living and one for the then surviving issue as a group of each such deceased child, for the benefit of such issue, per stirpes and not per capita;

D. Distribution before trust established. If any child shall be thirty (30) years of age at the time of the death of my wife, to pay over, deliver, assign, transfer, or convey to such child his share of the estate, discharged of trust;

E. Use of income and principal for child. As to any child under thirty (30) years of age, in the discretion of the trustees, to either accumulate or pay over to or apply the net income of such child's share for the benefit of that child in convenient installments, as nearly equal as practicable, and, in addition to income, to pay over to or apply for the benefit of each child so much of the principal of such child's share as the trustees, in the exercise of their uncontrolled discretion, shall deem needful or desirable for the support, maintenance, and schooling of such child, and for medical, surgical, hospital, or other institutional care;

F. Termination of trust. As each child shall attain the age of thirty (30) years, to pay over, deliver, assign, transfer, or convey to each child, discharged of trust, the entire remaining balance of the principal and the undistributed income of his trust:

G. Death of child before termination of trust. If any child shall die before attaining the age of thirty (30) years, at his death to pay over, deliver, assign, transfer, or convey the principal and the undistributed income remaining in such child's trust to those who will be his next of kin under the laws of the State of _____ at that time;

H. Separate trust for issue of each deceased child. To pay over, deliver, assign, transfer, or convey to each of the issue of a deceased child who shall be twenty-one (21) years of age at the death of my wife, his per stirpes share of the property in the trust herein established for such issue. However, if any of such issue shall be under twenty-one (21) years of age at the time his share becomes distributable, then, although his share shall vest immediately, the trustee shall hold his share in trust and use the income and any portion of the principal needful or desirable, in the uncontrolled discretion of my trustees, for the support, maintenance, schooling, and medical, surgical, hospital, or other institutional care of such issue until he shall be twenty-one (21) years of age, and then pay over, deliver, assign, transfer, or convey to such issue his portion of the trust property, discharged of trust.

Fifth: The interest of any beneficiary in principal or income of any trust under my will shall not be subject to assignment, alienation, pledge, attachment, or to the claims of creditors of such beneficiary.

Sixth: Each trust created under this will shall in any event terminate twenty-one (21) years after the death of the last survivor of such of the beneficiaries thereunder as shall be living at the time of my death and thereupon the property held in that trust shall be distributed, discharged of trust, to the persons then entitled to the income and in the proportions to which they are entitled to the income.

Seventh: In the event that my wife and I shall be killed or die under such circumstances that it will be impossible to determine which of us died first, it shall be conclusively presumed that she survived me; and this presumption shall apply throughout this will.

Eighth: I direct that my executors shall pay out of the family trust, established by the Fourth Article hereof, (without any right of reimbursement) all estate, inheritance, and succession taxes, and all other governmental charges which may be assessed against any gift made by me under this will and which may be determinded to be due against any property transferred by me in trust during my lifetime and against all property owned by me and any other person as tenants by the entirety or as joint tenants with right of survivorship and passing at the time of my death to such surviving tenants by reason of such ownership and any such taxes or other governmental charges as shall be assessed against any insurance issued on my life payable to named beneficiaries, whether in a lump sum or in trust or permitted to remain in the hands of the insurance company on optional settlement. It is my intention that all property passing under this will, except that passing as my residuary estate, and all property transferred by me in trust during my lifetime and all property passing at my death to a survivor by reason of ownership as tenants by the entirety or joint tenants with right of survivorship, and the proceeds of all life insurance payable to a named beneficiary whether in a lump sum, in trust, or under an option of settlement, shall pass undiminished by any such taxes or other governmental charges.

Ninth: I authorize my Executors (other than my wife), if they shall believe it advisable in order to reduce to the lowest possible figure the total of the estimated death taxes payable by or with respect to my estate and the estimated income and capital gains taxes payable to my estate and any one or more beneficiaries thereof, to elect (a) to value my gross estate as of a date that causes larger death taxes to be payable than would have been the case if my Executors had elected another date, and (b) to claim as income tax deductions expenses that would otherwise qualify as estate tax deductions. In the event of any such election my Executors (other than my wife) may, if they in their absolute discretion shall deem it appropriate, make such apportionment of the amount of income and capital gains taxes which my Executors estimate will be saved thereby among any of the trusts created by this Will and any of the persons beneficially interested in my gross estate whose interests have been adversely affected by any such election (including persons, if any, beneficially interested in property which is included in my gross estate but which passes outside of this Will), and to such extent, as my Executors (other than my wife) shall determine in their absolute discretion, either by making distributions outright to such persons or by augmenting or reducing any gift made in trust under this Will, provided, however, that my Executors (other than my wife) shall not be required to make any such apportionment if they shall decide in their absolute discretion not to do so, and provide further that my Executors shall have no power to make any apportionment that will reduce the principal of the marital deduction legacy created by the Third Article of this Will.

Bill of Sale for Motor Vehicle

Know all Men by these Presents,

That

the Seller,

whose address is

for and in consideration of the sum of $ paid by

the Buyer, whose address is

have bargained, sold, granted and conveyed and by these presents do bargain, sell, grant and convey unto the Buyer, and Buyer's successors (heirs, executors, administrators) and assigns, one

Model   Factory No.   Motor No.

To Have and to Hold the same unto the Buyer and Buyer's successors (heirs, executors, administrators) and assigns forever, and the Seller covenants and agrees to warrant and defend the said described motor vehicle hereby sold against all and every person or persons whomsoever.

☐ The motor vehicle purports to have been operated, as appears by the odometer,   miles.

☐ The Seller knows that the mileage indicated on the odometer is beyond its designed mechanical limits; the true cumulative mileage is   miles.

☐ The odometer mileage is known to the Seller to be less than the motor vehicle has travelled; the true mileage is unknown.

The Seller also certifies that the Seller owned the vehicle since   19

until the date of this Bill of Sale.

In Witness Whereof, the Seller has set his hand and seal or caused these presents to be signed by its proper corporate officers and caused its proper corporate seal to be hereto affixed, the

day of   19

Signed, Sealed and Delivered
in the Presence of   }

....
                                        Seller

How to Handle Your Own Contracts

CHAPTER 7

The Sales Contract

Introduction

After all of our discussion about contracts, many people might be surprised to find out that when the contract deals with the sale of goods, which is best described as anything other than realty and intangibles, the rules of the game change. For the most part, the offer to sell, coupled with the acceptance, cemented by valuable consideration and the transferral of goods from the seller to the buyer, is a contract; but states have enacted statutes which regulate such transactions under differing laws. The reason for this variation is that the everyday store purchase or wholesale or supply situation requires uniformity between states. Today all states, except Louisiana, have adopted the Uniform Commercial Code (UCC) as an answer to sales-related problems.

For the uniform statute to be triggered, certain requirements must be met. First, the item sold must be considered goods as stated above, and second, the contracting parties must consist of a consumer and a merchant or two merchants in the chain of producer-retailer. "Goods" is defined in the UCC as anything other than real estate (although goods linked to real estate, such as growing crops or movable fixtures, fall within the statute's purview) and intangibles such as services.

Formation

One of the first divergents from contract law occurs in the formation of the agreement.

Under common law contract rules, certainty of terms was a requisite, and if a term to the contract was left undetermined, the contract would necessarily fail. The sales laws grant greater latitude. Whereas, before the contents of the contract had to include the names of the parties, identify the subject matter, and quote the price and time of delivery, sales contracts need not satisfy price and time as long as both fall within the congenial limits of reasonableness. By permitting the going market price to control, where no price was agreed on, sales contracts do not fail for lack of certainty and the market place does not shut down. Basically, the test to determine whether a binding sales contract exists between the parties is not whether all the common law formalities of contracts have been adhered to, but rather is a two-fold test of (1) did the parties intend to contract and (2) does a basis exist for granting a remedy? If both of these contingencies are met, then the law avers that the parties have a binding sales contract. As mentioned before, price need not be pre-arranged but can be set by the marketplace at the time of delivery or by a reasonable conclusion. Also, whereas common law contracts must be definite as to the subject matter, be it toothpicks or Tiffany lamps, sales contracts need not be so specific as to detail every characteristic of the item such as quality or color. However, where these characteristics are bargained for and agreed upon, then, as will be seen, the terms of the contract must be met. Overall, as long as the two criteria listed above are satisfied, a contract is formed and the economy flows smoothly.

Offer and Acceptance

If you will recall the discussion in the introduction to contracts, perhaps the two basic elements of a contract, much like the subject and predicate of a sentence, are the *offer* and *acceptance*. The uniform sales statute in New York, known as the Uniform Commercial Code, or UCC, has had an impact on these two elements, which most likely also epitomizes statutory effects in other states. First of all, the UCC has eliminated the common law distinction between *unilateral* and *bilateral* contracts and treats both equally. As always, the parties can agree otherwise, thus permitting acceptance by the offeree's performance or promise, but where the latter conditions are not stipulated in the offer, the two concepts are merged. At common law, a unilateral contract was consummated upon the offeree's performance. If **X** promised to pay **Y** $100 to climb to the top of the Eiffel Tower, **Y**, merely by reaching the top, completes performance and is entitled to **X**'s $100. This result is so even though **Y** never communicated his intention to act or returned a promise to act. Since all that **X** bargained for was **Y**'s performance, his reaching the summit binds **X** to his promise to pay.

This seems all well and good and certainly just, but the next logical question is for how long does **X**'s promise remain alive. Can **Y** fail to communicate his plans to **X**, procrastinate for a fortnight, and then one evening, after mustering sufficient courage at the local bistro, stumble down to the Tower, heave himself to the top and claim his due? The answer, more likely than not, is no, judging from a standpoint of reasonableness. Under common law doctrines, an offer was only irrevocable if the offeree, in this case **Y**, paid consideration for the opportunity to delay his acceptance. Current law does not require the exchange of consideration if the offeror expresses in writing that his offer is irrevocable. The same rule applies if the *executory contract* is for the sale of goods, but is limited to offers from merchants and for a three-month period, unless a shorter duration is stated. If the typical consumer extends an offer

for goods on the other hand, then the UCC resorts to common law rules, and the offer is irrevocable only if he receives consideration in exchange.

So much for offer, how does the UCC alter the element of acceptance? In general, the UCC changes the concept of acceptance in two ways. The first occurs in the situation where the offeree in his acceptance modifies the terms of the original offer. The common law answer was to declare the modified acceptance a counter offer. No contract was formed and the offeror had the opportunity to refuse the new terms or accept as modified. In order to free market dealings with goods, the UCC eliminated this problem, which could result in a tennis-like volley of counter offers without a contract being formed. As between the merchant and non-merchant situations were differentiated. In the case of one party being a non-merchant, the newly-varied acceptance acted as an acceptance accompanied by an offer to the initial offeror on the modified or additional terms. The offeror could accept or reject these new terms as he pleased, but the contract was formed. If the parties were both merchants, then the return of an altered acceptance would act not only as an acceptance for the unchanged part of the offer, but would act as an acceptance for the altered terms as well. However, this law does not permit the offeree total leeway in modifying a contract offer and holding the offeror to different terms. The modified or additional terms became part of the contract, but only if the offer did not restrict acceptance to its original terms and the changes were not a material change in the original offer (in a common-sense application of the phrase). The offeror, within a reasonable time had the right to reject the offeree's modifications.

The UCC also changed the New York common law rule on the method of acceptance. Outside of the UCC, the law required that strict formalities had to be followed. If **S** offered **T** by cablegram an opportunity to enter a contract, the mirror rule mandated that the acceptance could be communicated only by cablegram; the reasoning being that the offeror's selection of a particular medium suggested the medium through which he wished to be notified of the offeree's decision. Exhorting the reasonableness standard once again, the UCC permits any medium to be utilized if reasonable. Although the courts would have the final determination, a contract would be enforceable then if an offer sent via a homing pigeon were accepted and communicated by telegraph, but not so if in reverse.

Consideration

All contracts, whether or not covered by the UCC, must contain consideration, the offeree's exchange of a bargained-for detriment for the offeror's promise to act. In general, any rule applicable to contracts is viable for sales contracts. One change, however, allows for the modification of sales contracts without additional consideration. Unless the contract expresses otherwise or unless the contract falls within the purview of the Statute of Frauds, the modification need not even be in writing. In New York, other statutory provisions have eliminated the need for consideration in the typical contractual arrangement, but unlike the UCC, these provisions required a memo signed by the person against whom the change operates. Additionally, should any cause of action arise out of a breach of the contract, the UCC pre-exempts the common law pre-existing duty rule and allows for a written discharge of the claim without consideration. New York applies a similar law for non-sale contracts, but not all states have enacted the same provision.

Performance and Breach

Assuming that a contract has been duly arranged with the requisite elements of offer, acceptance, and consideration, let us now look at differences in sales contracts under the UCC in regard to performance and breach. In any case, the contract will be considered satisfactorily completed as long as the substantial performance standard is met. The performing party need not comply with every detail of the agreement if the deviation from the terms of the contract does not impair the other party's position. This brings the concept of material breach into the discussion, for substantial performance and materiality of breach necessarily go hand in hand. Without the latter, the former occurs.

One factor in determining materiality, however, is whether the contract is one for goods. The UCC mandates that the tender of goods must be perfect. By this it is meant that the seller must deliver goods as specified. Partial delivery or a difference in quality or color from that specified is a breach of the contract. Since the seller retains possession of the goods until acceptance, the buyer simply rejects and then must hold and sell or return the goods to the seller. The perfect tender requirement arose because the seller was not subject to loss of his property. If, instead of a seller of goods, the promise was by a contractor who installed thousands of dollars of plumbing in an apartment complex, the loss of his property to the buyer because the pipe used was not the same as that agreed to although comparable in quality, would result in unbearable financial hardship. Thus, in the instance of a construction contract, not under the UCC, there is no need for perfect tender, and the court would be less likely to conclude that the seller materially breached the contract.

In discussing contracts for the sale of realty, mention was made that time was not implied as being of the essence. The parties could agree that such was the case, but without an expressed provision in the contract, failure to cure a minor tax encumbrance on the day of sale would not defeat the contract. Under the UCC, time is always of the essence as an implication of law. If the parties select a specific day for completion of performance and the day passes without completion, the seller is in breach.

Sometimes the buyer or seller need not wait for the day set for performance if it appears that the other party is not in a position to

85

Bill of Sale

Know all Men by these Presents,

THAT

part   of the first part, for and in consideration of the sum of
                                                ($) Dollars, lawful money of the United States
to   in hand paid, at or before the ensealing and delivery of these presents by

part   of the second part, the receipt whereof is hereby acknowledged ha   bargained and
sold, and by these presents do   grant and convey unto the said part   of the second part,
heirs, executors, administrators, successors and assigns

TO HAVE AND TO HOLD the same unto the said part   of the second part,
heirs, executors, administrators, successors and assigns forever. AND   do   for
heirs, executors and administrators, covenant and agree, to and with the said part   of the
second part, to warrant and defend the sale of the aforesaid

hereby sold unto the said part   of the second part,   heirs, executors, administrators,
successors and assigns, against all and every person and persons whomsoever.

IN WITNESS WHEREOF, the part   of the first part ha   set   hand   and
seal   or caused these presents to be signed by its proper corporate officers and caused its proper corporate
seal to be hereto affixed, this   day of   19 .

Signed, Sealed and Delivered ⎫
    in the Presence of   ⎬
                             ⎭

How to Handle Your Own Contracts

fulfill his commitment. This area of anticipatory breach was discussed under the introduction, but in a sales contract for goods, the UCC again imposes different rules. At common law, the issue of whether a party could hold the other in breach or suspend his own performance was conditioned upon the strength and merit of the information received. If it appeared, for example, that X would not perform, then Y could anticipate breach and hold X liable. But if it appeared that X could not perform, even though he attempted to, then Y could assume a failure of performance and withhold his own. Under the UCC, Y cannot suspend his own performance until he demands assurances from X that the latter's performance will be forthcoming. If written assurances are received within 30 days, then Y must continue fulfilling his bargain. Where 30 days expires without receipt of assurances on X's part, then Y can consider X in repudiation of the contract. Once Y does so and notifies X, or materially alters his own position (another common sense judgment), X cannot make demands by retracting the repudiation. Along these lines, Y cannot escape responsibility under the contract for such reasons as impracticality or impossibility of complying with the agreed mode of delivery. The UCC recognizes both of these impediments, but requires a drastic event to occur to invoke the doctrine of impracticality (e.g., war) and allow a reasonable substituted form of delivery if reasonable (e.g., tractor-trailer instead of freight train).

Assuming no premature breach, both parties have obligations which they must meet in order to demand return performance by or seek UCC remedies against the other. The seller's duties vary upon whether the goods are to be delivered by a carrier or tendered at the seller's place of business. In the first situation, the contract must be looked to in order to determine if the parties contracted for the delivery of the purchased goods at the buyer's place of business or at his home. In the absence of an expressed provision, the seller need only deliver the goods to a local carrier and notify the buyer, sending him whatever carrier papers

he might need to assume possession. As long as the seller acts reasonably, he will not violate the contract or the law. If delivery to the buyer is a condition of the contract, the seller must satisfy all conditions inherent in the mode of delivery. Typically, delivery contracts call for F.O.B. (free on board) or F.A.S. (free alongside delivery). F.O.B. or F.A.S. contracts can also be used both where seller need bear the risk only until the carrier takes possession and where seller remains liable until the goods reach their destination.

Once the seller places conforming goods at the site agreed upon by the parties, the buyer has the next move; he must pay for the goods in cash (check is considered legal tender, although possession does not transfer until the check clears) unless the contract extends credit. Again there is a distinction between carrier and non-carrier cases, but basically the buyer's duty is simply to pay when he receives the goods.

To protect the buyer, however, the UCC grants him the right to examine the goods before transfer of payment. As long as the contract does not restrict this right of inspection, the buyer can reject the goods by withholding acceptance even after delivery to him. The easiest way for the seller to curtail the right to inspect is by shipping C.O.D., thus forcing the buyer to make payment before he can examine the goods. The buyer should remember, however, that if a defect is obvious, he can reject the shipment regardless of his right to inspect.

Risk of Loss

Before discussing seller and buyer remedies, a brief note should be inserted on risk of loss. It is always possible, particularly where goods are shipped by carrier, that an unforeseen catastrophe could result in damage to or loss of the goods. In that event, one party must shoulder the financial onus of the loss. In determining which party must bear the burden, the concept of *risk of loss* has replaced that of *passage of title*.

The central factor in risk of loss is that of

breach; where risk of loss might have passed from seller to buyer if the seller had fully met his obligation in tendering conforming goods, a breach on his part will hold him liable until the buyer accepts in spite of the breach or until he cures. The provision in the contract and the status of the seller also are determining factors. If the seller is a merchant, as in a retail situation, the buyer does not become liable until he assumes possession. He can purchase the goods, paying cash, but if they are damaged before he picks them up, the seller suffers the loss. In a non-merchant sale of goods, such as when two friends transact a sale, the selling party need only tender the goods to the buyer in order to shift the risk of loss to him. Carrier cases pose different problems, but the basic rule is that risk of loss passes when the seller places the goods at the buyer's disposal, in compliance with the contractual terms. For example, if the contract called for F.O.B. at buyer's place of business, the seller would remain liable for the goods during transit. As mentioned, breach can alter the result. Thus, if in the above example, the contract authorized F.O.B. seller's place of business, so that normally the buyer would hold the risk of loss during the shipment, the seller remains responsible throughout until he cures the defect or the buyer accepts. In the event that the buyer is the breaching culprit, then the reverse holds true. He becomes liable once the seller earmarks or identifies the goods and ships them even though under the usual rules, the risk of loss had not yet shifted to him.

Statute of Frauds

Contracts of sale are governed by a specific Statute of Frauds provision under the UCC. Briefly, it provides that the only time a transaction is required to be in writing is if the sale equals or exceeds $500. Without an acceptable writing, the contract is unenforceable. Normally, the writing must be concurrent with the contract. However, as between merchants, the UCC relaxes the law. If a writing follows an oral agreement, it satisfies the Statute of Frauds and binds the parties to its terms, unless the recipient objects within ten days.

The requirements of the writing are lenient. Terms can be incorrect or omitted and the writing still will suffice, as long as the party to be charged signs it. The one limitation is that the quantity of goods needs to be stated and the parties should realize that the contract is enforceable only up to the quantity set out in the writing.

As with all laws, there are certain exceptions. If the contract is for specially manufactured goods which are not suitable to anyone other than the buyer, if the contract is admitted to in open court or if performance is consummated, then the contract is enforceable without a writing.

Parol Evidence Rule

Parol evidence rule, likewise, is expressly provided for in the UCC. As before, if the writing is intended to be the final statement of the agreement, then neither party can introduce evidence of prior or contemporaneous oral agreements contrary to terms in the written contract. However, the Code does allow the introduction of such evidence in certain instances.

The course of dealings between the parties and common trade usage can be offered in explanation of contractual terms. This can be done even if the writing is not ambiguous. Furthermore, the parties can supplement the contract with additional terms. However, the contract cannot be complete and the additional terms must be consistent with the writing.

Products Liability

It would be presumptuous to attempt to explain the rapidly evolving law of negligence and strict tort products liability. We should explain, however, that case law in many states is expanding the opportunities under which an injured consumer of a defective or dangerous

88

product can recover against the seller or manufacturer of a latently defective product. The manufacturer or seller is liable to an injured party (any foreseeable party, which includes consumer or a third party) if his lack of reasonable care caused the defect, a danger was foreseeable and the particular defect was the proximate cause of the injury. In fact, the injured party can sue not only the manufacturer of the product but anyone in the chain of distribution—e.g., middleman and retailer.

In some instances, however, the injured party need not prove that the manufacturer was negligent if he can prove that the product itself was unreasonably dangerous. Strict tort liability discards *privity of contract* and extends warranty theory to every party who might foreseeably be injured. The reasoning behind the theory is that the earlier discussed warranties of merchantability of fitness of use are breached if an unreasonably dangerous product is manufactured. The producer cannot disclaim liability or use the defense of contributory negligence which is available to him in negligence. Recovery is barred only where the consumer or third party's fault contributed to the injury. As in a negligence action, the injured party can sue anyone along the distributive chain.

This topic is mentioned only to alert the reader to possible actions he might have in case of injury from a defective product. Because of constant changes in product tort liability, an injured person should consult an attorney to be informed of his rights.

Warranties

Suppose that, in the hypothetical purchase situation at the beginning of this chapter, Henry's lamp failed to work after a short period of time. In disgust, Henry would most likely return to the store and demand repair, replacement or recompense. But suppose that the store refused to satisfy Henry's claim and flatly stated that it was its policy not to stand behind its products. In short, Henry is informed that he has been taken.

The reader may feel that Henry has no recourse, except to refrain from further patronization of the store. He had received no verbal assurances or written guarantees and seemingly has no viable cause of action. However, this is not true, for the authors of the UCC included within its provisions, implied warranties which every merchant or seller makes to the consumer. Unless these warranties are disclaimed in ways defined by statute, they operate to hold the seller liable for failure of the product.

The warranty of merchantability is implied in every merchant sale so as to protect the consumer against problems such as those of Henry. Several criteria exist in explanation of merchantability, but it can be simply stated: the goods must do that which they are supposed to do. If Henry bought the lamp for lighting, then light it must; similarly a toaster must toast and a vacuum cleaner must vacuum. Goods must be "fit for the ordinary purposes for which such goods are used." The warranty further contains requirements that packaging and labeling must meet contractual terms; goods must be acceptable as like goods in the trade; goods must not vary considerably within prescribed units and must not differ from promises expressed on the label.

Although all goods under the UCC carry the implied warranty of merchantability, a buyer must be cautioned that the merchant has not disclaimed his liability. To accomplish this end, the merchant must meet two statutory requirements; first he must specifically mention the term merchantability, and secondly, if the disclaimer is in writing (an oral disclaimer is effective), it must be conspicuous. The buyer also can lose the warranty by examining and failing to object to faults or by refusing to inspect the goods. If the defects are ones that would be uncovered by such inspection, the warranty is waived as of then. The warranty is also disclaimed by language stating that the buyer is taking the goods "as is" or "with faults."

In certain situations, a seller, whether a merchant or not, extends an additional warranty, one of fitness. In contrast with the

89

generic *warranty of merchantability*, the *warranty of fitness* applies to a specific purpose. To exist, the seller must be aware of a particular or special need of the buyer, and in return, the buyer must purchase the goods in reliance on the seller's affirmations. Again, in the hypothetical case of Henry and the lamp, if Henry needed a lamp capable of functioning with a 500-watt light bulb for prolonged periods, the warranty for fitness for a particular purpose would attach if Henry explained his need to the seller and bought a lamp which the seller selected for him.

The seller can likewise disclaim this warranty, but unlike the disclaimer of merchantability, he must do so in writing and it must be conspicuous. The disclaimer need not make a direct reference to the warranty, and thus, it can be stated in general terms. Identical with the warranty of merchantability, the implied warranty of fitness is defeated in those situations of buyer inspections or when expressions are included that the goods are taken "as is."

90   In addition, a seller may pass on to buyer any other warranty which he expressly makes, either orally or in writing. The buyer must prove that he could have relied on the seller's statements in purchasing the goods. However, if the buyer in fact does not rely on his statement, the warranty does not apply. Additionally, the seller cannot make an expressed warranty and attempt to negate its effectiveness by conduct or statements that are unreasonably contradictory.

The next question any buyer logically asks is: What is the impact of a breach of a warranty? The UCC expressly provides for the recovery of consequential damages as the result of a breach of warranty when no disclaimer exists, or if it does, is ineffective. Basically consequential damages include losses arising from failure of the goods to meet a buyer's requirements of which the seller was aware and personal injury or property damages which proximately result. To avoid the burden of such extensive damages, sellers frequently attempt to restrict their liability or to provide for liquidated damages. These limitations are permis-

sible unless they prove to be *unconscionable*, in which case the limitations will not be enforced by the courts. In one specific situation, the restriction is presumed to be unconscionable: A seller of consumer goods cannot waive liability for personal injury to the buyer or third parties who reasonably come into contact with the goods. However, there is no presumption of unconscionability of a limitation of commercial loss. Thus, parties can prearrange a fixed schedule of damages for failure of goods if it applies to such items as lost profits.

Remedies

Besides breaching warranties, a defaulting party can find himself in breach of the contract. When such a breach occurs, the other party naturally wishes to make himself whole by seeking and procuring one of the several remedies available to him under the UCC.

Which options are open to either the seller or the buyer is contingent upon whether or not the buyer has formally accepted the goods. From the perspective of both parties, one option has been discussed earlier in this chapter. Where the buyer or seller, through actions or words, casts doubt on his performance, the other may demand written assurances and suspend his own performance until the assurances are received. Unlike contract law, repudiation is not immediate in a case of anticipatory breach; however, if the assurances are not forthcoming within thirty days, the aggrieved party may then treat the contract as breached. If the conduct or words of the defaulting party do more than cast doubt—that is, make it certain that he will not perform, then the contract can be considered breached as of that time and the wronged party can pursue any remedy he wishes without requesting assurances.

Seller Remedies

The remaining remedies, which come into play only after one party has in fact failed on his promise, are particular to one party or the other. Since the reader is more frequently in the buyer's position, the seller's remedies will be discussed only briefly. Before the buyer has accepted and come into possession of the goods, the seller can usually recover his goods. If they are in transit, for example, he can halt delivery by so ordering the carrier or thy holder (such as a warehouseman) of the goods. He has this right up until the time that whoever has the goods notifies the buyer that they are being held for him or until the buyer receives a negotiable bill of sale. These rights belong to the seller and are not a breach on his part where the buyer breaches (such as in *anticipatory breach* or by failure to pay) or becomes insolvent. Once the buyer receives the goods, the seller may still recover the goods within ten days if he discovers that the buyer is insolvent or at any time if the buyer is insolvent and has also led the seller to believe otherwise.

Of course, in most instances, the seller does not want to recover his goods as much as he wants to receive his money. The question of damages is complicated and turns on the specific facts of the case. In general, the seller can demand the buyer to take the goods and pay the contract price, only if the risk of loss has shifted to the buyer and the goods are lost, ruined, or if the seller cannot find another ready buyer. If those situations do not exist, the seller has an option between three different measures: he can *select cover*, a UCC remedy, which is the difference between the price set in the contract and the price that the seller was able to obtain for the goods in a subsequent sale; or *common law damages*, which is the difference between the contract price and the market price (or going rate of same or similar goods); and finally, if none of these two measures make the seller whole, then lost profits. The last measure is based primarily on the seller's cost as offset against the agreed upon price. The seller also must take into account specific selling expenses which were eliminated since the sale fell through. At no time must he further decrease his recovery by subtracting whatever general overhead costs are attributable

to the goods covered by the breached contract. Other expenses which the seller incurred because the buyer breached his obligations can be tacked on to the final damages.

Buyer's Remedies

Most people however, are usually in the shoes of the buyer. Therefore, it would be more worthwhile and rewarding to examine the buyer's remedies in depth. Perhaps the best approach would be to review the law and then list its practicalities to the buyer-consumer.

Once again, acceptance is the crucial element in determining the remedies available to the buyer. Under the UCC, the buyer has the right of rejecting nonconforming goods prior to acceptance and a right of revocation after acceptance. In the latter situation, the right is qualified, it being required that the defect substantially impair the value of the goods to the buyer. What constitutes acceptance? For the most part, the buyer is not deemed to have accepted tendered goods unless he, (1) notifies the seller that all is well or that he will keep the goods despite defects (as will be seen, he can still seek damages for the defects); (2) exercises acts of ownership adverse to that of the seller; or (3) delays in rejecting defective goods. Acceptance can occur, in other words, either expressly through actual notification to the seller of the buyer's intent or impliedly by the buyer's failure to effectively reject (as evidenced by conduct inconsistent with the seller's ownership or retention of the goods). Up until the occurrence of any of these events, the buyer retains the right to reject nonconforming goods.

Acceptance, however, is conditioned on the buyer's right of inspection. Where the buyer has not had a reasonable opportunity to inspect the goods, his acts, which normally would be acceptance on his part, are negated. Thus, even a buyer who tells the seller, "Yes, I will take these goods," and who tenders payment, has not formally accepted the goods under the UCC. Upon later inspection and discovery of the defects or nonconformities, the buyer can reject and seek all available remedies.

Assuming that the buyer has not accepted, when and how can he reject the seller's goods? Basically, whenever the seller fails to meet the *perfect tender rule* under the UCC, the buyer can elect between either rejection or acceptance, in whole or in part. (The buyer should remember that whenever he rejects, accepts or revokes acceptance, he retains all his other remedies against the seller for breach of the contract.) Rejection, however, must be within a reasonable time after the buyer has had his opportunity to inspect. The seller also cannot unconscionably shorten this period of rejection by a provision in the sales contract. For the most part, the right to reject arises where the goods are not personally satisfactory to the buyer.

The buyer rejects by taking affirmative action. The UCC calls for the seller to be seasonally notified by the buyer. In addition, the buyer must particularize any and all defects determinable by reasonable inspection on which he bases his rejection. This requirement is highly important for the buyer, because if he fails to state the grounds for his rejection, he waives his right to justify his rejection on those bases. Since the seller has a right to cure the defects in the goods, the buyer cannot defeat this right by misleading or withholding information from the seller. As between merchants, a merchant-buyer must be more specific in listing his objections to nonconforming goods, but only after the seller requests such specifications in writing. In all arrangements, the buyer does not waive his right to base rejection or an action for breach on a defect which he cannot ascertain through reasonable inspection.

After rejection, the UCC imposes certain duties upon the buyer in his handling of the goods. Since the buyer rejected, the seller still owns the goods and thus the buyer must take reasonable care of them until the seller can effect reacquisition. The UCC again differentiates between consumers and merchant-buyers, thrusting the greater duty upon merchant-buyers. The typical consumer is cast in a role of a bailee or custodian, but otherwise has no duty

to return the goods. The merchant-buyer like-wise has no duty to return the goods, but he must comply with reasonable instructions sent to him by the seller if the seller has no local agent. If the seller does not advise the buyer how to handle the goods, the buyer can return, sell, or store them as long as his actions are reasonable. The buyer has a security interest in the goods and can enforce that interest to recover expenses and costs incurred in dealing with the justifiably rejected goods.

Assuming that after inspecting the goods, the buyer accepts, either expressly or impliedly, what is his position? Immediately upon acceptance, the buyer is bound to pay the seller the agreed upon price. He can no longer reject the goods per se, since he has already accepted, but rather must move under rules for revocation of acceptance if he is not satisfied. If after acceptance, the buyer is unable to revoke or does not wish to revoke, he is not precluded from asserting claims for breach of the contract or warranties. The mere acceptance, in other words, does not signify that the seller has satisfied all his obligations and that no breach has occurred. The buyer is only precluded from objecting to those defects of which he knew or should have known (opportunity to inspect) when he accepted the goods. However, where the defect is latent or the seller procured the buyer's acceptance by assuring him that the defects would be cured, the buyer retains his right to assert those claims.

To assert any claim, the buyer must notify the seller of breach within a reasonable time, although such notice is not applicable where the buyer's claim is based on a tort theory, (i.e., negligence or strict tort products liability). As with notification of defects under rejection, failure to notify the seller of breaches bars the buyer from recovering on those particular claims. If the seller sues the buyer, for example to recover the purchase price, the buyer can then assert his claim for breach against the seller.

Unable to reject because he has already accepted, the buyer does have a right, although not absolute, to revoke his acceptance. In order to justifiably revoke, the buyer must show that his value in the goods was substantially impaired by a nonconformity. In addition, he must show that he had no knowledge of the defect of which he complains, unless, as mentioned earlier, the seller coaxed his acceptance through assurances that the problem would be cured. Thus, he cannot revoke if he fails to inspect the goods and the defect is one which would have been ascertained upon such inspection. In addition, he cannot revoke if he accepts knowing of the defect and without being assured by the seller that the defect will be cured. Finally, and perhaps most importantly to both parties, the buyer cannot revoke if the seller in fact cures the problem within a reasonable time.

For the revocation to be effective, the buyer must notify the seller within a reasonable time after he discovers, or should have discovered the defect. Mere suspicion does not require the buyer to act. Also the buyer can effectuate the revocation without returning the goods to the seller. In fact, the buyer possesses a security interest in the goods as he does under rejection, and thus he can retain the goods in order to assure enforcement without endangering his right to revoke. The buyer, however, should be careful not to use the goods or act in any way inconsistent with the seller's ownership, or he may be barred from revoking.

The next question which must be asked, is what are the remedies which the buyer can seek when an incurable breach occurs? The buyer's remedies are the same whether the seller fails to deliver or repudiates, or whether the buyer rightfully rejects or revokes acceptance. The buyer is in an enviable position, for he has several options available to him which he can select concurrently. First, the buyer may cancel the contract upon notification to the seller. Unlike rejection or revocation, such action terminates the underlying contract. Whether the buyer cancels or not, he is entitled to recover any part of the purchase price which he has paid and money damages for the seller's breach. Secondly, where the breach is repudiation or nondelivery, the buyer may also obtain a court decree for specific performance if the goods are

unique or *replevin* if the goods are identified and *cover* (or replacement) cannot be procured. In essence, this means that because he needs the goods, the buyer wants to keep the contract in force and compel the seller to make delivery. In this situation, where the buyer is in possession and has justifiably rejected or revoked, he has a security interest and can recover his costs and expenses. If the seller refuses to reimburse him for these incurred costs, the buyer can resell the goods to enforce his interest.

Two different measures of damages are set out in the UCC for such situations. The first measure is based on the cost of replacement goods or "cover." The buyer's efforts to obtain cover must occur within a reasonable time and must be in good faith. Once the cost of cover is ascertained, the buyer's damages are the difference between it and the contract price. Thus, if the contract called for a price of $100 and an adequate substitute cost $105, the damages would amount to $5.00. The second measure does not require any positive action on the buyer's part and is the difference between the *going market price* as of the time of discovery of the breach and the *contract price*. Again, as a reminder, these measures are optional, and so the buyer should determine which affords him the greatest recovery before electing. In addition, the buyer also may recover any incidental or consequential damages as explained under seller's damages.

Where the buyer has accepted the goods and cannot rightfully revoke, his remedy is different. Upon the seller's breach of warranty or his failure to satisfy all of his obligations, the buyer cannot cancel the contract, but can collect damages, if he gives the seller reasonable notice of the problem. In a nonconformity situation, these damages amount to the loss sustained in the ordinary course of events, plus all incidental and consequential damages allowed under the UCC. Where the seller breaches either an expressed or implied warranty, the buyer can recover the difference in the value of the goods as they should have been (if properly tendered) and as they were when delivered (price

93

based on the time and place of acceptance), and again incidental and consequential damages. These measurements do not bar a higher recovery if in fact the buyer's loss was greater and the seller had been informed of the possibility at the formation of the contract. The buyer, however, cannot increase his recovery by using goods which he realizes are defective and thereby incurring further personal injuries or property damages.

Bills of Sale

This section contains no forms other than three special bills of sale. Although it applies to all purchases, whether goods or realty, the bill of sale is inserted here for the sake of convenience. Because many sales transactions include the transfer of a bill of sale, we should briefly explain the document, its requisites and effects.

The primary function of a bill of sale is to evidence a transfer of title. The document itself does not necessarily create immediate rights in the buyer. But neither does its absence defeat the buyer's title, once certain conditions have been met. Ostensibly, the bill of sale is not essential to the transfer of property. In the case of goods, for example, once the buyer accepts the seller's goods, he becomes the owner of the goods, whether or not a bill of sale is delivered to him. The only time that a bill of sale is mandatory is when both parties contract to provide for its execution and delivery, or when statutory law requires a bill of sale.

If a bill of sale is not essential, then why use one? Just as a diploma is not an essential part of a college education, it nevertheless serves its function in representing and evidencing a person's qualifications. In like manner, a bill of sale aids in establishing rights in property, by depicting the transfer of ownership. The bill of sale is a tangible symbol of the intentions of two persons to transfer title in a property or quantity of goods.

What are the requisites of a bill of sale? Like all contracts, it must be grounded in good

consideration. The property involved should be adequately identified so as to avoid later problems. When items such as taxi cabs, boats, planes, etc., are being transferred, registration numbers should be included in the description, along with color, make, model and other details.

The bill of sale must also state a present intent to transfer. It need not affirm delivery of the item. Delivery can be made at a preceding or succeeding time. The bill of sale must be duly executed which includes signing by the transferor and delivery of the document to the transferee. As a rule, the bill of sale accomplishes whatever the parties intend, since their intentions prevail.

In conclusion, usually a sale is covered by more than one document—a bill of sale and a *contract for sale.* Each has its own particular features and final results. The parties should note, however, that whereas a bill of sale is executed *after* the contract for sale, if the former is to be controlling, it should cover all matter and terms of the contract. Otherwise, for provisions not covered, the contract for sale remains effective and enforceable.

Commentary

So what does all this legalese mean to the consumer? Returning to the hypothetical case of Henry, who purchases a lamp from a retail store and back home discovers its defects, there are certain actions that Henry can pursue and certain dangers which he should have been alerted to from the start. It might be helpful to list some of these rights, some hints and some possible pitfalls:

(1)   If there is a sales contract, read it carefully. Beware of provisions which (a) limit remedies or change the measure of damages allowed by law. Such restrictions are permissible as long as they offer a reasonable (i.e., minimum remedy); (b) liquidate damages. Parties can con-

tract as they wish, and the buyer might unknowingly agree to a set sum, in case of damages. Again, these liquidated damages must not violate the rules of reasonability or conscionability.

(2) Remember that the consumer always has a right to inspect the goods before acceptance.

(3) If possible, always inspect and never accept goods which are known to be defective, unless the seller's assurances of cure are in writing.

(4) Remember that revocation of acceptance is unavailable for nonconforming goods known to the buyer at the time of acceptance and therefore, failure to inspect where the opportunity is present can lead to waiver of warranties.

(5) Signs of statements by sales personnel can lead to the conclusion that the consumer has been advised of his rights of inspection and has had his opportunity. In fact, without ever examining the goods (they could still be sealed in the box), the buyer could be deemed to have inspected and to have accepted the merchandise.

(6) If the goods are nonconforming or if a breach of warranty occurs, be sure to notify the seller as soon as possible.

(7) Always remember that although the law protects the buyer with implied warranties, it also makes provision for warranty disclaimer. The buyer should be wary not to waive any of his rights by accepting goods on which the warranties have been dis-

claimed. Avoid purchases which are labeled taken "as is" or "with all faults."

(8) Where goods are defective, return them to the store and ask for cure or an adjustment. Remember that the seller has a right to make a curative tender within a reasonable time. Other damages for breach are not available to the buyer until the seller fails to cure.

(9) Remember that if the seller does offer a curative tender, a consumer who improperly refuses to accept it (whether repair, replacement, or credit) is not entitled to damages for breach of contract.

(10) If the consumer has made a down payment and attempts to get out of the contract, he has a right to the return of any amount exceeding 20% of the purchase price, or $500, whichever is smaller. Seller is allowed to deduct from the excess the cost of any benefit bestowed upon the consumer or any damages which he incurs as a result of the breach.

(11) If damages are incurred, the buyer has options with the measure of damages. Make the most of the election.

(12) Overall, the UCC is couched in terms of good faith and reasonability. It is its general policy not to grant absolute rights to either party. Thus, where one party reserves an absolute right which seems oppressive and unreasonable, instead of being cowed, seek legal counsel in order to be fully advised of your rights.

(13) Always act in good faith.

95

Bill of Sale of Boat

Know all Men by these Presents,

THAT   as Seller,

of   County of

State of   for and in consideration of the sum of $ paid by

                                                                                                              as Buyer,

residing at   County of

State of   has bargained, sold, granted and conveyed and by these

presents does bargain, sell, grant and convey unto the said Buyer and the Buyer's successors (heirs,

executors, administrators) and assigns, the Boat hereinafter described.

YEAR BUILT	MAKE AND MODEL	NEW OR USED	LENGTH OVERALL	MAKE AND H.P. OF ENGINE(S)	ENGINE(S) NUMBER(S)	NAME OF BOAT AND REGISTRATION NUMBER

List extra equipment.

96

TO HAVE AND TO HOLD the same unto the said Buyer and the Buyer's successors (heirs, executors, adminstrators) and assigns forever; and the Seller covenants and agrees to and with the said Buyer to warrant and defend the said described Boat against all and every person or persons whomsoever.

IN WITNESS WHEREOF, the Seller has set his hand and seal or caused these presents to be signed by its proper corporate officers and caused its proper corporate seal to be hereto affixed, the

              day of   19   .

CHAPTER 8

Buying On Credit

Introduction

In this day and age, economic stability seems to be a major concern of most people. Many of us are walking in a daze resulting from high prices and no money. The dollar that purchased a sandwich and beer a couple of years ago entitles you to only the beer today. What is the solution? There might be many answers to the prevailing cash shortage which plagues everyone, but two of the more frequently used and least understood vehicles which manufacture instant cash are the credit card and the retail installment agreement.

Many of the people who use these methods do not fully understand the contractual ramifications of the transaction. What they do know is that they want a television and do not have the money to purchase it. The solution is to buy it with plastic money—the credit card; or if the person does not have one, the retailer will gladly suggest that he can pay for the television on time. Why not, the consumer reasons. Pay $50.00 down and $25.00 monthly for three years. Who thinks even of one year from now, much less three years? Out comes one agreement, the signatures are scribed, and suddenly potential problems loom.

Like many contractual situations, entering into a credit agreement is much easier than getting out. The beautiful television set appears to be there for the taking; the dotted line invites the signature; and what the hell, economic times are bound to get better. This logic is normal and as a result, most people frequently engage in this type of contractual credit agreement. This section is not intended to discourage

the use of credit cards and retail installment agreements. If understood and used properly, both are an effective means by which one can purchase goods.

Our main concern is to present the consumer with a guide explaining his rights and obligations under such agreements. Three statutes will be examined:

(1) Article 10 of New York Personal Property Law, § 401-419 (Retail Installment Agreements)

(2) Public Law 30-321, 82 Stat 146, 15USC § 1601-1681 (Consumer Credit Protection Act)

(3) Public Law 93-495, 88 Stat 1500, Title III, § 301, effective October, 1975 (The Depository Institution Act)

Article 10 of the Personal Property Law is applicable to New York State only. The other two statutes are federal law, and therefore are applicable on a national basis. Not every section of the three statutes will be discussed. Instead, they will be interwoven to allow the consumer to understand their basic tenor. When discussing Article 10 it will be cited as such, so that the reader will know it is applicable only to New York State.

Definitions

A model Retail Installment Agreement and credit card applications are abound with

97

reference to terms to which the consumer agrees when he signs. (Hopefully, the next time he sees that television on sale and they are always on sale, and temptation is overwhelming the will, he will hesitate for a moment and think about the headaches he might be purchasing along with that television). Where necessary, the statute will be quoted occasionally, with code sites for future reference. The following are some basic definitions which apply to all consumer credit transactions. 15 U.S.C. 1602 (Consumer Credit Protection Act) defines certain terms as follows:

"(e) The term 'credit' means the right granted by a creditor to a debtor to defer payment of debt or to insure debt and defer its payment.

(f) The term 'creditor' refers only to creditors who regularly extend, or arrange for the extension of credit which is payable by agreement in more than four installments or for which the payment of a finance charge is or may be required, whether in connection with loans, sales of property or services, or otherwise . . ., the term 'creditor' shall also include card issuers whether or not the amount due is payable by agreement in more than four installments or the payment of a finance charge is or may be required, and the Board shall, by regulation, apply these requirements to such card issuers, to the extent appropriate even though the requirements are by their terms applicable only to creditors offering open end credit plans." (This is an amendment, enacted by Public Law 93-495, 88 Stat 1500, Title III, § 303.)

(g) The term 'credit sale' refers to any sale with respect to which credit is extended or arranged by the seller . . .

(h) The adjective 'consumer,' used with reference to a credit transaction, characterizes the transaction as one in which the party to whom credit is offered or extended is a natural person, and the money, property, or services which are the subject of the transaction are primarily for personal, family, household, or agricultural purposes.

(i) The term 'open end credit plan' refers to a plan prescribing the terms of credit transactions which may be made thereunder from time to time and under the terms of which a finance charge may be computed on the outstanding unpaid balance from time to time thereunder. (Credit cards or open end credit plans.)

(k) The term 'credit card' means any card, plate, coupon book, or other credit device existing for the purpose of obtaining money, property, labor, or services on credit.

(m) The term 'cardholder' means any person to whom a credit card is issued or any person who has agreed with the card issuer to pay obligations arising from the issuance of a credit card to another person.

(o) The term 'unauthorized user,' as used in § 7644 of the title, means a use of a credit card by a person other than the card holder and who does not have actual, implied, or apparent authority for such use and from which the cardholder receives no benefit. (E.g., a person's wife is considered to have apparent authority if she does not have actual authority.)"

These definitions are taken from the Consumer Credit Protection Act.

98

Credit Transactions In General

In a credit transaction there is a general requirement of disclosure. This requirement is imposed upon any creditor who extends credit to a consumer and upon which a finance charge is or may be imposed. The disclosure must be clear and conspicious, containing all information required under the Act. (Disclosure requirements will not be discussed.) In cases of consumer credit transactions where a security interest is in real property, the obligor (consumer) shall have the right to rescind the transaction within three days of the transaction or the delivery of the disclosures required by the Act. Recision is made by notification to the creditor of the obligor's intention to do so. The creditor is obligated to clearly and conspicuously disclose this right to the obligor (in these types of transactions) and give the obligor adequate opportunity to exercise his right to negate the transaction. If the obligor exercises this right of recision, he is not liable for any finance or other charge, and any security interest becomes void. The creditor, within ten days of notice, must return to the obligor any money or property given as a down payment and do all that is necessary to terminate the security interest that was created. Once the creditor has performed these duties, the obligor must give back any property received from him. If it is impractical for the obligor to do so, he shall tender back its reasonable value. If the creditor does not take possession of the property within ten days after tender by the obligor, ownership in the property is deemed to be in the obligor with no further duty of payment.

The two most basic and popular forms for the extension of credit are credit cards and what are commonly known as retail installment agreements (time payment accounts).

Credit Cards (Open End Credit Agreement)

Under federal law, credit cards fall within the category of *open end credit agreements.* Simply stated, an open end credit agreement is one in which the purchaser (cardholder) agrees to pay the card issuer for the debt incurred on a monthly basis until his account is paid in full. Normally, this involves a minimum monthly payment. The end result of this type of credit is that there is no pre-set number of months, payments, or amounts which is intended to clear the account. Stated another way, one month a cardholder might put $15.00 towards his $75.00 purchase and the next month pay $35.00, depending upon his means. The interest charged the cardholder is determined on the basis of his average outstanding balance for the previous billing period (which by law is one month, but not necessarily one calendar month).

Periodic Statements

What must be contained in the periodic statements that are sent to the cardholder? Section 1637 and 1638 of the Consumer Credit Protection Act deal with these requirements. These sections are summarized as briefly as possible.

Before opening any account under an open end consumer credit plan (i.e., obtaining a credit card), the creditor shall disclose to the person to whom the credit is being extended the conditions under which a finance charge may be imposed, including the time period, if any, that the credit may be repaid without incurring any finance charge; how the balance is computed; the method of determining the finance charge; the periodic rates that may be used to compute finance charges and the balance ranges to which the rates apply; conditions under which any other charges may be imposed; conditions by which a creditor may acquire a security interest in any property which is to secure payment of the credit extended; and a description of the interest acquired.

It should be noted that in New York State, § 413 (12) of the Personal Property Law prohibits the creation of a security interest in any personal or real property (including any goods sold under such agreement) to secure payment of the buyer's outstanding indebtedness under such open end credit transactions. This statute further provides that while the security interest which the seller attempts to impose is void, the credit agreement is not otherwise impaired. Also, in New York State, an agreement between a purchaser and a retail seller (goods or services) for the purchase of a particular item, the payment for which is to be made in equal, pre-set, monthly installments, is called a retail installment contract. Basically, this is a one shot deal between a buyer and a seller for a particular item; here, all terms of payment are expressly set forth at the time of purchase. Federal law refers to this type of agreement as a *closed end credit agreement.*

Where the purchase of goods or services is contracted for through the use of an accepted credit card (this term means any credit card which the cardholder has requested and received or has signed, used, or authorized another to use, for the purpose of obtaining money, property, labor or services on credit), and the terms of payment call for varying monthly amounts over an extended period of time, with the imposition of finance charges based upon average outstanding monthly accounts, New York State labels this type of transaction a *retail installment credit agreement.* Under federal law, this is termed an open end credit agreement.

In an account, already under an open end consumer credit plan, the creditor must transmit to the obligor a statement containing the following items: the outstanding balance on the account; amount and dates of when credit was extended and a brief description of the involved transaction; the amount credited to the account during the period; the finance charge applicable to the period billed for; the balance on which the finance charge was computed and how the balance was determined; the balance of the account at the end of the period; and the date on which payment may be made to avoid further finance charge. In the case of an open end consumer credit plan, these items shall be disclosed in a notice mailed or delivered to the obligor not later than thirty days after last billing.

If the order of purchase is made by phone or mail without solicitation through a catalogue, advertisement or other matter printed by the creditor, the cash price and terms of the financing may be made at any time not later than the date the first payment is due.

If the creditor fails in his disclosure requirements, he can be civilly liable for his misconduct unless he remedies his failure within fifteen days after discovery of the error. A creditor must also make all appropriate adjustments to the account which are necessary to insure that the person will not pay finance charges at a rate in excess of the percentage rate actually disclosed. There will be no purpose in discussing the potential liabilities of the creditor, since if the reader is confronted with this problem, an attorney should be consulted and must be consulted if he wants to institute legal action.

Public Law 93-495: Credit Billing

Public Law 93-495 amends the Consumer Credit Protection Act by adding a complete new chapter entitled Credit Billing. This amendment becomes effective in October, 1975 and will be touched upon only briefly. If the obligor has a mistake in his bill, he must immediately send a written notice of the mistake (must be within 60 days of billing date) to the creditor. In this notice the consumer should state his name and account number, give the amount that he believes is in error, and set forth the reasons for his belief. Once that is done, he has met his obligations to put the creditor on notice. The burden to act now shifts to the creditor, who must pursue the proper steps. First, he must send acknowledgment within thirty days of receipt of the notice. He then has a choice of procedures, one of which he must follow to rectify the complaint. These will not be discussed since they are not applicable to the consumer. He has complied with his obligations to notify the creditor, who now must take the next step.

A "billing error" consists of a number of

items which the new Federal statute will require as of October, 1975; most of these items are grounded in common sense. Basically, it is when the obligor gets billed for an amount that he did not charge. However, one classification of a billing error that should be noted is the following as quoted from the statute:

"§ 161 (G) (3): A reflection on a statement of goods or services not accepted by the obligor or his designee or not delivered to the obligor or his designee in accordance with the agreement made at the time of a transaction." This particular item is pointed out because it is important for the reader to make sure that if he purchases a television or any other goods or services with a credit card, and he either does not receive them or they are defective, he should immediately write to the credit card institution and put them on notice. This notice, which is clarified as a billing error notice, must be sent to the creditor within sixty days of the statement which contains the contested charges. If the obligor (consumer) does not get proper notice to the creditor, he might encounter major problems later. Even if he has put the creditor, in the case of a credit card transaction, on notice of his billing error, the consumer might be confronted with some problems (discussed in the chapter on sales). However, to have a fighting chance to negate the obligation to pay for the defective goods, written notice is necessary. It is not hard to do and only costs the price of a stamp. This notice must be mailed separately and is invalid of made on the billing statement or stub. In fact, no part of the statement that the creditor sends the obligor should be returned in the notice. If the obligor wants to strengthen his position, the notice can be sent by registered mail with a return receipt requested. He should just make sure that he gets written notice to the creditor within sixty days of receipt of the erroneous billing statement.

In relation to the notice of billing error, the obligor need not worry that his future credit rating will be ruined. The new Act provides that a creditor or his agent may not report anything that would adversely affect the obligor's credit rating or credit standing because of his failure to pay a questioned amount. Only after the creditor satisfies his duties under the Act, and the amount in question is resolved, does the obligor become bound to make payment. Once made, these payments must be promptly credited to the obligor's account. No finance costs may be charged to the obligor's account, if payment is made within the time period agreed to between the parties. If excess payments are made (oh, to be that fortunate) in an open end consumer credit account, the creditor must refund the money upon request of the obligor or credit the obligor's account to the extent of the overpayment.

If a consumer uses a credit card to purchase goods or services and the seller allows for a return or debit, the consumer should make sure that the seller notifies the card issuer and sends a credit statement, if in fact the goods are returned. The credit card issuer must then credit the account. This duty is imposed upon the seller by statute, but it would benefit the consumer to remind him. It just might eliminate later hassles and save the consumer the trouble of having to notify the card issuer of a subsequent "billing error."

Another interesting note that is covered under the new statute (P.L. 93-495) deals with the prohibition against offsets (§ 169). It is important since many people who own credit cards also have checking and savings accounts at the same bank that issues the card. In essence, this section prohibits a bank from using the bank account funds to make payments on credit card obligations. Such action is expressly prohibited unless the card holder authorized it in writing. Thus, if the card holder in initiating his credit plan agrees that the card issuer may pay debts that are incurred through the use of the credit card by deducting all or a portion of such debt from the cardholder's deposit account, the bank is empowered to act. In conjunction with this provision, a card issuer cannot take action dealing with an outstanding disputed amount upon a request by cardholder. Of course, the card issuer can attach a cardholder's funds held on deposit with the card issuer, if that remedy is constitutionally available to creditors generally.

Cardholder Rights

The next area of discussion is of such importance that the actual section of the statute needs to be recited. Each and every credit cardholder should know his rights as spelled out by federal law. Any language that is confusing will be discussed after the citation of the statute.

170. Rights of credit card customers.

"(a) Subject to the limitation contained in subsection (b), a card issuer who has issued a credit card to a cardholder pursuant to an open end consumer credit plan shall be subject to all claims (other than tort claims) and defenses arising out of any transaction in which the credit card is used as a method of payment or extension of credit if (1) the obligor has made a good faith attempt to obtain satisfactory resolution of a disagreement or problem relative to the transaction from the person honoring the credit card; (2) the amount of the initial transaction exceeds $50; and (3) the place where the initial transaction occurred was in the same State as the mailing address previously provided by the cardholder or was within 100 miles from such address, except that the limitations set forth in clauses (2) and (3) with respect to an obligor's right to assert claims and defenses against a card issuer shall not be applicable to any transaction in which the person honoring the credit card (A) is the same person as the card issuer, (B) is controlled by the card issuer, (C) is under direct or indirect common control with the card issuer, (D) is a franchised dealer in the card issuer's products or services, or (E) has obtained the order for such transaction through a mail solicitation made by or participated in by the card issuer in which the cardholder is solicited to enter into such transaction by using the credit card issued by the card issuer."

"(b) The amount of claims or defenses asserted by the cardholder may not exceed the amount of credit outstanding with respect to such transaction at the time the cardholder first notifies the card issuer or the person honoring the credit card of such claim or defense. For the purpose of determining the amount of credit outstanding in the preceding sentence, payments and credits to the cardholder's account are deemed to have been applied, in the order indicated, to the payment of: (1) late charges in the order of their entry to the account; (2) finance charges in order of their entry to the account; and (3) debits to the account other than those set forth above, in the order in which each debit entry to the account was made." [P.L. 93-495, 88 Stat. 1500, C. 4, Credit Billing.] "

Upon close examination of this section, the reader can understand the importance of its meaning. It protects the cardholder from getting taken by shady sellers. Let us set up an example: The cardholder buys a $400.00 television from Sam Shadlay's Television and Appliance Store. The purchase is made through the use of an accepted credit card (e.g., Master Charge, etc.). The purchaser takes the television home and turns it on. Unfortunately, no picture appears; in fact, nothing happens. The television is not worth the box it came in. The purchaser returns to Sammy only to find that Sammy has closed for the day. Actually, Sammy has closed for good and has gone to Venezuela. The purchaser has a television that does not work and soon will receive a bill from the credit card company for $400.00, plus finance charges. Is he out of luck? No, because under this new amendment, all of his defenses that would have been good against Sammy for non-payment (such as breach of warranty of merchantability) are valid against the credit issuer. The purchaser does not have to pay the card issuer and can assert his defenses against the creditor (card issuer) as a result of this statute. This is quite different from the provisions of earlier laws and should be noted. One qualification, however, is that in any case, the purchaser must make a good-faith attempt to obtain satisfactory resolution of the disagreement or problem arising from the transaction from the person honoring the credit card. If his attempted resolution fails, he may then assert his defenses against the card issuer by informing him in writing that a billing error exists and the reasons why. This notification must occur upon receipt of the billing statement which includes the cost of the television. This law which became effective in October, 1975, will protect consumers from paying for defective goods.

Cardholder Liabilities

The rights of a credit cardholder have now been reviewed. What about the liability of a credit cardholder? A cardholder shall be liable for the debts incurred through the use of the credit card by him or a person whom he authorizes to use the card. This is obvious. If the card is lost or stolen however, a different situation arises and the liability imposed is greatly reduced. A cardholder shall be liable for the unauthorized use of a credit card only if it is an accepted credit card and then only to a maximum of $50.00 (this is actually stated on the back of the credit card). The cardholder is not held liable for any amount, even up to the $50.00 ceiling, that results from unauthorized use after the card issuer has been placed on notice by the cardholder that the card is lost, stolen, mislaid or otherwise. The key element to remember here is that liability is limited to $50.00 for the unauthorized use. However the card issuer should be notified promptly when the card is missing and the $50.00 might be saved if the card has not been used yet.

If the card issuer attempts to enforce liability for the use of a credit card, the burden of proof is upon the card issuer to show that the use was authorized. If the use was unauthorized, the burden of proof is still on the issuer and he must prove that the conditions of liability for the unauthorized use of a credit card have been met. These conditions are:

(1) The card is an accepted credit card;

(2) The liability is not in excess of $50.00;

(3) The card issuer gives adequate notice to the cardholder of the potential liability;

(4) The card issuer has provided the cardholder with a self-addressed, prestamped notification to be mailed by the cardholder in the event of the loss or theft of the credit card; and

(5) The unauthorized use occurs before the cardholder has notified the card issuer that an unauthorized use of the credit card has occurred, or may occur as the result of loss, theft or otherwise.

If these prerequisites are not met by the card issuer, the cardholder is not liable for even the $50.00.

The fraudulent use of a credit card can result in serious liability. One can be fined up to $10,000 or be imprisoned up to 10 years, or both. The fraudulent use of a credit card is a federal offense under this section.

Retail Installment Contract (Closed End Credit Agreement)

As stated previously, this is your run-of-the-mill consumer credit transaction. It is more commonly known as the "buy now, pay later" route to happiness. What distinguishes this type of transaction from a credit card purchase is the fact that at the time of the purchase, the seller must inform the consumer as to "total" cost of the purchase. "Total" means the purchase price, additional charges and finance charges. Normally, payments are in equal monthly installments and extend over a pre-agreed length of time. Each monthly installment is intended to pay part of the purchase price and part of the finance charge. When the last payment is made, the account is closed, and the goods or services purchased belong exclusively to the purchaser.

103

Application for a Master Charge

Firm Name or Employer	Telephone No.	Years There	Type of Business

Address (Number & Street)	Department	Employee Number

City, State & Zip Code	Position	Annual Income $

Name & Address of Previous Employer (If above less than 2 years)	Years There

Spouse's Employer and/or Source of Other Income	Annual Other Income $

Checking Account—Bank Name & Branch Address ☐ Regular ☐ Special ☐ Business	Account Number

Savings Account—Bank Name & Branch Address	Account Number

Real Estate Owned—Describe ☐ Home ☐ Other	Rent/Mortgage Payment $	Have you borrowed from Chemical ☐ No ☐ Yes—When

Indebtedness (List all current debts—attach additional sheet if necessary)

Name and address of Creditor	Account No.	Original Bal.	Unpaid Bal.	Monthly Pmt.

I represent that all the statements made by me in this application are true and correct, and authorize Chemical Bank to exchange credit information with others in connection with this application. I understand that the use of the Master Charge Card issued by Chemical Bank, is subject to the terms and conditions of the Chemical Bank Master Charge Agreement, a **New York Retail Instalment Credit Agreement.**

Date	Signature					
For Bank Use Only	Loan Control	Credit $	☐ SI ☐ DIS	Approved	Verified	Date

- - - - - - - - - - - - - - - Detach Here - - - - - - - - - - - - - - -

Here's the information on Master Charge costs:

PURCHASES

There is no **Finance Charge** on new purchases if you pay your indebtedness within **25** days of your billing date.

Payments may be extended by paying at least **1/36th** of the "new balance" shown on your Master Charge Statement or **$5**, whichever is the greater together with the **Finance Charge** included in the new balance each month. (The "new balance" is the total of the current month's purchases and any unpaid balance from previous months, less any "payments and credits" and plus any "debit adjustments" to your account, plus a **Finance Charge**.) A minimum payment is rounded up to the next highest dollar. A **Finance Charge** is imposed on the average unpaid principal amount of the previous month's new balance from time to time outstanding (an "average daily balance"), computed separately (i) for daily balances of **$500** or less at a periodic rate of **0.04931%** per day, for an **Annual Percentage Rate** of **18%**, and (ii) for daily balances in excess thereof at a period rate of **0.03287%** per day, for an **Annual Percentage Rate** of **12%**. The minimum **Finance Charge** in any billing period is **50¢** except that no **Finance Charge** is imposed on an average daily balance of less than **$5**.

COLLECTION

In the event your account is referred to an attorney for collection, a reasonable attorney's fee, not to exceed **20%** will be added to the amount due.

ADVANCES

You may repay advances on an extended basis by paying the instalment of (a) not less than **1/36th** of the total unpaid amount of advances (including **Finance Charges** and fines, if any) outstanding computed as of the time of the most recent advance or **$5**, whichever is greater, (b) a **Finance Charge** at a rate of **0.03287%** per day on the average unpaid principal amount of the advances from time to time outstanding from the date each written request therefor is posted to your account or, if made by check, after mailing thereof, and (c) a service fee of **25¢**, included in the **Finance Charge**, for each cash advance. A minimum payment is rounded up to the next highest dollar. A **Finance Charge** (including the service fee) as described above, is due whether or not payments are extended. The **Annual Percentage Rate** on an advance is **12%**.

(Continued on Other Side)

How to Handle Your Own Contracts

Security Interest and Default

In transactions of this type, the seller retains an interest in the goods purchased, and if the purchaser fails to make one of the prearranged payments, the seller may under certain circumstances take back the goods sold. This interest is technically a *security interest* or lien.

A security interest is generally defined as an interest in personal property (or fixtures) which secure payment or performance of an obligation. In non-legal terms, this essentially means that the seller retains a legal interest or right in the property which he sells and delivers to the obligor until he has made his final payment. If he fails to pay as agreed, the seller has a legal right to take back that property in order to satisfy the debt (i.e., the purchase price plus finance charges up to the time of nonpayment).

There is no express definition of "default" in the Uniform Commercial Code. Generally, those acts which will constitute the purchaser's default will be defined in the retail installment contract which he enters into with the seller. The consumer should be aware of the terms constituting a default before he enters into such an agreement. The law favors the creditor in protecting his rights once a default has occurred. If obligor finds himself in this position, the aid of an attorney is highly recommended.

Once the purchaser has paid more than 60% of the cash price of the goods secured, he is deemed to have an equitable interest in the goods and is entitled to notice from the seller of the manner in which those goods will be disposed to satisfy the debt. Unless otherwise agreed, the debtor may redeem the goods by tending full payment sufficient to meet the balance of the debt due and owing, plus any expenses reasonably incurred by the seller. Once the seller has disposed of the goods, he must notify the debtor as to the amount received for such goods. If the amount received is in excess of the balance due and owing, the debtor is entitled to the difference, less reasonable expenses incurred by the seller. If the amount recovered is less than the balance due

and owing, the debtor continues to remain obligated for that difference. In actuality, the disposition of goods after a default never results in a surplus. The debtor is always responsible for something more.

In light of the foregoing, the obligor should be sure of the terms and amounts to be paid, how they are to be paid, the definition of default, and if he has the financial means to meet his contractual obligation. If he does not follow these precautions explicitly, he is exposing himself to unimagined heartaches and legal entanglements. The law protects the buyer before he takes the goods home, and the seller after that.

Disclosure Requirements

If the sale is under a closed end credit agreement, the creditor must disclose the following: cash price of the property or services purchased; down payment credited; other charges that are part of credit extended but not part of the finance charge; total amount to be financed (purchase price plus other charges, less down payment); amount of finance charge in an annual percentage (except when finance charge does not exceed $5.00 and the amount financed does not exceed $75.00; or finance charge does not exceed $7.50 and amount financed exceeds $75.00); the number, amount, and due dates of payments for repayment; terms of default, delinquency, or similar charges payable in the event of late payments; a description of any security interest held or to be acquired by the creditor; and a clear identification of the property to which the security interest will apply. A creditor may not divide a consumer credit sale into two or more sales to avoid the disclosure of an annual percentage rate. The above disclosure must be made to the obligor before the credit is extended. This information may be contained in the contract which evidences the indebtedness of the purchaser. The obligor should be sure that he reads the retail installment contract carefully before signing it. If what is stated is unclear he should ask for an explanation. He should not sign the retail installment contract until he is certain of its terms and conditions.

The purchaser also is entitled to a filled-in copy of the retail installment contract. If it is not delivered to him at the time of the sale, it must be mailed to him at the address stated in the contract. Until the seller does so, the buyer who has not received the goods or services has an unconditional right to cancel and to receive an immediate refund of all payments made. [New York Personal Property Law, 405]. Most contracts of this type state on their face as follows, "I acknowledge receipt of a copy of this agreement." The obligor should be certain that he receives a completed copy signed by the seller. This acknowledgment means that he is presumed to have received a completed copy of the contract.

When the obligor has finished making all of the payments under the contract, and there is no balance outstanding, he may request in writing that the seller send him a release. This will acknowledge full payment and release of all security interests in the property.

Prohibited Terms and Conditions

There are certain terms and conditions which the seller may not include in the retail installment contract. If any one of the following clauses appear, the law considers them void, however, they do not invalidate the remainder of the contract. These clauses are as follows:

(1) The holder (seller) may not arbitrarily, and without reasonable cause, accelerate the amount owed in the absence of the buyer's default.

(2) The seller may not require a power of attorney to confess judgment or assign wages.

(3) The seller or holder of the contract is not given authority to enter upon the purchaser's premises unlawfully

or to commit any breach of the peace in the repossession of the goods.

(4) The purchaser is not required to waive or give up any right of action against seller or holder for any illegal act committed in the collection of payments or repossession of the goods.

(5) The purchaser is not required to give a power of attorney naming the seller or holder as the purchaser's agent in either collection of payments of repossession of the goods.

(6) The purchaser is not required to relieve the seller from any liability for any legal remedies which the purchaser may have against the seller.

Assignment

There may be occasions when the seller chooses to assign or sell the retail installment contract to a third person. Generally speaking, this is perfectly legal. However, the *assignee* (third party purchaser of the installment contract) must notify the obligor of the assignment. There are two important points he should keep in mind upon receipt of this notification. First, he is thereafter required to make his monthly payments to the assignee, since he now owns the contract. Also, if the obligor pays the original seller by mistake, he loses his money if he cannot locate the original seller and must still pay the assignee. (Don't throw away the notification of assignment.) Second, upon notification of the assignment, the purchaser has ten days to notify the assignee in writing of any defects of the goods received from the seller or of the seller's incomplete performance of all his agreements with the purchaser. If the purchaser does not do this he is obligated to pay the assignee the full price regardless of whether or not the goods or services received were defective. [New York Personal Property Law, 403 (3) (a).]

106

Door-to-Door Sales

Section 425 of the Personal Property Law of the State of New York deals with home solicitation sales. This is defined as a consumer transaction in which the payment of the purchase price is deferred over time and the seller or his representative is a person who does business by means of personal solicitation at a place other than the place of business of the seller or his representative.

In a transaction of this nature, the purchaser has the right to cancel the sale up until midnight of the third business day after the day on which he signs the agreement. The cancellation must be in writing, properly addressed with prepaid postage and deposited in a mailbox. This right of cancellation does not exist where the purchaser has requested the seller to provide the goods without delay because of an emergency, and where seller has commenced performance of the contract in good faith, before notice of cancellation is received. In the case of goods which cannot be returned to the seller in substantially the same condition as when received by the purchaser, the purchaser must reimburse the seller for the reasonable value of the goods. The seller must also provide the purchaser with a printed card which the purchaser may use to cancel the sale.

The purchaser is entitled to a return of his down payment. Under certain circumstances, the seller is entitled to a cancellation fee of 5% of the cash (purchase) price, but not to exceed the amount of the cash down payment.

The purchaser is required to return any goods received if the seller so requests after cancellation, but the purchaser need not deliver them at any place other than his residence. The purchaser must also take reasonable care of those goods for a reasonable time (defined as forty days).

Credit Card Application

This is an application for an open end credit agreement, commonly known as a credit card application. Most of the terms and provisions are self-explanatory.

In any of these applications the obligor should always remember two things:

(1) They are designed to protect the credit card issuer.

(2) Whatever information the obligor fills in should be as accurate as possible. Organizations that issue credit cards generally trade information on credit status and background. If he is dishonest, the issuer will probably discover it, and he will never again be considered for a credit card.

Page (1) is strictly informational and needs no explanation. Page (2) is the meat of the agreement.

No finance charge may be computed if the full amount of the purchase (indebtedness) is paid within the time stated. In this case, it is 25 days. This is a good example of wise use of a credit card. Having already been extended 25 days credit free, the obligor, through proper management of his finances can take full advantage of a prolonged period of credit.

Usually the obligor must make a minimum monthly payment, as stated in the particular contract which he has entered into. In this case, the minimum monthly payment must be 1/36th of the new balance or $5.00, whichever is greater, plus the finance charge.

The finance charge is determined on the basis of the average unpaid balance from the previous month. This is computed as follows: In New York State the charge may be:

(1) 0.04931% per day which is an annual percentage of 18% on an average daily balance of $500.00 or less; and

(2) 0.03287% per day which is annual percentage rate of 12% per annum on the average daily balance in excess of $500.00.

107

The minimum finance charge is 50¢ if the average daily balance is more than $5.00.

The attorney's fees which may be collected from you in the event your account is referred to an attorney for collection may be a maximum of 20% of the amount due and is to be added to that value.

In the event of a cash advance, the credit card issuer may levy a finance charge of 0.03287% per day (12% yearly) from the date of the advance, regardless of when it is repaid. In this instance, there is no grace period and interest will be charged from the moment the cash is advanced.

If the obligor defaults in any payment of a cash advance, the credit card issuer may charge a fine not in excess of 4¢ per dollar on the amount unpaid for a period in excess of ten days. In no event is the fine to exceed $5.00, and any fine imposed is, or will be, in addition to the finance charge.

Upon signature of the application and delivery to the credit card issuer, the obligor makes an offer. Upon receipt and signing of the credit card, the obligor accepts all of the conditions stated in the credit card application. This now becomes a binding contract. None of the terms are negatable. If the card is not returned, the obligor is bound by all terms and provisions.

Retail Installment Contract (Security Agreement)

This is the standard "buy now, pay later" time installment contract.

Page (1) begins with the identity of the parties to the contract. The clause begins with, "Buyer hereby purchases . . . and grants a security interest," to the seller in the property listed on the blank lines. The security interest discussed earlier is subject to the terms and conditions contained within this contract.

The clause beginning with the statement "This contract is not . . ." is the essence of a retail installment contract. It recites the buyer's obligation to pay the seller the total amount due under the contract. It breaks the payments down into equal monthly installments, with the first installment due and payable one month from the date of the transaction. Generally, a balloon payment will be the last payment due on the contract. Simply said, the final payment is a balloon payment, if it is more than twice as large as the normal monthly payment. The governing calculations appear in the box on the right hand side of page (1).

The seller has a right to require that insurance be obtained to protect the seller in the event of damage or loss of the goods, although the buyer may choose the insurance carrier.

In this particular contract, there is a default charge in the event of late payment. This provision is inherent in most installment agreements and usually cannot be avoided.

As for prepayment rebates, if the purchaser (buyer) pays the total outstanding amount due before the time required by the contract, he is entitled to recover from the seller a pro-rated rebate of the finance charge for that period of time when credit was offered but not used.

The Federal Truth In Lending Act, referred to under disclosure, is in fact, the Consumer Credit Protection Act, discussed previously.

If a person is asked to sign as a guarantor, he must remember that he becomes equally liable on the contract. In fact, the seller may recover from him alone without having to attempt collection from the buyer. It is recommended that a person does not sign as guarantor unless he personally knows the buyer and can be reasonably sure of his financial stability and responsibility.

Page (2):

Clause 1 and 2 are self-explanatory.

Clause 3 is clear and legally enforceable, with the exception of that portion relating to appointment of the seller as attorney in fact. In New York, for example, that portion has been invalidated by statute. If the purchaser (buyer) defaults in the insurance premiums required to insure the property, the seller may pay such premiums and charge the buyer.

108

Clause 4 deals with assignment of the retail installment contract. The obligor should remember that he has 10 days after notification of the assignment to inform the assignee in writing of any defects in the goods or failure of the seller to perform the contract.

Clause 5 is self-explanatory.

Clause 6 requires that the buyer care for the goods as if they belonged to the seller. In effect, they do. Remember, the seller has a legal interest in the goods until they are fully paid for. If any damage does occur to the goods, the buyer must notify the seller promptly.

Clause 7 requires honesty. When a person trades in something in order to buy something else, he is required to make sure that no one else has any interest in those goods.

Clause 8 is an acceleration clause. In essence, it states that if the buyer does not live up to his obligations called for in the contract, the entire unpaid balance shall, at the option of the seller, without demand or notice of any kind, become immediately due and payable. Other charges will be assessed to the buyer in the execution of this acceleration procedure. Other events listed in Clause 8 may also cause acceleration of payment (e.g., if the collateral is impaired). However, the main obligation of the buyer is to make payments as agreed. Failure to do this is the major reason behind defaults.

Clause 9 is self-explanatory and has been discussed previously.

Clause 10 allows the seller to accept one late payment without waiving his right to accelerate the debt if a late payment occurs again.

Oral agreements made before the contract is signed but not incorporated into the final contract are not legally enforceable and are useless. Oral agreements made after the contract is signed are just as useless. If the parties want a modification or change, it should be put in writing and the seller and buyer should sign it.

The first sentence of Clause 11 has been dealt with previously. To summarize it briefly, it states that any clause which might be prohibited or invalidated by later law will not affect the validity of the remainder of the contract. That clause, and only that clause, will be invalid. There is some question as to whether or not the second sentence of Clause 11 is valid as it presently appears, however warranties in sales contracts are discussed in another chapter of the book.

109

RETAIL INSTALLMENT CONTRACT (SECURITY AGREEMENT)

Dated..19........

Buyer...

Seller..

street address (residence)..

street address..

city & state.................................zip..........telephone

city & state.................................zip..........telephone

BUYER HEREBY PURCHASES the following articles of personal property and accessories thereto (hereinafter referred to as the "chattels") and grants a security interest in the chattels and proceeds therefrom to Seller

subject to the terms and conditions on the face and reverse sides of this contract:...

....

....

....

....

....

Cash Price	$.................................	
Sales Tax, if any	————————————	
Cash Price plus Sales Tax	$.................................	

THIS CONTRACT IS NOT PAYABLE IN INSTALLMENTS OF EQUAL AMOUNTS. BUYER HEREBY AGREES

TO pay Seller the Total of Payments in..............................equal monthly installments of

$............................ each, the first installment to be due and payable one month from the date hereof and all subsequent equal monthly installments on even date in each successive month thereafter, and

AN INSTALLMENT OF $....................... **WILL BE DUE AND PAYABLE ON**...............................**19**........

which payment ☐ is ☐ is not a BALLOON PAYMENT (a final payment is a balloon payment if it is more than twice the amount of the equal monthly installment).

(1) Cash Price (include taxes if they are to be financed)	$_____	
(2) Total Downpayment		
Cash	$_____	
Trade in	$_____	
(Items Traded:..........................)	_____	
(3) Unpaid Balance of Cash Price (1) minus (2)	$_____	
(4) Other Charges:		
physical damage insurance	$_____	
creditor insurance	$_____	
	$_____	
	$_____	
	$_____	
official fees	$_____	
(5) Amount Financed (3) + (4)	$_____	
Accrues from............19........		
(6) **FINANCE CHARGE**	$_____	
(7) Total of Payments (5) + (6)	$_____	
(8) Deferred Payment Price (2) + (7)	$_____	
(9) **ANNUAL PERCENTAGE RATE**	_____%	

INSURANCE AGREEMENT

(a) Cost of required physical damage insurance $........................ BUYER MAY CHOOSE PERSON THROUGH WHICH THIS INSURANCE IS TO BE OBTAINED.

(b) Cost of creditor insurance: ☐ Life $........................ ☐ Disability $........................ CREDITOR INSURANCE IS NOT REQUIRED BY SELLER
☐ I desire creditor insurance checked above ☐ I do not desire creditor insurance

....................19........   ....19........
date   Buyer's signature   date   Buyer's signature

SECURITY INTEREST Seller retains title to, and shall have a security interest and lien in and upon the chattels, the proceeds therefrom, all equipment at any time added thereto and returned or unearned premiums from insurance policies on the chattels, to secure payment and performance of Buyer's obligations in this contract. Any additional indebtedness representing amounts which may be expended by Seller (1) in release or discharge of taxes, liens and incumbrances and (2) to procure required physical damage insurance on the chattels shall also be secured by this contract.

DEFAULT CHARGE IN THE EVENT OF LATE PAYMENT If any installment is not paid within 10 days after it is due, a charge will be payable by Buyer as follows: **5%** of the unpaid installment or **$5** whichever is less.

ATTORNEY'S FEES CHARGE IN THE EVENT OF DEFAULT In the event of any default reasonable attorney's fees and costs of collection will be charged where permitted by law and as more fully set forth on the reverse side of this contract.

TIME IS OF THE ESSENCE OF THIS CONTRACT.

PREPAYMENT REBATE Upon prepayment in full Buyer is entitled to a rebate of the **FINANCE CHARGE** in accordance with the rule of 78. No rebate less than **$1** will be paid

Disclosure statements pursuant to state law that are inconsistent with the Federal Truth In Lending Act:........................

....

NOTICE TO BUYER (1) Do not sign this contract before you read it, or if it contains any blank spaces. (2) You are entitled to a completely filled in copy of this agreement (3) Under the law, you have the right to pay off in advance the full amount due and under certain conditions to obtain a partial refund of the credit service charge.

IN WITNESS WHEREOF, each Buyer signing below executes this contract and acknowledges receipt of a completely filled in Buyer's copy of this contract executed by Seller on the date and in the year first above written.

RETAIL INSTALLMENT CONTRACT

How to Handle Your Own Contracts

ADDITIONAL CONDITIONS AND AGREEMENTS FORMING PART OF RETAIL INSTALLMENT CONTRACT

1. The term Seller, as used herein, includes assignees and subsequent holders of this contract. The term Buyer, as used herein, shall mean all persons jointly and severally who sign this contract as Buyer.

2. Seller reserves the right to refuse to accept an insurer offered by Buyer, for reasonable cause, and if said right of refusal is exercised Buyer may choose another person through which the insurance is to be obtained.

3. Risk of loss or destruction of, or injury to the chattels shall at all times be in Buyer and no such occurrence shall release Buyer's obligations herein. Buyer hereby assigns to Seller, all moneys not in excess of the unpaid balance hereunder which may become payable under any insurance including returned or unearned premiums, and directs any insurance company to make payment direct to the holder of this contract to be applied to said unpaid balance and appoints said holder as Attorney in Fact to endorse any draft and to sign any proof of loss. Should insurance policy be cancelled, Buyer agrees to replace same with equivalent coverage before effective date of cancellation. Should Buyer fail to so replace such coverage, Seller may, but is not obligated to, obtain such coverage for the remainder of the term of this contract or such period beyond the term as is required by the insurance company issuing such replacing coverage, whereupon Buyer agrees to pay forthwith to Seller any additional premium incurred upon demand therefor.

4. Buyer hereby acknowledges notice that this contract may be assigned and that any assignee will rely upon the agreements contained in this paragraph, and agrees that the liability of Buyer to any assignee shall be immediate and absolute and not affected by any default whatsoever of Seller signing this contract. Buyer agrees not to assert any claim or defense arising out of this sale against any assignee who acquires this contract in good faith and for value and who has no notice of the facts giving rise to the claim or defense within 10 days after such assignee mails to Buyer, at his address as it appears in this contract, notice of such assignment identifying this contract. The foregoing shall not affect the rights of Buyer to pursue any remedies he may have against Seller. Seller shall not be deemed to act as agent of any assignee in the making of this contract or the collection of any moneys due herein, or for any other purpose.

5. Buyer agrees to pay all costs of filing any financing, continuation and termination statements necessary to perfect and keep perfected Seller's title to the chattels and to promptly pay all taxes, levies and other impositions levied thereon or imposed by reason of its use or in any manner assessed on this contract and the accompanying documents.

6. Buyer shall keep the chattels at the address of Buyer on the face of this contract and will not permit their removal without the prior written consent of Seller. Buyer shall maintain the chattels in good condition and repair and shall not use or permit them to be used for hire or any illegal purpose. Buyer shall not sell, abandon, exchange, lease or otherwise dispose of the chattels or any of Buyer's rights therein or under this contract or in order to grant any further security interest in the chattels. Buyer shall not injure, conceal, abandon, damage or destroy the chattels nor erase or deface any identifying marks, serial marks, serial numbers, or any identification thereon nor do or permit anything to be done which may impair the value of the chattels or of the security intended to be afforded by this contract. Buyer agrees to give immediate written notice to Seller of any loss of or damage to the chattels.

7. Buyer warrants the truth of all statements made herein and in any credit application in connection with this contract, and further warrants and represents that the chattels traded in, if any, are free from any lien, security interest, encumbrance or other charge.

8. If Buyer fails to comply with any of the terms and conditions or fails to perform any of the obligations of Buyer in this contract or if any statement, representation or warranty in any application in connection with this contract is untrue in any respect, or in the event of the death, incompetency, bankruptcy, or insolvency of Buyer, or if Seller with reasonable cause shall deem itself insecure or its collateral impaired, or in the event of the loss or destruction of the collateral, the entire unpaid balance shall, at the option of Seller, without demand or notice of any kind, become immediately due and payable, together with attorneys fees of 15% of the unpaid balance and costs and expenses of collection if this contract is placed for collection with an attorney not a salaried employee of the holder of this contract. In any such event Seller may, subject to any restrictions imposed by law, then or at any time thereafter, without demand or notice of any kind, enter upon any premises where the chattels may be found or may be supposed to be and take possession of and remove the chattels with the aid and assistance of any person without process of law. Upon demand by Seller, Buyer shall make the chattels available to Seller at a place designated by Seller reasonably convenient to Buyer and Seller. In the event of repossession of the chattels by legal process or otherwise, Seller shall have the remedies of a secured party under the Uniform Commercial Code including the right to retain from proceeds of the disposition of said chattels attorneys' fees and costs and expenses of collection as provided above and other legal expenses incurred for the purpose of retaking and disposing of said chattels.

9. Any requirement of notice to Buyer shall be met if written notice is mailed, postage prepaid, to the address of Buyer shown on the face of this contract or such other address as Buyer may specify in writing to Seller, at least five (5) days before the time of the sale or disposition or other happening requiring notice.

10. Failure or delay by Seller to exercise any right herein or acceptance by Seller of payment of any instalment due under this contract after the same has become due or after notice of any other default, shall not constitute a waiver of such default or of the right of Seller to exercise any right or remedy hereunder. No waiver of any default shall be deemed to be a waiver of any other or subsequent default, and all remedies hereunder are cumulative and not alternative. This contract may not be changed or terminated orally. Seller is authorized to correct any and all patent errors herein. Buyer hereby authorizes Seller to file such financing statement or statements as Seller shall deem necessary or desirable under the Uniform Commercial Code, signed only by Seller. No other extension of credit exists or is to be made in connection with this contract or the purchase transaction represented hereby.

11. If any provision of this contract shall be prohibited by or invalid under law, such provision shall be ineffective to the extent of such prohibition or invalidity without invalidating the remainder of such provision or the remaining provisions herein. This contract constitutes the entire agreement between the parties hereto; there are no oral representations, understandings or warranties. UNLESS OTHERWISE AGREED BETWEEN THE PARTIES HERETO IN WRITING, THERE ARE NO WARRANTIES WHICH EXTEND BEYOND THE DESCRIPTION ON THE FACE HEREOF; SPECIFICALLY THERE IS NO WARRANTY OF MERCHANTIBILITY OR OF FITNESS FOR A PARTICULAR PURPOSE.

ASSIGNMENT BY SELLER

FOR VALUE RECEIVED, receipt whereof is hereby acknowledged, undersigned hereby sells, assigns, transfers and sets over to

its successors and assigns (herein called the Assignee) the Retail Instalment Contract attached hereto (herein called the "Contract") together with all the rights and benefits of undersigned therein, hereby granting full power to Assignee either in its own name or in the name of the undersigned, to take all such legal or other proceedings which the undersigned could have taken but for this assignment. It is agreed, however, that undersigned shall remain liable under the Contract to perform undersigned's obligations thereunder or in connection therewith, and that Assignee shall not be required or obligated in any manner to perform any of the undersigned's obligations thereunder, nor shall Assignee have any obligation or liability by reason of or arising out of this assignment.

Undersigned represents and warrants with respect to the Contract that (a) it evidences a bona fide sale of the goods and/or services described therein to Buyer all as set forth therein; (b) the statements made therein are in all respects true and correct; (c) the down payment was made by Buyer in cash, unless otherwise specified, and no part thereof was loaned or paid either directly or indirectly to Buyer by the undersigned or any of the undersigned's representatives, (d) the sale of the goods and/or services was effected and performed in accordance with all laws and regulations affecting the same; (e) Buyer and Guarantor(s), if any, were over 21 years of age and had the capacity to contract; (f) the Contract and Guaranty, if any, are valid and enforceable in accordance with their terms; (g) the name(s) and signature(s) on the Contract and Guaranty, if any, are not forged, fictitious or assumed and are genuine in all respects; (h) no dispute with or claim by Buyer exists and there are and will be no defenses, set offs or counterclaims by Buyer; (i) a completely filled in copy was delivered to Buyer at the time of execution; (j) an executed copy of the Guaranty, if any, was delivered to Guarantor(s) immediately upon its execution, and (k) the goods and/or services have been delivered and/or furnished to and accepted by Buyer unless otherwise stated therein.

If any of the foregoing representations and warranties is breached or be untrue, or if Buyer gives notice to Assignee that Buyer is in any way dissatisfied with the goods and/or services or that Buyer has or may have a claim or defense arising out of the sale of the goods or services within 10 days after Assignee mails to Buyer notice of this assignment, or if any of the services described in the Contract are to be performed or rendered more than 10 days after Assignee mails to Buyer such notice of this assignment and Buyer gives notice to Assignor claiming that the undersigned has not furnished or rendered such services, the undersigned agrees, upon demand, to repurchase the Contract from Assignee and to pay therefor in cash the unpaid balance due thereon less unearned finance charges.

This assignment is made subject to all the terms, covenants, representations and warranties contained in any agreement in effect between the undersigned and Assignee on the date hereof.

Dated_____19_____ . _____ _____

                                          Seller - Agent   Title

Buying On Credit

CHAPTER 9

Assignments, Proxies, and Power of Attorney

Introduction to Assignments

One day, in need of a widget or two, Billie Buyer shuffles down to Willie's Widget Store and agrees with Willie that if he will deliver widgets, Billie will remit payment to him. A fortnight or two later, upon receipt of the first batch of widgets, Billie drafts a check payable to Willie only to be informed that Willie has assigned his rights to Cary's Collecting Agency and that his check instead should be made out to Cary. Must he do so? What if the widgets do not meet up to his expectations? Must he even pay at all? In short, what is an *assignment* and how does it affect the involved parties, Billie the debtor, Willie the creditor or assignor and Cary, the assignee?

It is always satisfying to have an historical perspective in attempting to understand any concept. At common law, assignments were invalid, the reasoning being that contracts were personal to the parties making them and one party should not find himself liable to a third party with whom he had not initially dealt. Eventually, a method was devised to circumvent the law by granting a prospective assignee a *power of attorney* (an agency relationship which will be explained shortly), to act as the assignor's collecting agent. The granting of the power gained further characteristics of modern day assignment when the courts began to consider the power irrevocable and the attorney an irrevocable agent of the creditor.

Today an assignment creates a definite legal interest which cannot be denied or go unrecognized. It is easily created by stating that,

"I, Willie, assign to Cary all my rights in my contract with Billie." In some instances, the assignment must be in writing, such as where the assignee is succeeding to rights in a signed security agreement, collateral, or contract covering goods exceeding $5,000 in value. In essence, an assignment simply transfers rights from one party to another; as between the assignor and assignee, a transaction is as final as a sale. After the event, the assignee has all of the rights that the assignor previously had and the assignor becomes totally divested of rights.

Assignments of Rights

To be final, an assignment must meet certain requirements of a contract. If the assignor transfers a right to the assignee, it logically follows that in return the assignor should be compensated for its loss. As in a contract, the assignor must receive consideration which consummates the assignment and makes it irrevocable. An assignment can be made by gift, if delivery of some object signifying the right is made to the assignee who thereby acquires dominion and control over the object. This control signals the irrevocability of the act, an essential element of an assignment. Thus, if a person wishes to assign a life insurance policy gratuitously, the assignment would not be complete until the assignee received the policy.

In order for a person to assign a right which he possesses, the right must be an assignable one. What is an assignable right? As in the widget case, the right that has been created is usually the result of a creditor-debtor relationship. The creditor has a right to payment which he can freely transfer to a third party, since by so doing the debtor's rights and duties are not affected. This test is administered to an assignment to determine whether or not it is valid. If the debtor's position is affected in any way, then the assignment fails. Examples of nonassignable rights are where the exercise of the right is personal, where the assignment materially changes the duty of the other party or varies his risk or where the other party's chance of receiving his bargained for return performance is materially impaired. Additionally, the parties can prohibit assignments at the outset, thus making all rights under the contract nonassignable. A mere promise not to assign, however, does not prohibit the assignment, but instead results in a breach of the contract in the event of such a transaction.

Delegation of Duties

A companion concept of the assignment of rights is the *delegation of duties*. Usually the possession of a right carries with it a concomitant obligation which must be fulfilled. In the widget case, Willie's right to receive payment is extinguished, if he fails in his duty to supply the quantity and type of widgets agreed upon.

The next question is whether the assignor in parting with his rights has also transferred his duties to the assignee. This does not mean that all duties can be delegated, for similar to rights, a duty cannot be delegated if it is personal to the assignor, mandatory under the original contract or substantially alters the performance to be received by one of the initial parties. For example, if the act alters the performance required of the assignor which involves specific skills or is based on a relationship of trust, it will not be delegable. Duties that are otherwise nondelegable can become so once the initial party to the contract agrees to the delegation or waives his right to object by accepting the assignee's services or goods.

Rights and Liabilities

Only the positions of assignor and assignee are affected by a valid assignment. As between themselves, the assignor confers implied warranties upon the assignee for value. These warranties are breached where the assignor did not possess the enforceable or genuine right that he claimed to have. In addition, the assignor cannot interfere with the assignee's newly acquired rights. Should the assignor intercede and receive payments which belong to the assignee as a result of the assignment, the assignee has several courses of action available to him in order to recover his due. An attorney can always guide a wronged assignee, assisting him in realizing his interest through an action for conversion, for restitution or breach of the warranties mentioned above.

The assignor and assignee both assume further responsibilities other than those to each other. If along with all rights, the assignor transfers his duties to the assignee, the assignee becomes liable for failure of performance to both his assignor and the other contracting party. This position occurs only where the assignee, now a delegatee, expressly assumes the duty. This assumption is implied, however where the contract assigned is one dealing with personal property. Otherwise, the general rule followed in New York and the majority of states is that no automatic assumption of duties results from an assignment.

Throughout the transaction, the assignor remains liable to the party with whom he contracted. The assignee may be bound to perform all of the duties to which the assignor agreed, but the assignor is still not released from his obligation. A *novation*, or complete discharge, can free the assignor from all responsibility and create a contract as between the original contracting party and the assignee, but only if the former agrees to the substitution.

Suppose in the widget case, Willie failed to perform as agreed and Cary began to demand payment; what rights does Billie have? In general, Billie should remember that the assignee has no greater rights than his assignor. Since non-

113

General Assignment

THAT

for value received, ha   sold and by these presents do   grant, assign and convey unto

TO HAVE AND TO HOLD *the same unto the said*

executors, administrators and assigns forever, to and for the use of

hereby constituting and appointing
true and lawful attorney irrevocable in   name, place and stead, for the purposes aforesaid, to ask, demand, sue for, attach, levy, recover and receive all such sum and sums of money which now are, or may hereafter become due, owing and payable for, or on account of all or any of the accounts, dues, debts, and demands above assigned

giving and granting unto the said attorney full power and authority to do and perform all and every act and thing whatsoever requisite and necessary, as fully, to all intents and purposes, as   might or could do, if personally present, with full power of substitution and revocation, hereby ratifying and confirming all that the said attorney or   substitute shall lawfully do, or cause to be done by virtue hereof.

    IN WITNESS WHEREOF,   *have hereunto set   hand and seal the* day of   *one thousand nine hundred and*

SIGNED, SEALED AND DELIVERED
IN THE PRESENCE OF

performance would have been a successful defense against Willie, it likewise would be a good defense against his assignee. This does not permit Billie to pay Willie after he knows about the assignment and claim fulfillment of his duties under the contract when Cary sues for payment. Failure of consideration, fraud or lack of an essential element which would lead to a defect in the contract between the original parties, will result in the same defect with the assignee as a party. The problem becomes overly complicated where the claim against Willie asserted by Billie is not one arising from the contractual arrangement itself, and is being used to reduce or offset the assignee's claim. Local law varies and legal counsel would be able to explain the viability of one's position in a particular situation.

This discussion of assignments is a brief overview. At best, the reader now has some knowledge of what occurs as a result of an assignment and, in particular, some of the rights and liabilities of the parties. The list is by no means exhaustive and was offered in an effort to give more credibility to the documents. The specific examples of assignments shown in the text are also brief and for the most part follow the general rules outlined. This is not to say that the law governing the substantive transaction is not intricate and massive, for each assignment mentioned carries with it legal implications beyond the range of this book. Still, a basic comprehension and review of the forms should benefit the reader.

Examples of Assignment

General Assignment

The general assignment is the example of Willie, Billie and Cary and the purported assignment between the latter. The declaration of an intent to assign is sufficient and the transfer of the right is "for value," thereby becoming irrevocable. The form embellishes upon the basic concept only to the extent that the assignee appoints another person to be attorney-in-fact, to demand, receive, and perform "all and every act . . . necessary." to meet the purpose of the assignment.

Mortgage Assignment

A mortgage is like other rights under law or chose in action in that it may be freely assigned in most instances. One problem with mortgages, however, is that it is either an equitable or legal land interest and, as such, state law may require it to be in writing. In New York, statutes outline other essentials, illustrate short form mortgage assignments and dictate rules of construction such as the words of assignment in a mortgage and bond or note which grant the assignee full power of attorney to act in the assignor's stead. Other states require that the assignment meet all the formalities of deeds.

This particular mortgage assignment states the parties involved in the immediate transaction, the assignor and assignee, the maker of the mortgage initially, and the information identifying it:

(1) amount of original mortgage with interest

(2) date of execution

(3) date and place of recordation

(4) description of encumbered property.

Additionally, since the debt and mortgage in many jurisdictions, such as New York, must follow one another, reference is made to the assignment of the "note or obligation described in said mortgage." Finally, the assignor warrants that the amount of the current mortgage is accurate.

Lease Assignment

A lease assignment is explained adequately in the discussion of leases. Examination of the form reveals the essentials: the entirety of the lease term is covered and the assignee ac-

Assignment of Proprietary Lease

Know That

Assignor,

in consideration of the sum of

($) dollars,

paid by

Assignee,

and for other good and valuable consideration, does hereby assign unto the Assignee a certain proprietary lease dated

19 by and between

Lessor, and

Lessee,

covering apartment in the building known as

To Have and To Hold the same unto the Assignee and Assignee's personal representatives and

assigns, on and after 19 the effective date, for the balance of the term of the proprietary lease, and any renewals or extensions thereof, and subject to the covenants, conditions and limitations therein contained.

In order to induce the Lessor to consent to this assignment and Assignee to accept this assignment, the Assignor represents to Lessor and Assignee that:

a) Assignor has full right, title and authority to assign the shares and the proprietary lease appurtenant thereto,

b) Assignor has fully performed all the terms, covenants and conditions of the proprietary lease on Assignor's part to be performed to the effective date hereof,

c) Assignor has not done or suffered anything to be done which might impose any liability on the Lessor or Assignee, and

d) There are no claims, security interests or liens against the proprietary lease, or the shares in the Lessor corporation allocated to the apartment to which the proprietary lease is appurtenant, or to any fixtures and/or personal property installed by Assignor in the apartment.

Assignment of Mortgage With Covenant

KNOW THAT

, assignor,

in consideration of

dollars,

paid by

, assignee

hereby assigns unto the assignee, a certain mortgage made by

given to secure payment of the sum of

dollars

and interest, dated the   day of   , 19   , cepts all covenants and conditions of the assign-or's lease. The assignor also makes several warranties to both the lessor and assignee which are independent covenants having no impact on the efficacy of the assignment.

Assignment of Wages

The assignment of wages, salaries or other forms of earnings or compensation have been held to be assignable, since, generally, the assignor has vested interest in the payment. The vested interest and assignability disappear where payment is conditional and no current contract evidences the obligation out of which the interest rises or no existing arrangement indicates the availability of a pool of funds to satisfy the interests.

As for wages, theory holds that the right to one's income is assignable although it is a right which for many unexpected reasons may not vest. Obviously, if the assignor terminates his employment at any time and terminates his income, the assignee possesses a hollow right. An employment contract will avoid the dilemma by vesting the otherwise potential interest.

An assignment of wages in a state which does not regulate the practice can have a debilitating effect on the welfare of the assignor if he is unable to manage his affairs on the lower income. Most states, fortunately, protect wage earners from possible myopia by limiting the assignment to a particular amount or percentage of the total salary or wage income. Other statutes void assignments for failure to stand up to statutory requirements.

The assignment form is straightforward, but the assignor should be certain to distinctly identify the goods and clearly describe the transactions involved, so as not to authorize the employer to pay out money to other potential creditors. Beyond that, the laws of most states have erected sufficient safeguards for the consumer-wage earner.

Assignment For the Benefit of Creditors

It would be hoped that no one need ever be in a position to make a general or special assignment for the benefit of creditors. In such an assignment, an assignor transfers rights to an assignee, the rights are in specific properties of the assignor and the assignee acts as trustee holding the property or proceeds for the benefit of the assignor's creditors. In short, it is a method by which a debtor can repay his creditors voluntarily without submitting to bankruptcy. Once the property is put in trust with the assignee, title passes irrevocably and the assignor retains no rights.

The law governing assignments for the benefit of creditors is too involved for discussion in this book, but examination and explanation of the form should answer minor questions which the reader may have. Since the final step is drastic and final, an attorney should always be consulted before the commitment is made.

Statutory law, for the most part, controls the operation of assignments for the benefit of creditors. Generally, the lack of exact compliance with the governing statute will not defeat the conveyance to the trustee unless the statute so dictates. In New York, the assignment must be in strict accordance with the statute and the law mandates that the entire instrument must be in writing, although other states permit oral assignments. In any case, the statutes must be checked for specific requirements.

The form allows for the identification of the parties, the assignor and assignee, and mention of the debtor's business and location. The creditors need not be included in the form and are not parties to the assignment unless so expressed. The area of concern is in the description of the property conveyed. If the property passing into the trust is to be only partnership property, for example, the assignor should be cautious not to be ambiguous and risk inclusion of personal property which he did not intend to

Assignment of Wages

KNOW ALL MEN BY THESE PRESENTS, THAT, I

being over 21 years of age, residing at

do hereby transfer, assign and set over unto

having a principal place of business at No.

herein referred to as "Assignee", and to said Assignee's legal representatives, successors and assigns, all of my salary, wages, commissions and compensation for services now or hereafter due and payable to me from

of   my present employer
and from any future or other employer, to the extent of 10 per centum thereof, payable on
of each *week, month,* until the obligation herein below described shall have been fully paid, satisfied and discharged, together with all lawful charges and interest thereon and I hereby authorize my said employer to pay 10 per centum of my salary, wages, or compensation as and when the same would become due and payable to me.

At present, I receive compensation in the sum of $ per

The consideration for this assignment and the transaction out of which it arises and to which it relates, together with a description of the goods sold or services rendered or other basis of indebtedness and the date on and place at which payments are to be made, is as follows:

This assignment is security only for above described transaction or series of transactions and no other assignment or order for the payment of my salary, wages, commissions or other compensation for services is subject to payment or exists in connection with same transaction or series of transactions, or in connection with any other transaction, and no levy on execution against said salary, wages, commissions or other compensation is in force.

I hereby acknowledge receipt of a copy of this assignment and of all papers executed by me attached to said assignment, together with a copy of all papers executed by me pertaining to the transaction or series of transactions herein described. This instrument may not be changed orally.

IN WITNESS WHEREOF, I have hereunto executed this assignment this   day of
          19   .

This is an Assignment of Wages, Salary, Commissions or Other Compensation for Services.

Witness: ....
                                                                Assignor

STATE OF   COUNTY OF   ss.:

On this   day of   19   , before me personally appeared
                                   to me known and known to me to be the individual described in
and who executed the foregoing assignment and   he duly acknowledged to me that   he executed the same.

The foregoing is a true and accurate copy of an original assignment duly executed by said
                              on   19   now in possession
of   and I so certify under my hand and seal this
           day of   19   .

....
                                                                Notary

General Assignment for Benefit of Creditors

WHEREAS *the part   of the first part   indebted to divers persons in sundry sums of money, which   unable to pay in full, and   desirous of providing for the payment of the same, so far as it is possible by a general assignment of all property for that purpose:*

NOW, THEREFORE, *the part   of the first part, in consideration of the premises and of the sum of one dollar paid by the part   of the second part, upon the ensealing and delivery of these presents, the receipt whereof is hereby acknowledged, ha   granted, bargained, sold, assigned, transferred and set over, and by these presents do   grant, bargain, sell, assign, transfer and set over, unto the part   of the second part   successors and assigns, all and singular the lands, tenements, hereditaments, appurtenances, goods, chattels, stock, promissory notes, claims, demands, property and effects of every description belonging to the part   of the first part, wherever the same may be, except such property as is exempt by law from levy and sale under an execution.*

TO HAVE AND TO HOLD *the same, and every part thereof, unto the said part   of the second part,   successors and assigns.*

IN TRUST, NEVERTHELESS, *to take possession of the same, and to sell the same with all reasonable dispatch, and to convert the same into money, and also to collect all such debts and demands hereby assigned as may be collectible, and out of all the proceeds of such sales and collections, to pay and discharge all the just and reasonable expenses, costs and disbursements in connection with the execution of this assignment and the discharge of the trust hereby created, together with the lawful commissions or allowances of the part   of the second part for   services in executing said trust;* THEN

AND *then to pay and discharge in full, if the residue of said proceeds is sufficient for that purpose, all the debts and liabilities now due or to grow due from the said part   of the first part, with all interest moneys due or to grow due thereon; and if the residue of said proceeds shall not be sufficient to pay the said debts and liabilities and interest thereon in full, then to apply the said residue of said proceeds to the payment of said debts and liabilities ratably and in proportion.*

AND *if, after the payment of all the said debts and liabilities in full, there shall be any remainder or residue of said property or proceeds, to repay and return the same to the said part   of the first part,   executors, administrators or assigns.*

AND, *in furtherance of the premises, the said part   of the first part do   hereby make, constitute and appoint the said part   of the second part   true and lawful attorney , irrevocable, with full power and authority to do all acts and things which may be necessary in the premises to the full execution of the trust hereby created, and to ask, demand, recover and receive of and from all and every person or persons all property, debts and demands due, owing and belonging to the said part   of the first part, and to give acquittances and discharges for the same; to sue, prosecute, defend and implead for the same; and to execute, acknowledge, and deliver all necessary deeds, instruments and conveyances: and for any of the purposes aforesaid to make, constitute and appoint one or more attorneys under him and at his pleasure to revoke the said appointments, hereby ratifying and confirming whatever the said part   of the second part or   substitutes shall lawfully do in the premises.*

AND *the said part   of the first part hereby authorize   the said part   of the second part to sign the name   of the said part   of the first part to any check, draft, promissory note or other instrument in writing which is payable to the order of the said part   of the first part, or to sign the name of the part   of the first part to any instrument in writing, whenever it shall be necessary so to do, to carry into effect the object, design and purpose of this trust.*

THE *said part   of the second part do   hereby accept the trust created and reposed in   by this instrument, and covenant   and agree   to and with the said part   of the first part that   will faithfully and without delay execute the said trust, according to the best of skill, knowledge and ability.*

assign. Such partial assignment, however, may not be a general assignment as covered by the form, since in most states a vital element of the assignment, whether executed under statute or common law, is that the transaction must divest the debtor of substantially his entire property and close out his current estate. Certain of debtor's property is exempt under the statutes, so this voluntary act, like forced bankruptcy, allows a person to retain some of his necessities for living such as clothes and working tools.

The trust arrangement is an explanation of the assignee's powers as trustee. These powers are generally spelled out by statute. The assignee must receive all property, give an accurate accounting to all those having a direct interest in the trust and then discharge the assignor's debts as set out in the agreement.

At this juncture, the assignor must list all debts and demands against him, making such provisions for preferences between creditors as the statutes permit. Whether preferences are prohibited within the assignment itself or within a specified time period prior to the assignment, are questions whose answers are so varied by local law that even general statements would be insufficient. Reference to local law in all of these instances is necessary. Once the preferential creditors are repaid, the remainder is used to pay remaining creditors in whole or ratably, depending on the amount of available funds.

The remainder of the instrument provides for a return of all unused proceeds or property to the assignor and appointment of the assignee as attorney-in-fact under a power of attorney for the assignor.

Powers of Attorney

In order to fully explain powers of attorney, one would have to run the gamut of agency laws. Such an endeavor would by impractical and not entirely necessary. Basically, a power is the authority to do that which the grantor of the power could legally do. Without it, the donee of the power does not have any right, actual, apparent or inherent, to perform the act for the grantor.

By now you may be confused by the mention of actual, apparent, or inherent authority. Suffice it to say for our purpose that a power of attorney is a form of actual authority in that the grantor formally expresses the agency relationship within a written agreement with the donee. Actual authority can be divided itself into expressed and implied authority; the former being the actual communication between the principal or grantor and agent or donee of the power; the latter being the extent of that power as the agent views it. Implied authority, in other words, is the agent's power to pursue all reasonable channels which in his estimation are necessary to fulfill the expressed authority.

A power of attorney, then, is delineated by the expressed grant of authority which the principal confers on the agent. These expressions of authority are construed just as all other contract provisions. The major difference with a power of attorney, however, is that the agency created is a special power and as such is restricted for all practical purposes to the four corners of the agency agreement. The reason for this is that the primary function of the written power is to evidence the existence and scope of the agent's authority to third parties. In his dealings with the agent, then, the third person should request to examine the written power in order to determine for himself whether the agent is within his authority. This becomes more apparent when the third party realizes that he is charged with full knowledge of the power of attorney regardless if he reads it or not.

Looking at the power of attorney in the text, the reader first notices the reference to New York Law. Besides the general rules offered here, statutory law further defines the limits of granted powers in most states. Before granting an agent any authority, the principal should consider the extent of his own words.

Next, the two parties, the principal and agent, are named. As the note suggests, if two attorneys-in-fact are designated, the principal should be careful to specify whether the power is to be exercised jointly or independently. This can be accomplished by inserting the word

121

Revocation of Power of Attorney

my attorney(s)-in-fact TO ACT

(a) If more than one agent is designated and the principal wishes each agent alone to be able to exercise the power conferred, insert in this blank the word "severally". Failure to make any insertion or the insertion of the word "jointly" will require the agents to act jointly.

First: in my name, place and stead in any way which I myself could do, if I were personally present, with respect to the following matters as each of them is defined in Title 15 of Article 5 of the New York General Obligations Law to the extent that I am permitted by law to act through an agent:

[Strike out and initial in the opposite box any one or more of the subdivisions as to which the principal does NOT desire to give the agent authority. Such elimination of any one or more of subdivisions (A) to (K), inclusive, shall automatically constitute an elimination also of subdivision (L).]

To strike out any subdivision the principal must draw a line through the text of that subdivision AND write his initials in the box opposite.

(A) real estate transactions;   [   ]

(B) chattel and goods transactions;   [   ]

(C) bond, share and commodity transactions;   [   ]

(D) banking transactions;   [   ]

(E) business operating transactions;   [   ]

(F) insurance transactions;   [   ]

(G) estate transactions;   [   ]

(H) claims and litigation;   [   ]

(I) personal relationships and affairs;   [   ]

(J) benefits from military service;   [   ]

(K) records, reports and statements;   [   ]

(L) all other matters;   [   ]

Second: with full and unqualified authority to delegate any or all of the foregoing powers to any person or persons whom my attorney(s)-in-fact shall select.

Third: To induce any third party to act hereunder, I hereby agree that any third party receiving a duly executed copy or facsimile of this instrument may act hereunder, and that revocation or termination hereof by operation of law or otherwise shall be ineffective as to such third party unless and until actual notice or knowledge of such revocation shall have been received by such third party, and I for myself and for my heirs, executors, legal representatives and assigns, hereby agree to indemnify and hold harmless any such third party from and against any and all claims that may arise against such third party by reason of such third party having relied on the provisions of this instrument.

In Witness Whereof, *I have hereunto signed my name and affixed my seal this.....................*

day of..., 19.........

....(Seal)
(Signature of Principal)

How to Handle Your Own Contracts

General Power of Attorney Short Form

Whereas,

in and by   Letter of Attorney, bearing date the   day of
one thousand nine hundred and   did make, constitute and appoint

as by the aforesaid Letter of Attorney may more fully and at large appear.

Now know ye, That   the said
have revoked, countermanded, annulled and made void, and by these presents do revoke, countermand
annul and make void the said Letter of Attorney above mentioned, and all power and authority thereby
given, or intended to be given, to the said

In Witness Whereof,   have hereunto set   hand   and seal the
          day of   one thousand nine hundred and

Sealed and delivered in the presence of

State of
County of   } ss.
                    of
before me,
a Notary Public in and for the State of
duly commissioned and sworn, dwelling in the

personally came and appeared

to me personally known, and known to me to be the same person   described in and
who executed the within Revocation of Power of Attorney, and

acknowledged the within Revocation of Power of Attorney to be   act and deed.

In Testimony Whereof, I have hereunto subscribed my name and
affixed my seal of office, the day and year last above written.

Be it Known, That on the   day
one thousand nine hundred and

Assignments, Proxies, and Power of Attorney

"severally" or "jointly" after the words "to act."

Little guidance can be offered in completing the next section. How much authority the principal wishes to confer upon the agent is up to him. He should remember, however, to keep an eye on the statute and if any questions exist, to seek legal advice. Where the principal desires to restrict the power as to any subdivision he should be explicit in the blank space in explaining the restrictions. The principal should also consider if he wishes to allow the agent to further delegate the power to subagents. The final paragraph simply states that once the third party acts in response to the power of attorney, he may continue to act under its authority in confidence of its validity until he receives an expressed revocation of the power. The power is then notarized.

While on the subject of powers of attorney, one additional form should be noted—the revocation of the power form. Since man often likes to undo that which he has previously done, the general rule is that a principal can always revoke his grant of authority and leave the agent or attorney-in-fact powerless. The two basic exceptions exist where the authority was originally given as security or where the agent has an interest in the subject matter. If either situation prevails, the authority as a matter of law is irrevocable.

The power to revoke and the rights to revoke are not synonymous. Thus, if the granting of a power of attorney or any analogous agency relationship was established under contractual agreement, the principal still would have the power to revoke, but simultaneously would breach his contract.

As for the method of revocation, the principal may exploit any medium at his disposal to convey to the agent and third parties that the agent's power has been terminated. In New York, revocation is complete if the manner unequivocally communicates the intended result. The form here accomplishes this requirement by first citing the source of the agent's power (the "Letter of Attorney") and then averring that the principal does "revoke, countermand,

annul and make void the said Letter of Attorney . . ." The principal should remember that although the revocation terminates the agency relationship, he remains liable to third parties who transact business with the agent prior to being notified of the revocation.

Proxy

Even in these times of recession, as market values cascade downward, many people continue to invest in the stock market. Regardless of the sanity of such a financial program, shareholders of voting stock are always the recipients of proxy solicitations. With an important shareholders' meeting imminent, factions within the corporation, in efforts to secure the upperhand, or even congenial groups with the power structure wishing to attain the necessary majority, must solicit proxy authorizations from those holders who otherwise would not attend the meeting.

Many of the corporate law consequences of proxies are of little importance for our purpose. Still, a general background would be worthwhile to shed light on the "whys" and "whats" of your action in signing a proxy statement.

Authority to vote by proxy is usually conferred by statute or by the corporate charter. Whether a by-law can grant the same power is a question which can only be answered by reference to local law. Once the right is conferred, no further attempts by corporate officials to restrict the power can prevail.

If a person is the legal holder of the stock, meaning that he has requisite legal title on the corporate transfer, he alone can appoint a proxy. Rules vary, contingent upon the holder's status (i.e., corporation, infant, executor, etc.), but for our purposes, it is settled that the holder of title on the day of record possesses the right to vote and concurrently the right to vote by proxy. By satisfying all formal requisites, the shareholder may confer his voting rights onto another shareholder or any other legally competent person in the absence of a statute to the contrary.

What then are the formal requirements? In essence, all the shareholder is doing is appointing an agent to act on his behalf. The writing, then, should state unequivocally both the legal owner of stock and the person who is to act as proxy, as well as the declaration of the creation, of an agency relationship and the delegation of power. As the proxy ballot indicates, the latter requirement is satisfied by the words "do hereby constitute and appoint." The shareholder should then sign his name at the end. As long as the proxy meets these requirements and on its face is free from illegality, the proxy becomes effective, unless local laws mandate additional requisites. These additional directions, for example might include the name of the corporation, the date, acknowledgment by one or more subscribing witnesses, a seal and filing the proxy with powers to be. Once completed, the proxy is vested with all powers that the stockholder legally enjoyed and can exercise them in accordance with whatever general or special authority was granted.

One final note on the finality of a proxy: Laws differ among the many jurisdictions. Generally, a proxy is revocable at any time unless the authorization declares the proxy irrevocable or the proxy is considered coupled with an interest such as payment of valuable consideration. Should this question ever arise, advice of counsel should be sought.

Proxy

𝕶𝖓𝖔𝖜 𝖆𝖑𝖑 𝕸𝖊𝖓 𝖇𝖞 𝖙𝖍𝖊𝖘𝖊 𝕻𝖗𝖊𝖘𝖊𝖓𝖙𝖘,

That *I* **125**

do hereby constitute and appoint ....
Attorney and Agent for me and in my name, place and stead, to vote as my proxy at any election

....
according to the number of votes I should be entitled to cast if then personally present.

In Witness Whereof, *I have hereunto set my hand and seal this* ....*day*
of ....*one thousand nine hundred and*

Sealed and delivered in the presence of

....

How to Handle Your Own Contracts

CHAPTER 10

Conclusion

Various rights, obligations and remedies involved within particular transactions already have been discussed. Hopefully, the reader has been helped by those explanations. For the most part, in the text we only have scratched the surface of the subject, because the law dealing with these particular contracts is both expansive and intricate; in particular transactions (e.g., forming a partnership), an attorney should be consulted, if at all possible. Nonetheless, some knowledge of the law can be helpful if applied with caution. This chapter will deal with four different, but related areas of contract law—breach, remedies and discharge of a contract, theories based on general common law. It should aid the reader to develop a full picture of a contractual transaction from start to finish. The chapter will close with some general comments.

Breach of Contract

A breach of contract is an unjustifiable failure to comply with the obligation assumed by a party to contract. Simply, it means that one party, the promisor, does not honor his promise to the other person, the promisee. Breach of contract may occur in three basic ways: (1) non-performance of the duty imposed by the contract; (2) repudiation; and (3) hindrance or prevention of performance by one party upon the other. Breach of contract is not a difficult concept, or at least not as difficult a concept in contract law as some discussed earlier in the book. Breaches of contract are very common. However, a brief explanation may help the reader understand an overall contractual transaction.

Conditions

Failure to perform a contractual duty can be confused with conditions stipulated in the contract. Failure of a condition by one party does not create a liability. It is breach of a promise, not of a condition that creates liability. There is no problem with understanding breach of promise. If the contracting party fails to perform the promise contracted for, the promisee has an action for breach of the contract. However, many contracts contain conditions, the breach of which may not constitute a breach of contract; rather, it allows the other party the right to non-performance without incurring liability.

Conditions are sub-divided into three classes: *condition precedent, subsequent*, and *concurrent*. A quick look at each will bring the point home.

A condition precedent is a fact or event which must occur before a duty of performance becomes mandatory. Let us illustrate: "In consideration of your taking me to the game, I will buy you a beer if the Knicks win," is an example of a condition precedent. If the Knicks do, in fact win, then I have to buy you a beer; the condition precedent, that is, the Knicks winning, has been satisfied and that condition precedent is now elevated to an unconditional duty. If I do not buy you a beer, I have breached the contract. If the Knicks did not win, I have no duty to perform and, hence, no contractual liability.

A condition subsequent is very rare. When it exists, a condition subsequent terminates the obligation to perform the contract and the possibility of incurring liability for any breach. In essence, it discharges a previous absolute duty of performance. For example, an obligation agreed to in a contract may be subject to a condition if notification within a period of time, such as an insured notifying the insurance company of a loss within twelve months. If he fails to satisfy the condition, the insurance company's obligation is terminated because the condition subsequent in the contract has occurred. It discharges any obligation of performance under it.

A condition concurrent must be in existence at the time when both parties are required to perform their obligations. An example: You purchase a motorcycle at Mike's Motorcycle Shop. The motorcycle is to be delivered C.O.D., (cash on delivery). Thus, payment is conditional on delivery and delivery is conditional on payment.

Express conditions, which can be any of the above three, are created by agreement of the parties to the contract. The reader should look for words or phrases like "on condition that," "provided," "if," etc. Also, a condition may be reasonably implied.

What should be noted by the reader is to be on the lookout for conditions in a contract. Remember, a breach of a condition is not a breach of the contract. The conditions must be satisfied to impose a duty to perform, breach of which performance is breach of the contract.

Repudiation (Anticipatory Breach)

Repudiation is a statement by a promisor that he will not undertake his future promised performance. There are a number of ways that breach of contract by anticipatory repudiation may be effectuated. A positive statement issued by the promisor to the promisee, proclaiming

that the promisor does not intend to perform, results in a breach of contract. A simple example will illustrate the point: "I will sell you my car on June 5, 1975 for $500." You accept my offer and are ready to tender the $500. We have a contract. On June 1, I tell you, "I am not going to sell the car to you." You are mad, but also wise. You consult an attorney and sue for damages. You win. There was a breach of contract. (Damages are discussed later.)

A voluntary act on the part of the promisor which makes rendering performance impossible, or apparently so, is a form of repudiation and gives rise to breach of contract. Consider the same example, except instead of informing you on June 1 that I will not sell the car, I sell the car to Paul, a third party, who does not know of our deal. Is this a breach of contract? Yes, and you may sue for damages for breach of contract on the theory that performance is now impossible because of the sale to Paul.

A repudiating party always has an opportunity to retract the repudiation if it is done before the promisee (you) has sued or changed his position in reliance on the repudiation. An example will illustrate the point. On December 1, a contract is entered into between X and Y for the sale of X's car to Y for $500. It is in writing and duly executed. The date of performance is December 25. On December 15, X tells Y that he is not going to perform. Y does nothing about this. (Y could sue then if he wishes, but chooses not to). On December 20, X notifies Y that he intends to perform the contract as agreed to. This retraction is effective, the contract is reinstated and the parties, X and Y, are both bound by its terms. Y's inaction allows X to retract the repudiation and perform as required under the contract's terms.

There are other remedies available to promisee after promisor's repudiation (anticipatory breach). It has been mentioned that the promisee may sue for damages immediately upon the issuance of the repudiation. The promisee may accept the promisors repudiation as a discharge of his own contractual obligation and simultaneously recover for his own performance in restitution (discussed later), or the

128

promisee may wait until the actual date that performance was to take place, and upon non-performance, sue the promisor then. And, finally, the promisee may always attempt to urge the promisor to perform.

The common law concept of anticipatory breach (repudiation) has been incorporated into the Uniform Commercial Code with respect to sales. This theory was discussed in the chapter on sales and an explanation was developed there. It is worth noting that a repudiation is not considered a breach when the defendant (promisor) is under a unilateral obligation to pay a sum of money at a future date. The repudiation of the obligation does not give rise to a course of action, and the doctrine of anticipatory breach cannot be used to accelerate payment of a debt (e.g., installment payments). Therefore, the party who entertains this type of repudiation must wait until the due date of payment and then sue for non-performance.

Prevention of Performance

One party's hindering or preventing the performance of the other party is self-explanatory. X and Y contract for the sale of X's car to Y on December 25 for $500. On December 15, Y destroys X's car. X obviously cannot perform. However, since Y caused X's non-performance, Y cannot sue for breach of contract. More accurately stated, Y could sue for breach of contract, but X would have a valid defense to non-performance.

Remarks

This concludes the discussion of breach of contract. For all practical purposes, the reader will know when a breach occurs. It is not difficult to know when you have been wronged. The key questions to ask when negotiating a contract are:

(1)   Are there any conditions contained in the contract?

(2)   When are these conditions to be performed?

(3)   When performed, what legal obligations arise under the contract?

Another key point to note is that in the event of a repudiation, the wronged party has many courses of action, all of which should be acted upon immediately, with aid of legal counsel. Examination of remedies is our next task, since it is important that a party realizes what can be done when a contract is, in fact, breached.

Remedies for Breach

After one party has breached his duties, the other has three alternative recourses available to him which he can pursue in order to be *made whole*. These three basic remedies are damages, restitution and specific performance.

Damages

As a general statement, the purpose for remedies for breach of contract is to put the injured party in the same position after the breach as he would have been had the other party fully performed. The most common means to accomplish this end is to award the party money damages in an amount sufficient to offset the losses incurred. The only difficulty in achieving this just result is in the measurement of damages.

Different legal theorists attach different labels to the type of damages recoverable by an aggrieved party. As a general rule, the party is allowed the difference between the price called for in the contract and the cost of his own performance. These damages are strictly compensatory and are recoverable only to the extent foreseeable by the breaching party at the time of the formation of the contract.

Extraordinary or consequential damages which proximately arise as a result of the breach, can be recovered only where the breaching party can reasonably foresee their occurrence. Example: X agrees to sell Y 100 widgets. On the day set for performance Y fails to accept delivery of the widgets, and X sells them elsewhere, at a lower price. Obviously X has a right to be compensated for his lost profits and whatever additional incidental cost incurred from selling the widgets to a third party. If the later sale results in a price greater than that agreed to in the contract and X suffers no pecuniary loss, then he is entitled to nominal costs at best.

To illustrate extraordinary damages, let us assume that X breaches, and because of this non-delivery, Y is unable to complete a deal from which he would have made an unusually high profit. In addition to the compensatory damages, is X liable for Y's loss of these high profits? The answer is no, unless X had knowledge of Y's subsequent deal at the time of contracting. The determining factor again is foreseeability and since X could not be reasonably expected to foresee the later contract, calling for an incredibly high profit level, he is not liable to Y for that particular loss.

In order to recover at all, the injured party must be able to calculate damages with some certainty. If his measure of damages is purely conjecture, at best he can recover nominal damages (a token amount) or his costs in performing his part of the bargain. One additional burden on the injured party is that he must attempt to mitigate. Even after proving damages with utmost certainty, he cannot recover any damages that he could reasonably avoid. In the above example where Y refused to accept delivery of the widgets, X has a duty to sell the widgets to another party. If to do so would require an unreasonable effort (e.g., if the only other user and purchaser of widgets was three thousand miles away), then he is excused. Where he does act to mitigate the damages, he is allowed to recover for any costs which he incurs.

Restitution

Restitution is a remedy for an aggrieved

party who has not fully performed his side of the bargain before learning of the other party's breach, and when the other party's duty requires something else or more than an agreed price. To seek restitution, a valid contract must be in existence, one party must totally breach it and the aggrieved party must be in a position to rescind. Since the injured party has not given his full consideration as stated in the contract, he is unable to seek damages—a calculation in which the contract price is always a factor. Still, he has suffered a measurable loss for which he should be compensated. In short, he should be restored to the position he was in before partially performing under the contract.

The measure of damages for restitution is limited to the actual cost of the partial performance which the injured party has rendered, less whatever value of returned performance he has received. If X pays Y $1,000 for a super widget, which is capable of doing more tasks than an everyday widget, and uses it in performing everyday tasks for several weeks only to have it fail in its first extraordinary job, X can recover his $1,000 less the value received from the widget in its normal duties. One highlight in the area of restitution is that the contract price does not restrict recovery, as it does under damages. Thus, even though an aggrieved party would have lost money under the original contract price, he can profit in an action for restitution—because the court is not limited to an award based on the agreed to price.

Specific Performance

One final remedy is specific performance or *specific restitution*. Sometimes, money damages will not make an injured party whole. In such an instance, he naturally would like a court to mandate that the contract be performed or in the alternative, that the specific object of the contract (e.g., a section of realty) be returned. If money damages are not satisfactory, the court will so order as long as it can supervise the performance and if its decision does not unjustly prejudice the other party. It should be remembered that a court can grant specific performance at its discretion and if it decides not to do so, the other remedies remain available to the injured party.

Discharge

Discharge is the end of the line. The parties, in effect, state that they are happy with each other and everything has been performed as agreed to. Performance is the usual method by which discharge becomes effective.

There are many methods of discharge. Discussion of them will be listed here and explained in greater detail later. Methods of discharge of a contractual liability may take the following forms:

(1) new agreement

(2) substituted contract and novation

(3) accord and satisfaction

(4) cancellation and recision

(5) merger

(6) release and covenant not to sue

(7) occurrence of a condition subsequent

(8) payment

(9) discharge by operation of law

Method (3), accord and satisfaction, and (7), occurrence of a condition subsequent, were discussed previously. Let us begin with (1), a new agreement.

A *new agreement* has to be in the same form as the original contract. If the original contract was in writing, the new agreement must also be in writing, if required by the terms of the original contract or by law. The new agreement should state that the parties discharge each other from any contractual liability arising out of the original contract.

A *novation* involves the substitution of a new party into the contract with a discharge of one of the original parties. The other original party, however, must agree to this substitution.

In essence, a new contract is executed between the new party and the old party with all the same terms of the original contract. For example, X and Y have a valid contract. Y decides to substitute Z in his stead. If X accepts this substitution, a novation has occurred, and Y is relieved of his liability. A novation results as long as all the parties, in this case X, Y and Z, are involved in the new agreement and Y's original liability, is extinguished.

In a two party situation, an original contract can be discharged with the substitution of a new contract. This can be effectuated either by an express intention in the new contract to that effect or by a new contract which is inconsistent with the original one. The former situation discharges through an expressed provision. The latter situation discharges impliedly.

Recision of a contract, by mutual agreement of the parties, discharges their respective obligations and liabilities. The parties, in essence, are restored to their original statuses. Cancellation is the destruction of a document (e.g., a note which is the debt (and not merely evidence of the debt) is destroyed by the party owed the money) or its surrender to the party subject to the duty or to someone on his behalf.

A *merger* involves a discharge of the contractual obligation by operation of law. Basically, a merger is the acceptance by one party of a higher contractual right, such as a judgment, which by law, discharges the lesser right (contract right) by incorporation into the judgment.

A *release* or a covenant not to sue, unlike recision, involves the surrender of a right by only one party under the contract. In return, therefore, the other party must supply good consideration in return for that surrender.

Payment is simply meeting one's obligation under the contract. X owes Y $100 on the contract. X pays Y $100. X is discharged.

Discharge by operation of law, includes not only merger, but certain actions of the parties, such as a material alteration of a negotiable note or a specific proceeding of law, such as bankruptcy, which acts as a discharge by preventing the obligee to recover.

131

Conclusion

A Reader's Checklist

Hopefully, the text has been helpful in illuminating pitfalls which the layman may confront in the daily management of his affairs and in suggesting remedies which he can seek. In all honesty, the book was written in that spirit. Time and again, it has been suggested that advice of an attorney is the best solution to any contractual problem. In some areas, such as wills, mortgages and partnerships, only a skeleton of the law was offered because of the intricacies involved. In all likelihood, a person will and should consult an attorney before executing these agreements or documents. It should be remembered that knowing how to "handle your own contract" at times can mean knowing when to seek counsel.

Other topics covered, however, are those confronted much more frequently and in which consultation with a lawyer would prove impractical. For example, the layman cannot be expected to seek legal advice in ordinary contractual transactions such as signing a lease, applying for credit, buying on time and purchasing personal use goods.

It is in these areas that the book has been focused in depth. In conclusion, a reiteration, in checklist form, is presented here for use when engaging in any contractual situation. If the reader remains alert, and follows these 15 bits of advice he may detect these latent dangers and avoid them where possible—he will not sell his soul, as did Doctor Faustus.

(1) Always receive a copy of every document involved in the transaction that is signed by either party.

(2) Retain all receipts, envelopes, and any other tangible evidence of communication between the parties until satisfaction.

(3) Preferably pay by check—this, in itself, is a record of payment.

(4) Never sign a contract that contains blanks that could possibly be filled in at a later date.

(5) Remember, everyone has a right to a completed copy of the agreement.

(6) Carefully read every contract and search for certain clauses that might prove detrimental. Examples are: (a) waiver clauses; (b) a wage assignment clause; (c) provision for cooling-off periods; (d) acceleration clauses; (e) power-of-attorney; (f) submission to particular court jurisdiction or compulsive arbitration; (g) waiver of right to trial by jury.

(7) In a contract for services to be performed in the future (e.g., health spas, dancing schools, vocational schools, judo classes, etc.) determine what cancellation privileges exist.

(8) In retail installment agreements, always determine who is financing the credit extended to you. Is it the seller or a third party? If it is a third party, determine who it is.

(9) In any consumer transaction, generally beware of certain rights that the consumer might forfeit by signing the agreement.

(10) Goods should never be purchased through a post office box. However, if you are "taken" and the post office box is used for commercial purposes, you can find the company's true name and address through the post office.

(11) Not all contracts are enforceable. Numerous provisions in contracts are determined to be unconscionable, illegal, etc., and therefore unenforceable. Whenever this problem arises, an attorney should be consulted.

(12) Certain agencies exist in most metropolitan areas whose primary functions are to deal with unfair practices in the consumer market. Although these agencies do not ad-

judicate rights, they may expedite an equitable resolution. These organizations and agencies, such as the Better Business Bureau, American Arbitration Association, Federal Trade Commission, Consumer Protection Agency, etc., should be utilized by the consumer; these agencies were created for your use and protection; do not hesitate to use them. This list of organizations and agencies is incomplete—each locality may have one or more of these, or other agencies which perform similar functions.

(13) Consultation with an attorney has been recommended throughout the book. However, many people lack the monetary means to avail themselves of personal legal advice. In many communities, excellent organizations exist such as Legal Aid, Inc. and Legal Services (Community Action for Legal Services) that were created to aid those with minimal or no income. These organizations were founded on the theory that every person deserves to have his legal rights adjudicated properly. Do not hesitate to use them.

(14) In New York (and possibly in your state) there is a small claims court. The main purpose of this division of the state court system is to offer the aggrieved party a forum to present his "side of the story." The claim cannot exceed $500, and the remedies available are refunds and damages. A point to be noted is that the action can be brought cheaply (under $5.00) and will be heard generally within one month after filing. Also, representation by an attorney is not necessary. Informality is the tenor of the proceeding.

(15) In transactions for the purchase of goods in which the goods prove to be unsatisfactory, a course of action not often used, but sometimes effectual, is a personal letter to the president of the corporation. Do not discard this recommendation as frivolous, since the price of a stamp might bring an equitable solution to the problem.

133

In closing, one point is emphasized: the book is meant to be an aid to the layman in contractual situations; it is not intended to be used as an affirmative tool with which to negotiate in bad faith. If a flaw is discovered in a contract, it should be made known to the other party and not be used later to avoid the legal obligation. There is no substitute for fairness and honesty in contractual dealings.

Conclusion

To all to whom these Presents shall come or may Concern,

Greeting: *KNOW YE, That*

for and in consideration of the sum of

dollars ($)

lawful money of the United States of America to   *in hand paid by*

the receipt whereof is hereby acknowledged, have remised, released, and forever discharged and by these presents do   for
heirs, executors, and administrators and assigns, remise, release and forever discharge the said

heirs, executors, administrators, successors and assigns of and from all manner of actions, causes of action, suits, debts, dues, sums of money, accounts, reckoning, bonds, bills, specialties, covenants, contracts, controversies, agreements, promises, variances, trespasses, damages, judgments, extents, executions, claims and demands whatsoever, in law, in admiralty, or in equity, which against

134   *ever had, now ha   or which   heirs, executors, or administrators, hereafter can, shall or may have for, upon or by reason of any matter, cause or thing whatsoever from the beginning of the world to the day of the date of these presents.*

This release may not be changed orally.

In Witness Whereof,   *have hereunto set   hand   and seal*

the   day of   19
Sealed and delivered in the presence of

....*L.S.*

State of   **County of**   *ss.:*
          On the   day of   19   before me personally came

to me known, and known to me to be the individual   described in, and who executed the foregoing instrument, and duly acknowledged to me that   he   executed the same

....

How to Handle Your Own Contracts

Bibliography

Anderson, R. Anderson on the Uniform Commercial Code, Vols. I and II. Rochester: Lawyers Cooperative Publishing Co., 1971.

Benden, Richard Roy and Rohan, Patrick J. Powell on Real Property. New York: Matthew Bender and Co., 1968.

Bicks, A. Contract for the Sale of Realty. Student Edition (as revised). New York: Practicing Law Institute, 1972.

Black, H.C. Law Dictionary. Fourth Edition. St. Paul: West Publishing Co., 1951.

Bromberg, Alan R. Crane and Bromberg on Partnership (Hornbook Services). St. Paul: West Publishing Co., 1968.

Burby, William E. Handbook of the Law of Real Property. Third Edition (Hornbook Services). St. Paul: West Publishing Co., 1965.

Calamari, John D. The Law of Contracts (Hornbook Services). St. Paul: West Publishing Co., 1970.

Casey, W.J. Estate Planning. New York: Institute for Business Planning, Inc., 1973.

Consumers Report, A Guide for Renters, Pts. I-III, Vols. 39, No. 10; 39, No. 11; 40, No. 1. Consumers Union of the United States, Inc., Mount Vernon, New York, 1974.

Corbin, Arthur Linton. Corbin on Contracts. St. Paul: West Publishing Co., 1952.

Corpus Juris Secundum. Agency, Vol. 3; Assignment, Vol. 6; Assignment for the Benefit of Creditors, Vol. 6; Compensation and Salaries, Vol. 15; Contracts, Vol. 17; Contracts, Vol. 17A; Deeds, Vols. 26-28; Landlord and Tenant, Vols. 52-53; Mortgages, Vol. 68; Sales, Vols. 77-78; Wills, Vols.

94-96. Brooklyn: The American Law Book Co., 1936 to date.

Ferser, Merton. Principles of Agency. Brooklyn: Foundation Press, 1954.

Friedman, Milton R. Contracts and Conveyances of Real Property, and cumulative supplement (1972). Second Edition. New York: Practicing Law Institute.

Friedman, Milton R. Friedman on Leases. New York: Practicing Law Institute, 1974.

Hawland, William Dennis. A Transactional Guide to the UCC. Philadelphia: Joint Committee on the Continuing Legal Education of the American Lawyers Institute and American Bar Association, 1964.

Kratovil, Robert. Modern Mortgage Law and Practice. Englewood Cliffs, N.J.: Prentice-Hall, 1972.

LeBlanc, Nancy E. A Handbook of Landlord-Tenant Procedure and Law with Forms. Third Edition. New York: MRY Legal Services, Inc., 1966.

Mandel, Ludwig. The Preparation of Commercial Agreements. New York: Practicing Law Institute, 1973.

Marks, Edward; Maloney, Richard J. and Paperno, Lloyd. Mortgages and Mortgage Foreclosure in New York. Massapequa Park, N.Y.: Acme Book Co., 1961.

McKinney's Consolidated Laws of New York Annotated. Real Property Law, Bk 49. St. Paul: West Publishing Co., 1968.

Moynihan, C.J. Introduction to the Law of Real Property (Hornbook Services). St. Paul: West Publishing Co., 1962.

Nordstrom, Robert J. Handbook of the Law of

Sales. St. Paul: West Publishing Co., 1970.

Osborne, George Edward. Handbook on the Law of Mortgages (Hornbook Services). St. Paul: West Publishing Co., 1970.

Restatement of the Law. Agency, Vols. 1, 2. Second Edition. St. Paul: American Law Institute Publishers, 1958.

Rowley, Scott and Sive, David. Rowley on Partnership. Second Edition. Indianapolis: Bobbs-Merrill Co., 1960.

Scoles, E.F. Problems and Materials on Decedents' Estates and Trusts. Second Edition. Boston/Toronto: Little, Brown and Company, 1973.

Seavey, Warren Abner. Handbook of the Law of Agency (Hornbook Services). St. Paul: West Publishing Co., 1964.

Simpson, L.P. Handbook of the Law of Contracts. Second Edition (Hornbook Services). St. Paul: West Publishing Co., 1965.

Sugarman, Robert Reuben. The Law of Partnership. Second Edition. Brooklyn, 1947.

United States Code Annotated. Commerce and Trade. Title 15. St. Paul: West Publishing Co., 1974.

United States Code Congressional and Administrative News. 93rd Congress. Second Session. No. 12, Dec. 25, 1974. St. Paul: West Publishing Co., 1974.

Walsh, W.F. A Treatise on the Law of Property. Second Edition. New York: Baker, Voorhis and Co., 1937.

Williston, S. A Treatise on the Law of Contracts, Vols. 1-15. Third Edition. Mount Kisco, N.Y.: Baker, Voorhis and Co., Inc., 1957.

Wincor, Richard. The Law of Contracts. Dobbs Ferry, New York: Oceana Publications, 1970.

136